T0354383

THREE IRON HORSES
and a
BUTTERFLY

Arthur H. Bolden

authorHOUSE®

AuthorHouse™
1663 Liberty Drive
Bloomington, IN 47403
www.authorhouse.com
Phone: 1 (800) 839-8640

This book is a work of non-fiction. Unless otherwise noted, the author
and the publisher make no explicit guarantees as to the accuracy of
the information contained in this book and in some cases, names of
people and places have been altered to protect their privacy.

© 2015 Arthur H. Bolden. All rights reserved.

No part of this book may be reproduced, stored in a retrieval system, or
transmitted by any means without the written permission of the author.

Published by AuthorHouse 03/06/2015

ISBN: 978-1-4969-6818-0 (sc)
ISBN: 978-1-4969-6817-3 (hc)
ISBN: 978-1-4969-6816-6 (e)

Library of Congress Control Number: 2015902036

Print information available on the last page.

Any people depicted in stock imagery provided by Thinkstock are models,
and such images are being used for illustrative purposes only.
Certain stock imagery © Thinkstock.

This book is printed on acid-free paper.

Because of the dynamic nature of the Internet, any web addresses or links contained in
this book may have changed since publication and may no longer be valid. The views
expressed in this work are solely those of the author and do not necessarily reflect the
views of the publisher, and the publisher hereby disclaims any responsibility for them.

CONTENTS

Acknowledgements 6
Preface..10

Chapter One: Darlington And South Carolina History.................24
Chapter Two: Elias Bacote 40
Chapter Three: The Bacote Side 108
Chapter Four: The Kelly Side 152
Chapter Five: Shadrack Kelly 242
Chapter Six: Shadrack Kelly/John Carolina................................274
Chapter Seven: Evelyn Kelly Bolden Brown 296

Epilog 330
Sources Of Information...340
Appendix...344
Index 347

ACKNOWLEDGEMENTS

M any readers may not appreciate the difficulties and obstacles encountered during the penning and ultimate publishing of a treatise of this nature. It requires support from a cadre of alliances that assist in the research, writing and publishing aspects, as well as those who render ideas, insights, encouragement, understanding, as well as mental and financial support. I am eternally grateful to my fruitful alliances for their contributions, patience and understanding during the last four years.

I embarked on this project with inspiration from my wife, Ms. Jacquelyn (Jackie) Bolden and daughter, Ms. Sydne Long. It began with the intent to compose a brief Word document on my computer from an assortment of documents and notes relating to our family history that my mother had maintained for as long as I can remember. In addition, I sought to pen in ink some family lore I retained from numerous conversations with her. The goal was to make the information available for my children, however, it evolved into a much larger than anticipated treatise on family history. They were patient and tolerant of my mood changes at that time as well as my clutter as I moved between rooms in the house with piles of papers and books. I wish to extend my loving thanks and appreciation to Jackie. Her support especially throughout the latter stages of this project has been invaluable. To my sons, Arthur and Troy, who expect nothing less than 100 per cent commitment and effort, I say "thanks for sharing your ideas."

Whatever merit this treatise possesses it owes to my daughter Sydne. Her faith in my idea encouraged me to toil with the many required details, and her generosity enabled me to enlist the services essential to produce a respectable work.

Kudos to Mrs. Evelyn K.B. Brown for possessing the discipline, insight and wherewithal to serve as an unofficial griot of these families for nearly a century and for maintaining much family lore in written form.

Acknowledgement is made to my dear cousins, Ms. Patricia Bacote James and Ms. Gladys Bacote Hunter for entrusting to me cogent details of incidents and events at the Bacote enclaves in Darlington County during the last century, and for providing insight into the lives of the offspring of Elias and Matilda Bacote. Their input was invaluable in the preparation of the manuscript, as they provided details many family members had no knowledge of, had forgotten, or were reluctant to release or discuss.

The author wishes to extend heart-felt thanks to Ms. Vivian Guyton for helpful discussions and emails and for leading me to Roseville Plantation. It is clear that our by-chance meeting was pre-ordained. I also thank genealogy researcher and historian Scott Wilds, an authority on Darlington, South Carolina history, for uncovering and sharing vital information from the bondage era, as it relates to the ancestors cited here-in. Without his assistance, the scope of this project would have been virtually unattainable. Thanks to the writer, Charles Stansbury, for inspirational and educational discussions involving the publishing process and to my son in-law Lewis P. Long for his inspiration and helpful discussions.

The author is forever indebted to the Director, Doris G. Gandy, and her staff at the Darlington County Historical Commission for their cooperation in providing historical Bacot and Kelly materials and assistance in locating related materials in their vast archives located in the former city jailhouse. Sincere appreciation is extended to Ms. Kay Williamson, Ms. Gail Gandy, and Ms. Nanny Diggs for their efforts. Thanks are also extended to Ms. Mirenda Douglas and the staff at the historic Mechanicsville Baptist Church for opening their archives and providing CDs of church files during the era of bondage.

To the authors of the "2003 Kelly Reunion Booklet," Ms. Rene' Peterson, Ms. Catherine Kelly, Bishop Jerry Kelly, Dr. Brenda Kelly, Pastor Bessie Kelly-Jones, Mrs. Aleemah Spence and Mr. La'Ray Peterson, your inclusive, genealogical, document provided much needed foundation for this endeavor. Nearly complete Kelly genealogical data was placed at the author's fingertips enabling the project immensely.

Thanks are extended to the widow of Mr. Carl Tucker, Mrs. Eleanor Tucker, the owner of Roseville Plantation, who provided the author insightful history of the plantation and allowed me to briefly tour the restored manor and grounds, unannounced. I visited them a few years ago before Mr. Tucker passed away. They expressed much kindness and understanding.

I would be remiss if I failed to acknowledge the suggestions, proof reading, comments and editing of an early draft of the manuscript by my dear friends, Ms. Annette Baker and Ms. Jacqueline Antoine.

Ms. Robin Stennet and my wife Jackie provided the same critical and inspirational services on later versions. Each of them improved the presentation immensely with their corrections, recommendations and thoughtful comments, and to them I am eternally grateful. Ms. Stennet's diligence and interest during the project's latter stages provided vital impetus and inspiration to the author to continue when the going got difficult and the task seemed unsurmountable. Her precise, grammatical, and flow corrections were particularly critical to the process. Ms. Stennet secured the final edition. Her writing skills and firm grasp of language allayed all of the author's fears. Thank you Robin. Grateful acknowledgement is also made to Ms. Diane Gerard for her professional rendition of the illustrative figures presented herein. Her diligence and interest over the entire span of the project provided inspiration to the author.

I am particularly indebted to my deceased brother, Chester Bolden, who, during our formative years, diligently tried to develop in me a fuller appreciation of the significance of extended family. Chester had a firm grasp of our genealogy, from core family to extended cousins. All I wanted to do was play ball. Thanks Chester, I think I finally got it.

I also thank the staff at Authorhouse for their unwavering support throughout the entire process. To my coordinator, Jessa Paxton, to the book designer, and the art director, all who worked tirelessly to design the book and make it an appealing, visual beauty, I offer sincere, heartfelt appreciation.

PREFACE

This is a treatise on Bacote and Kelly family history and is primarily about three gentlemen and a woman. They represent ancestors from three different generations, who nobly carried their family torch and established high standards for succeeding generations to aspire. I wish to state quite definitively that it is by no means my intention to generate an all-inclusive genealogy driven survey of Bacote and Kelly family histories. Additionally, I wish to state quite definitively, it is not my intention to specifically omit, demean, dishonor, disrespect, or under-represent any members of these large families. Many ancestral as well as contemporary Bacote and Kelly family members may not appear in this treatise. Nevertheless that does not reduce their importance or significance to the family, or to the author.

I seek to participate in the preservation of these Kellys and Bacotes most valued and revered possession, their history. There are only a few entities as powerful and important as a family firmly steeped in their history. A portion of this history has already been systematically deleted from the deepest receptacles of our brains as our ties with our African heritage were dramatically severed during the era of bondage. It would be a tragic, irresponsible, mistake to let another interruption occur so quickly. It is very important that we document as much as possible about this history now, because as generations pass on, we will be left with unanswered questions. A continuing debate about the past will ensue. What happened? Who was the first to come to America? Who shaped the course of our family history? Who in our family were drum majors for justice and equality? Who fought in the wars, for America? Who were the pioneering college graduates and businessmen/women? What did she do? Who was his father? What are the names of her children? How did our family history of involvement in Christianity evolve? What were some of the major contributions of the family to American society? By definition, and as I am discovering, the reconstructed past is contestable territory as it involves skepticism, contingency, presumption, interpretations, and truths as well as untruths. I have discovered there are already some simple discrepancies in some of the information that I have amassed from different sources, such as ages, birthdays, first names etc.

My humble intent is to feature **Elias Bacote**, a Bacote gentleman, **John Kelly Sr.**, a Kelly gentleman, **Shadrack Kelly**, a Kelly gentleman, and **Evelyn K.B. Brown**, a Kelly/Bacote woman. These ancestors respectively, were two male slaves, the son of a freed slave and a daughter of the son of a freed slave. Their lives spanned three vastly different eras of American history, and each of them remarkably, exhibited immense courage, patience, intelligence, insight, resourcefulness, the ability to endure, the willingness to struggle and the faith to sacrifice against all odds. Embedded in their landscapes were enormous setbacks, perils and personal tragedy, but they moved forward in a grand fashion. At a juncture in American history when our individual futures are severely challenged, they are featured because their stories are very illuminating, because they were, under the circumstances, heroic ancestors who withstood many of the challenges of their eras, because they possessed great character, and not because of any amount of materiality they accumulated. Their stories serve to memorialize the victims of bondage and Jim Crow and to communicate Kelly and Bacote history, culture and values. There are other noted ancestors of these families, and ancestors of other families across this great country that deserve a similar distinction, and maybe this treatise will inspire such an undertaking.

This project really began with the idea of generating a document/ treatise for me and my descendants about Kelly and Bacote family history, but it instantly became so interesting and enthralling that I knew I had to share it. It began as a passion and gradually became a mission that I am honored to perform. So because of my unselfishness, I feel obligated to state what my intentions are for self-benefit as well as the benefit of others. It also helps establish some guidelines for the author, as well as for you, the reader. I will address some accomplishments and actions of a core Kelly/Bacote family as presented herein, up to and including the generation born during the 1930s and 1940s, but that generation only to a limited degree.

I do not have the information, desire or knowledge to discuss a larger percentage of the events that occurred in the lives of these ancestors. I seek to document the truth about what transpired in only a few instrumental cases. A backlash of the perilous journey they endured was the lack of adequate discussion or dialogue regarding the past. Don't be misled here, numerous important facets were acknowledged over generations, but there were just as many that were filed in some obscure folder of their brains and eventually deleted. As a result there are holes in the family landscape that merit attention, if only for the sake of history.

When the time came to generate a title for this treatise I felt severely challenged. Somehow I wanted it to depict something about the venues where these ancestors toiled, to be descriptive of their existence, and to honor them. During a conference call with members of my immediate family numerous brain-stormed considerations were generated. The list was narrowed to a few which came to the forefront, for example, the name of the plantation of their bondage, the catchy name of a farm tract owned by the Bacotes, simply a History of the Kellys and the Bacotes and a few others. However, all of them seemed too mundane and unassuming, as we felt these were powerful individuals with powerful stories.

During the course of the call one participant remarked that he was taken aback by the role the railroad played in Bacote lore and how some of its virtues paralleled those of some ancestors I sought to feature.

The development of the railroad industry changed many aspects of life in America. In the 1860s railroad lines were constructed across the country connecting the East to the West. Locomotives conquered the prairies, tamed contested territories while more firmly connecting and bonding the Union. In the process, the industry displayed the credible virtues of courage, integrity and tenacity.

The iconic term "Iron Horse," which refers to trains during that period of time, serves as a perfect metaphor for the three male ancestors featured in this treatise. Just as that machinery transformed the American landscape and economy by playing a major role in labor, land development, transportation of goods as well as passengers at a critical stage in American history, so too did the deeds of Elias Bacote, John Kelly Sr. and Shadrack Kelly alter many aspects of the South Carolina landscape as well as create a paradigm in the evolution of these families. These pioneering ancestors exhibited many of the traits attributed to that iconic term. They were steadfast, immovable and abounding in endurance. As you will see, they implemented initiatives that expanded the family horizons for generations. As it was with the "Iron Horse," in each case the concept was bold and adventurous and a symbol of hard work and indestructibility. We all liked the concept of iron horses.

In an analogous sense, a parallel can be drawn between the iconic Evelyn K.B. Brown and the butterfly. When one thinks of this ancestor, in addition to her strength and vision, a gentleness emerges, a caring and loving persona. In many regards she was very much like the beautiful, colorful Monarch Butterfly which is known for its endurance and ability to gracefully migrate long distances. Unlike her counterparts from above she did not stay put. From the farm, to "uptown" Darlington, to college, to New York City, to international destinations; Evelyn exhibited a strong desire and disposition to travel and explore faraway places. She was known for going to different places, experiencing different cultures while spreading goodwill, compassion and love. Similarly, the butterfly gracefully migrates, transporting things like seeds, nectar and pollen in the eco-system, enabling fertilization and reproduction. Evelyn's life was a perpetual portrayal of love, love of her family, love and respect of her fellow man. It is very interesting that in Chinese culture butterflies symbolize love. The butterfly serves as a perfect metaphor for this family icon.

From the conference call, the concept of *Three Iron Horses and a Butterfly* evolved and was a unanimous choice for the title of this ambitious work.

I am truly inspired by the actions of these icons and I seek the knowledge to comprehend why and how they ascended to the heights they soared. To simply contend that they overcame adversity is indeed an understatement.

I endeavor to develop a relatively superficial, unbiased, historical, narrative about important sub-units of each of these relatively large families, intertwined with a listing of much of the broader family that I have gained knowledge of via historical research and informal interviews with family members.

I endeavor to record relevant facts based primarily on documents of Evelyn Kelly Bolden Brown, Mechanicsville Baptist Church records, U.S. Census Reports, Darlington County Historical Commission Papers, 2003 Kelly Reunion Booklet "Reviving the Legend to Live the Legacy," Bacot Family Papers, genealogy researchers, historians, and information generously provided by family members et al, over the years. In some cases I will be forced to make, at best, a modest interpretation of a particular event or action. If inaccurate, it will be an honest mistake.

In focusing on these four ancestors, some important ancestors and contemporary family members will not be included herein; hopefully that will not lessen the significance and impact of this document to readers. To go into detail about a larger segment of the Bacotes and Kellys would require too much research and work for me. I would much rather be out hitting the golf ball, working on my game.

It is my goal to provide a beneficial reading experience for family members as well as the public at large, where one becomes fascinated and excited while digesting the historical information. I seek to generate a broader perspective of the bondage and post-bondage periods, from an African-American standpoint, based on interesting information pertaining to the lives of four icons of these families. Within this framework, it is my desire that the reader develops a sense of the Mechanicsville, South Carolina landscapes and an insight into the psychology of the featured individuals.

It is very insightful that Evelyn K.B. Brown possessed a cache of old family documents and notes pertaining to the history of these two families. These documents, some of which were inherited from her parents, some which were legal in nature, or notes scribbled on pieces of paper, old personal family letters etc., were archived in a locked cedar chest that she kept at the foot of her bed for decades. Only a selected few knew the location of the key to that chest. Evelyn felt that as a devoted at-large Kelly/Bacote family member, it was incumbent upon her to maintain these invaluable records so that the history of the family passed on is as true as possible. This treatise is an attempt to take that storehouse of information, along with further historical research, and break new ground while unearthing heretofore unknown, vague, and forgotten aspects of that history. I will bring stories to life that have never been adequately penned. The history of every core sub-unit of the Kelly and Bacote families is significant as it relates to those families at-large. For a more in-depth Kelly genealogical perspective, a comprehensive listing of Kelly genealogy, I refer you to the valuable and informative *2003 Kelly Reunion Booklet.*

This research is not nearly completed and this treatise will undoubtedly present some questionable dates and assertions. I continually seek to motivate myself to search aggressively for more historical data, and in the process hopefully inspire and motivate the youth of these families, as we toil to preserve the legacy of some extraordinary ancestors.

Some may say, "Arthur dealt primarily with love, property accumulation and education and did not adequately address issues like devotion, fellowship, spiritual accomplishments, death, sex and other issues." That is another project. Some of the very young family members may say "Arthur devoted too much attention to the slavery issue." As noted author James Baldwin so brilliantly stated in his 1963 novel, The Fire Next Time, "to accept one's past, one's history, is not the same thing as drowning in it, it is learning how to use it." My goal is to provide a brief historical sketch of the professional lives of the featured individuals, to bring some of their accomplishments to the public forum, to illustrate some of their distinctive traits of character, not to extol or deify them, but to illustrate some models that may be of benefit to future generations.

We must endeavor to recognize, celebrate and honor the historical significance of the successes of our ancestors. For centuries these brave and courageous individuals contributed immeasurably to the culture, independence, wealth and history of this great nation. Regrettably, from a historical and public relations perspective, many African-Americans feel that those contributions have not been afforded the measure of recognition that they deserve, and that they have been systematically downplayed, if not completely omitted, in our literature, classrooms and museums. Some members of these families may contend that there is no inherent value in pursuing the history of these ancestors. They have made statements like, "it's too ugly, let's forget about it and move on." I respect their decision in that regard, but I strongly disagree. It is paramount that this information is disclosed.

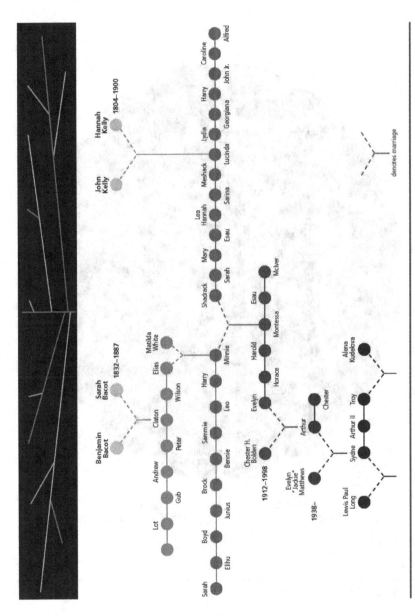

Figure 1. Genealogy: Lineage of a Kelly/Bacote Family

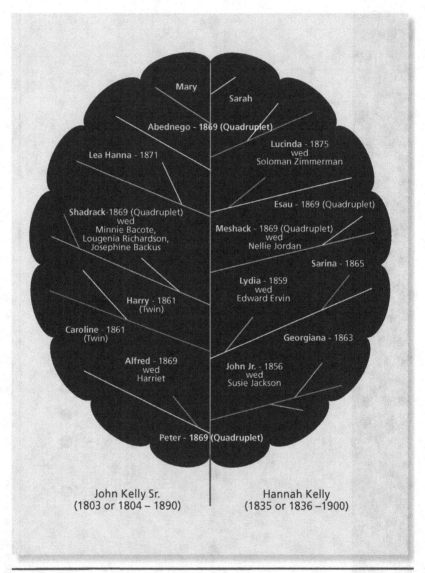

Figure 2. Kelly Family Tree

In a sense my sentiments here are an echo of the rhetoric expressed many centuries ago by the brilliant Iranian scholar, Abu'l-Rayhan Muhammad Al-Biruni (973-1050), whose writings encompassed a vast field of knowledge. Al-Biruni wrote, "It is our duty to proceed from what is near to what is distant, from what is known to that which is less known, to gather the traditions from those who have reported them, to correct them as much as possible and to leave the rest as it is, in order to make our work help anyone who seeks truth and loves wisdom."

I contend that, to a large degree, the more true knowledge individuals possess of their family history the stronger they and their contemporary family are as a people, socially, mentally and psychologically. The mental and psychological aspects of our individual existence are very critical. The more we know and understand about ourselves as young individuals the greater our chances of personal development and fulfillment. Knowledge of the past is a form of experience.

I cannot overstate the relative importance of this link to the past. That is the essence of history. It is what makes history the important discipline it is today, and why the library is stacked to the ceiling with history books. If we feel we came from greatness we will aspire for greatness. By the same token, if we feel our family survived successfully for generations on welfare, handouts and incarceration, chances are we may not diligently aspire to break those chains.

The more I became engrossed during the creation of this treatise the greater my realization became of its potential importance as a historical document, but more importantly as a source of information for future generations. What can we say about the nature of family history and the important role it may play in our development as individuals? Knowledge of our history, the successes, pitfalls, disasters and humbling moments that befell our ancestors, and not just the ones who experienced the wrath of bondage, but also succeeding generations, can facilitate the avoidance of a lot of negative duplication. We can amass the negatives, learn from them and convert them into positives. If we're strong enough mentally we can simply erase them from our system. We additionally have the option of embellishing the strong positive facets of this history and utilizing them as models for our present existence.

It is important to have knowledge of the past in a text of documented facts. Some individuals will retain more oral history than others without distorting it. But what happens when these retainers are no longer on this side of the Golden Shore? The knowledge is lost and we are forced to delve into the realm of speculation. I can recall as a young man hearing discussions and stories about some family members who preceded me, even having discussions with family conscious older relatives as they related what they knew regarding the past. However, now to my chagrin, I cannot recall much of the gist of those conversations. In hindsight, if only somehow they had been put in print, zeroxed or recorded, my knowledge today would be greatly enhanced.

In addition, from a medical standpoint, the importance of past family medical history cannot be overstated. Today, the first piece of information doctors want is the medical history of your family. "Is there a history of cancer, diabetes, high blood pressure, alcoholism, drug addiction, mental disorders, leukemia, sickle cell anemia, etc. in your family," they typically ask? Presently, this information may be more important than ever, because with current technology the human genome (DNA) has been fully sequenced, analyzed and partially interpreted. The interpretation process of specific sequences is ongoing. However, a definite correlation between the content of one's DNA and the presence of specific gene-related illnesses in one's family has already been identified. What this means is that in the very near future society is going to benefit more greatly from knowledge of long term, ancestral, medical family history, with the saving of lives and possible prevention of unnecessary distress, suffering and trauma.

I believe it is critically important that we remain cognizant of the fact that our behavior and posture today, to a large extent, was shaped by the lives of the people who preceded us; that we are a product of our own experiences as well as those of our ancestors. Their history is indeed a legacy that should not be covered in the sands of time. We honor these individuals and illuminate their legacies when we preserve the history of their emancipation and individual struggles for self-realization. However, ultimately their true measure will be determined by how they handled adversity, the tough times, not how prosperous or how much materiality they espoused.

As it is the responsibility of each generation of humanity to improve on mankind's existence, so is it the responsibility of each generation of a family (a sub-unit of mankind) to weed out the bad stuff, improve on the good things and generate novel ideas. Of course that does not always occur, but I do believe that that's what the Creator had in mind. Classic examples of this model are families that moved from one end of the self-reliance and responsibility spectrum to the other, from sharecroppers to farm owners, from apartment building maintenance men to apartment building owners, family businesses that thrived and developed over two, three, and four generations, optimizing the original idea or concept and taking it globally to even greater heights.

It is my sincere desire that this discourse, thus penned, is worthy of preservation, and will be viewed with pride and veneration by the Kelly and Bacote families at large, however remote they may be removed from the homes of their fathers. It offers some behind the scenes glimpses at four, significant, African-American figures and their unsung contributions to this nation's story. In addition, it is hoped that it will provide inspiration, knowledge and insight for younger family members, as well as the public at-large, as they relive the barriers and challenges these individuals encountered. Perhaps it will open minds, hearts and eyes to the richness of the broad African-American experience, culture and history, which could induce an enhancement of the spirit of healing, reconciliation and more importantly better understanding between the many diverse cultures in America. Hopefully, as importantly, it will encourage discourse on the contributions of other family icons and promote the preservation and protection of their legacies.

I challenge each and every young Kelly and Bacote descendant, who has the opportunity to peruse this treatise, to develop a sense of pride and respect for the Kelly and Bacote traditions, respect for who they are, where they originated and what they've accomplished. This history, of course, is filled with unspeakable tragedy, but it also features enormous accomplishments, prolific memories, and above all faith and hope. Hopefully, this new-found knowledge will serve to re-affirm their rich heritage, foster a spirit of reconciliation and enhancement of character, as well as assist in the reinforcement of individual identity and continuity.

To have the opportunity to discover, explore and examine portions of the lives of such illustrious ancestors of these families, individuals who exhibited legendary capabilities and adroitness, is a privilege and indeed a pleasure frequently unavailable to us in this great nation, due to the unfortunate scarcity and limited availability of detailed records from these historic eras.

John Hope Franklin, the noted historian, touched eloquently on this issue in his autobiography, *Mirror to America,* when he talked about the history of a nation not only being imbedded in the records of legendary wars, or the lives of the rich and famous, but also in the lives of the most consistently despised, improvident, underserved population.

The late, iconic, poet emeritus, Maya Angelou, addressed the relevance and importance of a documented family history in a very powerful manner in her poem *A Black Family Pledge.* In a concise manner the poem highlights and supports many of the premises and ideas I have put forth in this Preface. From it one experiences a sense of the relationship and connectivity of this history and the future. One very eloquent line reads; "Because we have forgotten our ancestors our children no longer give us honor."

As a descendant of these ancestors, I offer this brief look into history, for the benefit of my own family and all students of history. Only because I consider that some readers will want to know who the author is or what are the author's credentials, will I offer tidbits of information about myself throughout this treatise. Having published over 30 international Biochemical Research papers, I am an experienced writer who fully understands the importance and significance of substantiating facts and data before putting them out in the air waves for public scrutiny.

CHAPTER ONE

———————

DARLINGTON AND SOUTH CAROLINA HISTORY

It is well documented that the slave trade made South Carolina the powerhouse that it is today in agriculture. The state was built on the backs of many remarkable individuals, both black and white, and it is clear that the strong, courageous African-American Bacote and Kelly families made exceptional contributions to the development of Darlington County, South Carolina. With the never ending forest, majestic pine trees, billowing oaks and vast swampland that we have here, it must have been a monumental task just clearing the land to develop thousands of acreage for crops.

Charles Cotesworth Pinckney, noted Charles Town lawyer, planter and politician put it very succinctly when he stated at the Constitutional Convention, "while there remained one acre of swamp land uncleared in South Carolina, I would raise my voice against restricting the importation of negroes." He boldly continued this exploitive diatribe, declaring "I am ...thoroughly convinced... that the nature of the climate, and the flat, swampy situation of our country obliges us to cultivate our lands with negroes and that without them South Carolina would soon be a desert waste."

From the earliest settlements, Kelly and Bacote ancestors [shown in Figures 1, 2, and 2A] served on the primary workforces for that task and many other labor intensive endeavors. They grew cotton and tobacco in the historic Cotton Belt and the "Back Swamp" of South Carolina during the 18th and 19th centuries.

Sometimes when I close my eyes and let my mind freely roam, I can visualize them out there working diligently in the hot fields of Mechanicsville or at scenic Lourdes Lake, fishing, singing and just having a good ole time. I see them casually walking through the woods, engulfing the serenity of the forest, sweating yet being cooled by the shade of the unspoiled massive oak and longleaf pine trees.

One cannot fully comprehend the plight, accomplishments and history of ancestral Kelly and Bacote family members without an appreciation of the history, topography and geography of Darlington County as it relates to the State of South Carolina and indeed America at large. This is the terrain they traversed daily for over 200 years, that we have documentation of. They traveled along narrow, newly made, muddy paths and crude roads, when the only light was the light of the moon above, not the state of the art, well lit, ten lane interstates, turnpikes and toll roads that exist today.

Before these ancestors or the first European settlers came to Darlington County in 1736-1737, northeastern South Carolina was occupied by the Cheraw, Pee Dee, and Waccamaw Indian tribes. The Cheraw, a Sioux speaking tribe, were located along the banks of the Great Pee Dee River near the present town of Cheraw. They lived in small round dwellings constructed of sapling trees covered with bark and animal skins.

During 1711, they fought against the Tuscarora alongside the British and Catawba Indians. From 1715 to 1716, they united with other Native American tribes to fight against the colonists and traders in the Yemassee War. In the 1730s many Cheraw Indians united with the Catawba, while others merged with other Sioux speaking tribes in North Carolina, as their lands were being overrun by the settlers from across the ocean, compromising their safety and survival. They reasoned there was greater security and safety in numbers.

In 1759, small pox, an eastern disease which the European settlers brought to America, and to which the Indians had no immunity, killed many of the remaining independent Cheraw in South Carolina. In 1600, there were an estimated 2,000 Cheraw in the state, today they are almost entirely extinct.

English settlements in Charles Town date back to 1670. Charles Town, now called Charleston, situated between the Ashley and Cooper Rivers was a center of vigorous export and import activity and served as the seat of the provincial government. Since law, order, stability and continuity was very crucial to the success of the early settlements, South Carolina was divided into eight circuit judicial court districts, shown in Figure 3, to handle legal matters such as settlers, immigration, relocation etc.

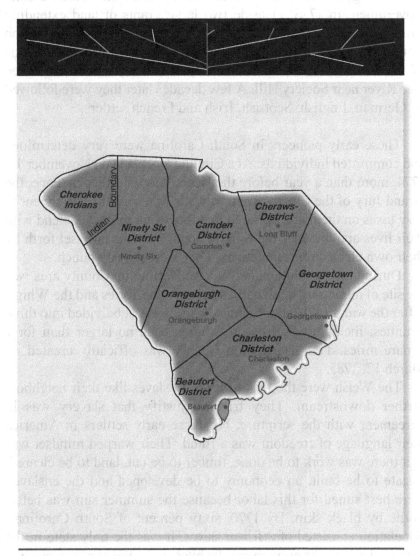

Figure 3. South Carolina Circuit Court Districts - 1769
Compiled by Historical Records Survey, W.P.A., 1938

However it would be sixty years later before the Europeans ventured deep into the "Back Swamp Country," as it was called, into Cheraw Indian territory shown in Figure 4 and Figure 5. In order to encourage settlements in this area of South Carolina, the Colonial Government in 1736 set aside two large grants of land extending along both sides of the Pee Dee River. The entire length of Darlington County as it exists today lies within these two royal grants. The Welsh were the first to come and they settled at the bend of the Pee Dee River near Society Hill. A few decades later they were followed by German, English, Scottish, Irish and French settlers.

These early pioneers in South Carolina were very determined and committed individuals. At a Circuit Court held on November 15, 1774, more than a year before the Declaration of Independence, the Grand Jury of the Cheraw District denied the right of Parliament to levy taxes on them and declared that they were ready to defend with their lives and fortunes the right to honor only the laws set forth by their own elected representatives. They were a feisty bunch.

During the Revolutionary War, the Darlington County area was the site of numerous small battles between the Tories and the Whigs. After the war, in 1783, the Cheraw District was subdivided into three counties, including Darlington County, each no larger than forty square miles. Thus Darlington County was officially created on March 12, 1785.

The Welsh were the first to bring in slaves like their neighbors farther downstream. They tried to justify that slavery was in agreement with the scripture. For these early settlers in America their language of freedom was a fraud. Their warped mindset was that there was work to be done, timber to be cut, land to be cleared, a state to be built, an economy to be developed and the enslaved were best suited for this labor because the summer sun was better borne by black skin. By 1770, sixty percent of South Carolina's population consisted of African slaves. It was the only state in the Union where blacks outnumbered whites. First, the money crops like cotton, indigo and rice were planted as the settlers capitalized on the large investment in their imported labor force. In addition, numerous food crops were also planted as many of the large plantations were essentially self-sustaining.

The settlers spoke in stirring terms of liberty, justice and religious freedom, but these privileges were attainable for the privileged settlers and never quite within reach of their enslaved labor force for generation after generation.

The European Rogers, Bacots, Kelleys and Brockintons were early settlers in the middle to late 1700s in the "Back Swamp Country." By 1820 numerous villages had arisen throughout the area. Among these was Kelly Town, located near Black Creek in the northwestern portion of the county, Springville which was more of a summer resort area than a village, and the historic Colfax/Mechanicsville area, located about fifteen miles south of Society Hill. Each of these areas played a significant role in Kelly and Bacote history as outlined in this treatise.

The early settlers were primarily farmers who raised cattle and hogs and grew rice and indigo. Most of the plantations were vast, as large as 400-4,000 acres, and most of the lands are still inhabited by descendants of the original owners. [See Figures 4 and 7.]

Africans from the West African rice-producing nations of Senegambia, Angola, Ghana, Gambia and Sierra Leone arrived in the "Back Swamp" with vast knowledge and experience in growing rice and indigo, an asset that would later prove to be very valuable to the landowners. An article on the history of Mechanicsville penned by Chapman J. Milling relates that the slaves in Mechanicsville, "for the most part were tall, dark brown people, many of whom had the regular features of the north-central African. Some were from the West Coast, West Africans and Guinea Negroes, who were looked down upon with disdain by the taller, lighter colored Africans. Many spoke with a Gullah accent, having been brought up the river from Charleston or Georgetown, but not the classical Gullah of the sea island and tidewater slaves."

Indigo was a huge export product for South Carolina that made many early settlers wealthy. With the ever-expanding acreage of farmland devoted to the cotton industry and the labor of the enslaved labor force, the overall wealth of the area grew considerably during the first half of the nineteenth century. Evidence that there was a lot of wealth in that area, can be observed by taking a tour of Cheraw, Society Hill and Darlington and noticing the numerous old streets lined with huge majestic mansions and palatial homes still standing from the Colonial and Antebellum periods.

The Pee Dee River played a very important role in the early development of Darlington County as some of the very earliest settlers established themselves as traders on the river, which served as a shipping venue for exports and imports via the port at Charles Town. Flat barges propelled by enslaved Africans pushing them with long poles were commonplace along the river. They hauled cotton to the coast and returned with coffee, sugar, spices, and manufactured goods. Later small steamboats used the river, stopping at locations like Roseville Plantation, and other plantations bounded by the river, to exchange cargo and goods, until the early 1900s.

The river actually begins as the Yadkin River in the western mountains of North Carolina, where it is presently utilized in the production of hydroelectric power and also as a drinking water reservoir. From North Carolina it meanders through the mature bottomland hardwood forest, longleaf pine sand hills and floodplain forest of South Carolina, along the northeastern border of Darlington County and connects with the Little Pee Dee River in Marion County.

In 1809, the Darlington District was almost enlarged via annexation with the Marion District, but the petition was denied. Darlington was incorporated in 1835, and Society Hill in 1880. Nearly eighty years later Marion County was finally formed and it included a portion of the lower part of old Darlington County.

In 1868, under the South Carolina Constitution, the Darlington District became Darlington County, and was divided into 21 townships under the New England Plan. None ever operated as a bona fide political entity, the move was purely for geographical identification. The names were changed again in 1878 to some present day names like Timmonsville, Hartsville and Darlington townships as shown in Figure 5.

The industrious city of Florence was formed in the 1850s as a stop for the Wilmington & Manchester Railroad and was home of a confederate prison camp during the Civil War. It was incorporated in 1888 and also took about one-third of the original old Darlington County territory. In 1901, the county lost an additional fifty square miles of territory in the new formation of Lee County.

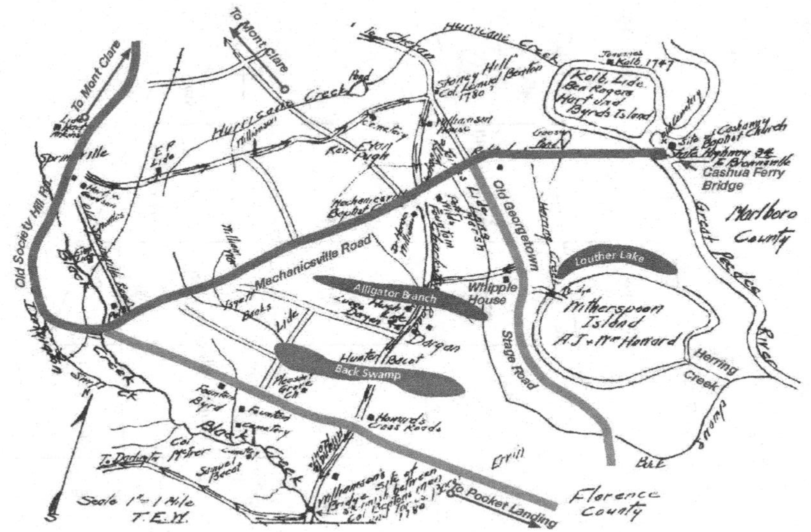

Figure 4. Old Darlington Area Map

Darlington County Historical Society - Fall Tour - October 1959

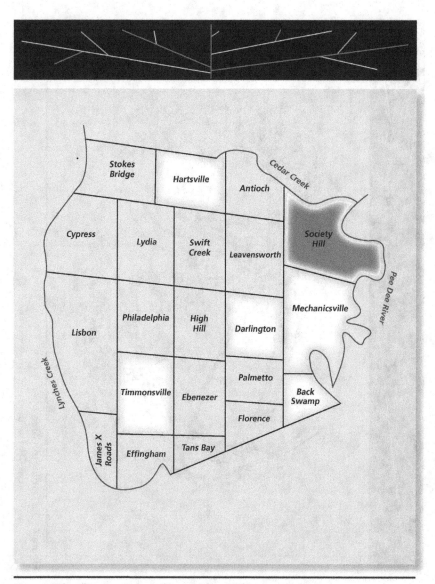

Figure 5. Darlington County Township - 1878

The Mechanicsville section of Darlington County was once called Colfax Township as shown under the New England Plan [see Figure 6] and then Riverdale later in its historical development. This beautiful area, which also essentially connected Florence County and the Pee Dee River, is a sportsman's paradise. It contains Louthers Lake [sometimes written Lowthers Lake, and shown in Figure 4] known for its assortment of great, fresh water fish such as wide mouth bass, sunfish, bream, carp, catfish and eel. Of the 36 lakes in Darlington County, Louthers is one of the most popular and I am certain along with the Pee Dee River served as a favorite recreational area for many of the ancestors cited herein.

Scenic Witherspoon Island, shown in Figure 4 and Figure 7, which features a fifty foot elevation, is also located there. A.J. Howard and William Howard were among the early land owners on Witherspoon Island. Richard Howard, a distinguished timber and forestry expert currently in Darlington County, who has performed timber and forestry work for numerous Bacotes in Mechanicsville, is a direct descendant of these two pioneers. Much of the island is currently residentially developed and features large estate homes and manors. It does not contain any commercial enterprises and has retained much of its natural beauty, eco-system and wild life.

During the Colonial and Antebellum Periods the primary route from Cheraw to Georgetown went through the "Back Swamp" via old Georgetown Road (sometimes also referred to as "Kings Highway") where early Kelly ancestors resided. [See Figures 4, 5, 7] Ancient live oaks cast rugged shadows on the spanish moss laden trees that lined this beautiful old, red clay, stagecoach route or lane. Kelly Place, the post slavery home of some Kelly ancestors covered in this treatise was located at what is presently 557 Georgetown Road. Georgetown Road is highlighted in yellow in Figure 7.

Figure 7, a 1955 rendition of a section of the Darlington County map, is a very important as well as informative source in terms of the information discussed throughout this treatise. Many references will be made regarding sites located therein. The highlighted names represent post-slavery Bacote and Kelly ancestors and the location of their homesteads. The location of Alligator Branch is highlighted. Cashua Ferry Road, also known as Route 34 or Mechanicsville Road is highlighted. Black Creek is shown as it meanders through the

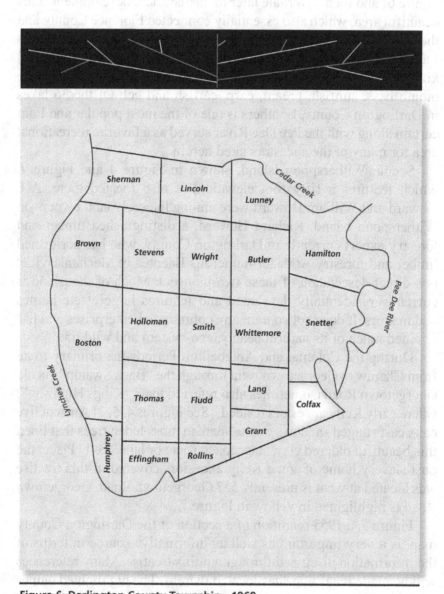

Figure 6. Darlington County Township - 1868
Darlington County Historical Commission, 204 Hewitt Street, Darlington, SC 29532

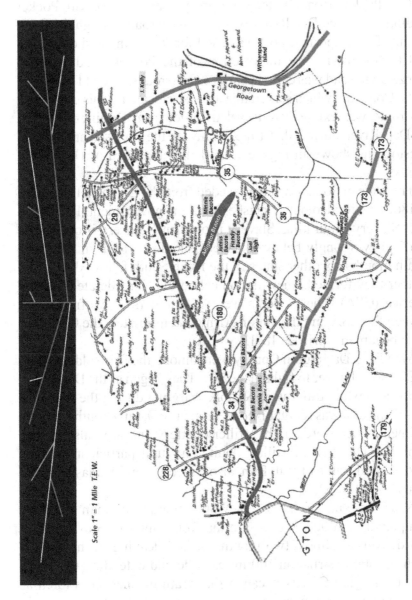

Scale 1" = 1 Mile T.E.W.

Figure 7. Darlington County Map - 1955   Note Bacote and Kelly Family Homesteads

southwestern section of the County. The well-known Pocket Road and Georgetown Road, formerly known as Old Georgetown Road, are highlighted.

The Pocket Road, named for its passage to McCall Pocket Landing at the Pee Dee River, was a primary road through the Back Swamp. This important port was used for importing and exporting via Charles Town. The intersection of the Pocket Road and Old Georgetown Road was called Clarke's Crossroads. The old McCown Clarke Company which served that area was located at this crossroad. This route was extensively traveled to get from Darlington to the Pee Dee River during that time. Many of the post-slavery Bacote ancestors, as shown in Figure 7, settled in that area of Darlington County.

The State of South Carolina seceded from the Union on December 24, 1860 due to ideological clashes with the government. Its mantra was: "Slavery is our king. Slavery is our truth. Slavery is our divine right." They strongly believed slavery should be legal in America. Within months six other states in the Deep South followed suit, and together they formed a new nation called the Confederate States of America (CSA). These events were forerunners of confrontations between the CSA and the Union Army and ultimately the Civil War which began on April 12, 1861.

Men from Darlington County were among the first soldiers from the CSA to volunteer to fight in the war. They began as the Darlington Guards and while training in Suffolk, Virginia during the winter of 1861-62 the unit was reorganized as Company D, First South Carolina Regiment. They were a light artillery battery and were also known as the Pee Dee Light Artillery Unit. This unit participated in the noted Second Battle of Bull Run, also called Second Manassas, from August 28-30, 1862.

Near the end of the Civil War General Sherman marched triumphantly through South Carolina from January 15 to March 9, 1865 delivering almost two months of hell, leaving in the wake a swath of total destruction 100 miles wide and extending the entire state. Darlington County escaped the wrath of Sherman's torch as cabins and palatial mansions were left intact. Darlington was not in the direct line of his advance through the state. No battles were fought here, only minor skirmishes. Detachments of the Union Army passed through Kelly Town and New Market and in the process executed a former slave on the Public Square in Darlington for what they called insurrection. After the war, Darlington was occupied by federal troops until 1871.

After the Civil War ended and the era of bondage was abolished, South Carolina, and indeed America at large, sought to provide relief and assistance to the newly freed in their quest for self-sufficiency.

The Bureau of Refugees, Freedmen, and Abandoned Lands, also known as the Freedmen's Bureau was established in the U.S. War Department by an act of Congress on March 3, 1865. This was the Federal Government agency that aided the freedmen, freedwomen and white refugees after the war and during the Reconstruction Era. A branch of this much needed agency was headquartered in Darlington County and operated from 1865 to 1872. It was responsible for supervision and management in issues involving housing, employment, medical care, and rations in the county. It also assisted in the re-uniting of displaced families and served as legal advocates at both the local and national level.

This Bureau is also widely recognized for its efforts in developing educational opportunities for the newly freed who, not surprisingly, demonstrated a strong thirst for knowledge. It partnered with missionary and aid societies to provide much needed opportunities at the elementary, high school and college levels not only in South Carolina, but throughout the South.

An enduring product of this initiative emerged not far away in the bordering state of Georgia. In 1867, the nation's first historically black college for men was founded as Augusta Institute in the basement of Augusta, Georgia's Springfield Baptist Church. It eventually became known as Morehouse College, named in honor of Henry Morehouse, a white, liberal minister and secretary of the Northern Baptist Home Mission Society. This important institution would profoundly shape the lives of newly freedmen and their prodigy for generations.

Much of the college's international scholarship and service acclaim was garnered under the dynamic leadership of Dr. Benjamin Elijah Mays, noted educator and mentor to Dr. Martin Luther King Jr.

Morehouse has a rich tradition of appointing its own graduates to the prestigious presidential position, including the current president, Dr. John Silvanos Wilson Jr., a 1979 graduate. Located on a 66 acre campus in Atlanta, Georgia, Morehouse is home to students and faculty from over forty states and eighteen countries. It has produced outstanding men and extraordinary leaders, among them three Rhodes Scholars, and has been recognized for its achievements by a cadre of U.S. publications.

In 2003, *The Wall Street Journal* named Morehouse College one of the top fifty most successful schools across the nation. In 2004, *Black Enterprise* magazine ranked Morehouse the number one college in the nation for educating African-American students for the third year in succession. Without sounding pompous, I think it is fitting and proper to mention that, over the last 150 years numerous Kelly and Bacote young men have traversed the hallowed grounds of this highly successful institution.

The industrial success of Darlington County during the 20th century came primarily from its brickyards, saw mills, oil mills, Sonoco Products Company and the Dixie Cup Company. However, despite the successful industrialization of the county, agriculture still plays a primary role in the economy as it has done since its inception. The principal players have changed from relatively small or large farms to Mega-Farms with only a few farmers, like Jimmy Norwood, Ben Williamson, Dorla Lewis and Ned Dargan monopolizing the industry there. The county still boasts some of the most fertile and best type of soil for growing corn, cotton and tobacco in the Pee Dee area.

During the era of bondage and for nearly two decades after the Civil War, cotton was king. With the invention of the cotton gin, which automated the separation of cotton seeds and hulls from the cotton fiber, cotton became one of South Carolina's premier exports. During the late summer, a glance at the sloping terrain of Old Georgetown Road or the flat landscape of Pocket and Bull Roads reveals a sea of cotton, thousands of acres of the white, soft, fluffy stuff.

Darlington County evolved into primarily a rural, farming, residential, bedroom community. Newsworthy events throughout the county have historically chronicled the happenings of ordinary people. Events like weddings, deaths, births, celebrations, winter blizzards, tornadoes, hurricanes and crop harvests generally dominated the headlines. It has always been a great community to raise a family and to live to a ripe old age while enjoying good ole Southern hospitality.

Flue-cured tobacco was introduced in the 1880s and quickly emerged as the premier cash crop for many Kelly and Bacote ancestors, as sharecroppers or primary land owners. In 1896, within a five mile radius in the Riverdale section there were greater than 420 acres of tobacco planted. As of the year 2010, there were no Kelly or Bacote descendants actively farming in Darlington.

The celebrated county, located in the northeastern quadrant of South Carolina, as stated earlier, was carved out of the original Cheraws District shown in Figure 3, and chartered in 1785. The city of Darlington is the county seat of this historic area and according to the 2010 census boasted a population of 6,289 citizens. It is believed to have been named for a Revolutionary War General or Darlington, England. In more recent years it has become internationally known for the stock car races at the famous Darlington Raceway.

Notable Darlingtonians who helped shape the Darlington landscape include The Honorable David Rogerson Williams, former member of the United States House of Representatives (1804) and South Carolina Governor (1814-1816). He is also credited with establishing a water- powered cotton mill on Cedar Creek near Society Hill for the manufacture of cotton bagging, oznaburgs, etc. Other notables include Civil War General Evander M. Law, early settler and planter Samuel Bacot II, bandleader, pianist and songwriter Buddy Johnson, industrialist James Lide Coker, builder Leroy Stubbs, World War II hero Lieutenant Billy Farrow, Major League Baseball player Orlando Hudson, educator Bennie Gary, PGA Tour golfer Tommy Gainey, sports coach and educator Virgil Wells, writers James Patrick Kilgo and Elizabeth Boatwright Coker, and Harold Brasington of Darlington Raceway fame.

CHAPTER TWO

ELIAS BACOTE

The vast majority of the material presented herein was amassed primarily from the collection of Evelyn K.B. Brown papers, U.S. Census reports, Darlington County Historical Commission documents and papers, Darlington County Court Records, Mechanicsville Baptist Church records, the "2003 Kelly Reunion Booklet," reports provided by South Carolina historian, Scott Wilds, as well as family members over the years.

The earliest reference to sub-units of the large, diverse, African-American Bacote Family (Figure 1) and the Kelly Family (Figure 2) that I have been privilege to, dates back from the late-1700s to the early-1800s in the Back Swamp/Colfax section of Darlington Township, Darlington County, South Carolina. Therefore for the purpose of this treatise I say, "in America it all started in the Back Swamp" but in reality we know it probably started earlier at another location.

This is the first detailed written account and in depth documentation, of these eras, of the history of these two important families as they relate to the evolution of the Back Swamp/Colfax/ Riverdale/Mechanicsville area. The early history of their Caucasian counterparts is well documented, as much has been recorded regarding their families, travails and contributions. It is equally important that history accurately reflects details of all aspects of the early beginnings of African-American families in America also.

Most contemporary Bacote and Kelly descendants have grown up knowing that their early ancestors were enslaved. However, until this thesis was researched and assembled with stories and documents relating to these iconic individuals brought to the public arena, they had very little specific documented information about anyone or about what has transpired. One day historians will have the capability and technology to trace the ancestral beginnings of the Kellys and Bacotes, cited in this treatise, deeper into the 18th and 17th centuries, and ultimately into African and American Indian civilizations with details that provide a broader perspective.

The starting point for this documentation of a significant portion of Kelly and Bacote family history begins on the Bacote side with the enslaved **Benjamin and Sara Bacot.** Their names were originally observed by the author on a document of their son, **Elias Bacote,** which has survived in the capable hands of family for over a century. It consists of a list of names etched on a decorated metal sheet. The list includes Elias' wife Matilda, numerous of their deceased children, as well as living children, plus two names from an older generation, **Benjamin** and **Sara Bacot.** From a family viewpoint the belief has always been that they were the parents of Elias. Their surnames of Bacot of course, at that time, inherently suggested that they had been housed at a Bacot Plantation during their years in bondage, a significant assertion that seems to be true.

A segment of the rigorously important Bacote family lore that was entrusted to the minds of numerous generations of descendants has been re-visited in this treatise. As of the year 2014, they are the oldest known patriarch and matriarch of this Bacote family and serve as the starting point for Bacote history herein. Benjamin was born around **1825** and passed away in 1870 at age 45. Sara was born in **1832** and passed away at the age of 55 on July 4, 1887. They spent the major portion of their lives in bondage. Both survived that ordeal and eventually became free citizens.

We cannot fully comprehend the history of America without knowing the history of our enslaved ancestors, as they, like the rest of America, including whites, struggled with bondage, resistance, opportunity, segregation, poverty, survival and freedom. We can acquire a vast amount of knowledge simply by studying their lives as it relates to the history of this country.

There are a few observations of the bondage and post-bondage periods, which fascinate my mindset, that need to be brought to the forefront here, as I attempt to relate some of the issues, the ancestors, highlighted in this treatise, had to manage and navigate.

The dehumanization of Africans, portraying them as unskilled beings of minimal intelligence and low moral capacity led to the legitimization of the inhumane Trans-Atlantic slave trade. Slavery in North America began with the English colonization of Virginia in 1607, although African slaves were brought to Spanish Florida as early as the 1560s. This tragic industry which lasted from the 16th to the 19th century was responsible for the relocation of millions of Africans, against their will, from their homes in central and western Africa to toil as unpaid laborers on cotton, sugar, coffee and cocoa plantations in North, South, and Central America, and the Caribbean. Most of these Africans and their descendants were forced into slavery and in many cases, savagely brutalized, humiliated, dehumanized, and subjected to the extreme indignity of being disconnected from their illustrious heritage and stripped of their real family given names and identities.

The prevailing pro-slavery, anthropology based arguments were that Africans, as a race of people, were inferior, barbaric, superstitious, and incapable of governing themselves, hence best served by enslavement. This arrogant viewpoint along with the economic demands for cheap labor, not just in North America, but throughout the Western Hemisphere, provided the warped basis for the institution of slavery.

As contemporary generations, nearly 150 years removed from the era of bondage, attempt to comprehend and challenge assertions and postulations from that era, it is important that we have in our grasp as much of the truth as possible regarding what really occurred. However brutal bondage in America was, in many cases it simply was not what many history books most often portray. Numerous mistruths have been proclaimed. In addition, a vast amount of truth has just not been cast in the public's eye, or made common knowledge. In my opinion, historical viewpoints have been presented, in many cases, to validate certain individual actions and behaviors, to appease the prevailing populace, to market the writings, or to simply enhance an author's position in the community and unfortunately in many cases, by design, do not to represent the total truth.

As more contemporary academicians address the issue and as more research is conducted many interesting viewpoints are emerging. Many older historians and academicians have left the public with a slanted declaration. There are numerous events and actions, in my opinion, that occurred during slavery that, simply put, have been misrepresented. Many myths perpetuated by historians eager to placate and glorify the defeated southerners after the Civil War are finally being dismantled and corrected.

There is no dispute that slavery was a momentous tragedy, a catastrophic institution that reeked unprecedented havoc throughout the western hemisphere. Although this treatise is by no means intended to be a document on slavery, nor an attempt to support or condone it, there are many observations, old and new, that fascinate me. They merit consideration. A few are presented herein.

One fact often understated is that many slave owners were not supremely overbearing, nor guilty of the physical mistreatment or brutality, as depicted in many history books and Alex Haley's blockbuster, bestselling book *Roots*. At some plantations selected slaves were afforded the luxury to come and go as they saw fit as long as they took care of their business and obeyed the wishes of the owner. Some owners did not "work their slaves to death," as we read in some articles, because then they would have to replace them and basic economics argues against that. These owners were not crass or imperceptive; they managed and maintained the things that made life easier and profitable for them.

One astonishing statistic not often mentioned in Eurocentric history books is the numbing reality that of the twenty-thirty million Africans loaded onto slave ships, only nine-twelve million survived the oceanic passage across the Atlantic Ocean. This computes to a surprisingly low survival rate of only 40%, from the oceanic passage alone, which speaks volumes about the profit margin and the inhumane nature of that devastating industry.

Another under-presented fact is that rather than being linked exclusively to the growth of cotton in the Cotton Belt, or the Black Belt of Alabama, African slaves helped build Washington DC, including the White House, the current residence of President Barack Obama and his family. The White House construction began in 1792 with the use of free black men and slaves as laborers. New York City also relied heavily on the slave labor force between 1629 and 1827.

This work force contributed greatly to the construction of Manhattan, the financial capital of the world. Many slaves and free Africans were also engaged in maritime work. Slaves were the pioneering work force in the growth of tobacco in the Chesapeake Virginia region at the end of the 17th Century and were very instrumental in the development of rice as a money crop in the wet coastal plain or low country of South Carolina at the beginning of the 18th Century.

In addition to playing a major role in the building of America, these men and women also had a huge presence in the protection of this country. Many African slaves and former slaves were active warriors in the War of 1812, the Civil War and the Revolutionary War. As a matter of fact, approximately fifteen percent of the Continental Army was black.

Although Washington's forces were a mixed multitude there was also an all-black regiment consisting of former slaves, called The Bucks of America, in that legendary group. They fought courageously in the Battle of Rhode Island preventing the British from infiltrating the American line. The presence of this extraordinary regiment was also felt in the Siege of Yorktown, where it is said that without the service of James Lafayette the Americans would not have been victorious in that battle, which led ultimately to the defeat of the British.

When we think of slavery in America our minds generally recall images of hundreds of Africans packed on European slave ships crossing the Atlantic Ocean, or of blacks donning bandanas, picking cotton or harvesting tobacco under the scorching sun in large fields throughout the South. Sometimes we fail to recall that American Indian slavery and slave trade was also ubiquitous throughout the South. Tens of thousands of Native American Indians were also subjected to the inhumane condition of enslavement, placed in bondage in their own country. Throughout the history of the world, when a country has been explored, invaded, and settled, the natives were, in many cases, subjected to this horrible fate. The literature is laden with such occurrences.

Although their numbers paled when compared to the number of Africans in the same situation, Native American Indians lived, married, toiled and endured side by side with our African ancestors on the plantations of South Carolina.

It has been transmitted through family lore that **Benjamin and Sara** had at least seven boys, and an uncertain number of girls. The names of the known children of Benjamin and Sara Bacote are:

    i.   Claton
    ii. Wilson
    iii. Peter
    iv. Gub
    v.   Lot
    vi. Andrew
    vii. Elias

It is very interesting that the names of three of their sons, Lot, Peter and Elias appear on an 1865 Cyrus Bacot Plantation Work Agreement Contract that lists the freed slaves who committed to the agreement. An excerpt from this document is presented and discussed in detail later in this chapter. Except for Elias, Lot and Peter, we have limited information about Benjamin and Sara's other offspring at this time, and someone should pursue that critical issue.

Elias Bacot was a man many spoke of, but few possessed in-depth knowledge about his life. Although scant literature exists in regard to this man, the available bits of information reveal an extraordinary story.

Elias stands very prominent in Bacote family history. He had an interracial heritage. Family lore has it that there was Blackfoot Indian in his lineage, that one of his parents was of Blackfoot extraction. It appears from a large auto-chrome photograph of Elias, which exists in the family treasures, that he was a handsome gentleman of average stature, and indeed not entirely of African descent. His sharply chiseled features were not typically African. He possessed a relatively sharp nose, thin lips and there were no curls in his coarse hair. His complexion had a golden, light brown tint.

It is unclear at this time whether one of Elias' parents, Benjamin or Sara, was pure Blackfoot Indian or not. What does appear clear, from family lore and his photograph, is that Elias had Indian ancestry connecting the history of this specific Bacote family in America to the famed Blackfoot Indian tribe.

Information gathered narrows his date of birth to 1847- 1850. This was just a few years before the infamous *Dred Scott Decision of 1857* was enacted. That law was probably one of the most prominent legal decisions other than the Thirteenth Amendment that impacted the lives of Elias and other ancestors of that era. Chief justice Roger Taney penned the majority opinion which described "negroes as being far below the scale of created beings" and concluded that the constitution did not provide them any rights which society was mandated to protect or ensure.

Although the Decision was not a positive law for young Elias and his peers, it demonstrated that unrest was prevalent. Many slaves were not as content as some historians would have us believe. They were not seeking any protection; they were rebelling, escaping and agitating. There was also constant on-going pressure from the Quakers, the Underground Railroad, John Brown and his peers, as well as a cadre of abolitionist movements.

During the antebellum the South Carolina Militia was very active in the Darlington District, and indeed the entire state, patrolling the countryside, attempting to counteract rebellious acts and discourage run-away slave activity. History will eventually confirm that they were very unsuccessful in this venture as the runaway slave phenomenon was a serious issue for slave owners, one they could not control, contrary to what we see in the media and many history books today.

Over the years, it has been generally accepted among family members that Elias Bacot resided at a Bacot Plantation, but no one knew which specific one. As elucidated in detail throughout this treatise, some enslaved blacks adopted the sir names of their owners and it has been assumed that Elias falls into that category. The primary question has been, in which specific Bacot plantation was he domiciled?

The European Bacots were members of a group of settlers that migrated to America from France for religious reasons. They were known as Huguenots, members of the Reformed Church that were persecuted by Catholics and the French government because of their scriptural doctrine. Pierre Bacot, born in Tours France around 1647, was one of the first Bacots to settle in America, around Charles

Town, South Carolina in 1694, when one hundred-seventy seven Huguenots arrived ashore.

The Darlington branch of these Bacots began with Samuel Bacot I, who was born in 1716 and married Rebecca Foissin. Early land records indicate that Pierre's great grandson, Samuel Bacot II (1745-1795) settled in the "Back Swamp" in about 1770. Samuel Bacot II was a war hero, having served in the South Carolina State Militia during the Revolutionary War. He was taken prisoner by the British in 1780. The story goes that Samuel managed to escape and in the process freed his fellow comrades from a Charles Town prison.

Samuel had six children, including three boys, Samuel Bacot III, Cyrus Bacot and Peter Hannibal Bacot.

Since Elias was born around 1850, mathematically his years in bondage had to occur under one of the three Samuel Bacot II offspring, like Cyrus Bacot et al, or one of their descendants like Cyrus Bacot II, or Richard Brockington Bacot (b.1805) and Peter Samuel Bacot (b.1810), sons of Peter Hannibal Bacot or another Bacot plantation owner of that era. There were a few Bacot plantations, including Roseville Plantation, the Cyrus Bacot Plantation, the E.L. Bacot Plantation, and two or three other smaller Bacot plantations operating at that time in the Darlington District.

Evidence presented later in the chapter identifies **Elias Bacot's** plantation address as the Cyrus Bacot Plantation.

This is a very important discovery as it relates to the history of this Bacote family in America. Before this information was uncovered there was uncertainty regarding Benjamin and Sara's plantation address, as well as Elias', because of the compelling story in Bacote family lore that Elias had been a runaway slave.

Among the legendary tales pertaining to **Elias,** perhaps one of the most revered according to family lore, is that he had a history as a run-away slave, that he was difficult to "contain." So greatly did he appreciate the difference between bondage and freedom as a young man? As the story goes, he ran away from the plantation and while attempting to traverse the dense forest it became more and more difficult to stay comfortably ahead of the dogs that the search party was utilizing. He could hear the dogs barking and the search party gaining ground and decided to take a chance and hide in Black Creek until they passed. The beautiful, well known, Black Creek, which is noted for its ice cold, dark, murky, snake laden water, extends harmoniously through Darlington County, including a portion of the Bacot land holdings. Legend is, the armed party searched the woods diligently, as he perched patiently in the cold creek for hours until darkness prevailed, to make his move. Under the cover of darkness he was able to evade his potential captors. From there the lore gets murky. It has been said that he was found by some of his peers from the plantation, who were also searching for the young man under the pretense that he was simply disoriented or lost in the virgin forest. He was whisked with haste to the plantation before the search party could locate him. There is no mention in family lore that he was punished for his defiance. It is a compelling story that receives high ratings within family ranks. Elias made his position clear.

This escape or attempted escape, this prodigious act of defiance, made him a family icon, an "Iron Horse," as a young man, as it spoke volumes about his mindset, bravery and courage.

It also refutes another interesting myth regarding slavery in America; the idea, among some, that the enslaved did not desire freedom, hence were content in bondage. This represents a gross misconception of American history. I was on a tour of Daufuskie Island, a small South Carolina coastal island, in 2007 and the tour guide made the statement that slaves had been very content in their situation. I was shocked at his lack of knowledge and expressed my dismay. The reality is that slaves were constantly running away, not in the thousands, but in the tens of thousands according to noted historian John Hope Franklin and Loren Schweninger's, <u>The Quest for Freedom, Runaway Slaves and the Plantation South.</u>

It has been conservatively estimated that in the South there were about 50,000 runaways annually. Virtually every medium-sized-to-large plantation complained about run-away problems, as slaves like **Elias Bacot** bravely risked the lack of safe hiding places, recapture and severe punishment to attain their freedom.

It seems evident now that both Elias and his parents had the same plantation address. The significant implication is that Elias was dissatisfied with his state of affairs and was willing to put it all on the line in his quest for freedom, against all odds.

These established linkages are important as they may provide clues to the behavior patterns and modus operandi of the "Iron Horses" later in their lives. **Elias Bacote's** persona was influenced by Cyrus Bacot. On the other hand (one of the other "Iron Horses") **John Kelly Sr.'s** [See Chapter Four] life, personality and persona was impacted by Richard Brockinton as well as Brockinton's adopted son Peter Samuel Bacot at Roseville Plantation. There is at present no evidence to suggest either a positive or negative effect resulting from the actions of either of these planters, however history, sociology and psychology has demonstrated that a positive as well as a negative trickle-down effect from leadership personalities can occur in these type of situations. I believe that some slave owners were more humanitarian than others, that some of them actually exposed selected slaves to the business side of farming, the art of selling, trading and exporting and how to run a large operation like a plantation. It is well documented that many of the enslaved South Carolinians who fought in the Civil War on the Union side as well as the Confederacy, returned to their former plantations that had been overrun by the Union Army where the former planter/landowner had been killed in combat. In numerous cases they single handedly re-organized, managed, and returned those miniempires to productivity and profitability. These men undoubtedly had been privileged to some on the job training.

Elias's story would be remarkable in any era. But from being born into the world of bondage, navigating the treacherous Reconstruction and Jim Crow Eras in that toxic climate of intense repression where many African-Americans and American Indians were essentially psychologically and mentally silenced, while confined to the degrading lowest class status, makes his achievements simply astonishing. **Elias Bacot(e)**, was a young man when president Abraham Lincoln signed the historic Emancipation Proclamation on January 1, 1863. This oft-misrepresented document marked what some historians would deem as the apparent beginning of new hope for him and other enslaved ancestors in South Carolina. At least in their minds, hope existed that their day of release from bondage was impending.

That proclamation was directed only to the states that had seceded from the union and South Carolina was one of them. Slave holding states that remained with the Union were not affected. It also did not apply to the Border States of Kentucky, Missouri, Maryland, and Delaware, Tennessee, as well as portions of Louisiana and Virginia.

Although the proclamation freed only a small percentage of slaves, it did alter the character of the bloody Civil War and enhanced the faith of the enslaved. It gave President Lincoln a legal basis to free the enslaved in areas of the Confederate States of America (CSA) that were still in the rebellion mode. It promised military action by the Union military to free people in bondage. After the signing, every advance of Union troops through the South expanded the domain of freedom, except in cases where captured blacks were returned to their owners. In most cases, however in the Union Army-occupied areas of the CSA the enslaved were deemed free.

Can you imagine or fully comprehend the thought of the possibility of being a newly freed man or woman, being essentially a new person, free to live a life as a bona fide human being? However words on a parchment would not be enough to deliver these courageous souls totally from bondage. What would be required was a victory of the Union Army and total annihilation of the CSA. In actuality, the Proclamation played a major role in that victory by declaring the acceptance of black men and women into the Union Army, enabling nearly 200,000 black soldiers and sailors to join and fight for their freedom.

After the surrender of the CSA, new progressive legislation by the re-united Congress of the United States of America was required to free our ancestors. Actually, the Thirteenth Amendment, approved by Congress and ratified by the States in 1865, is the legal document that really secured the freedom of Bacote and Kelly ancestors in South Carolina, featured in this treatise. Benjamin and Sara Bacot, Elias and Matilda Bacote, and John and Hannah Kelly were finally freed from bondage.

History has shown us that total freedom is rarely freely granted. In the minds of many Americans, both black and white, there has never been a real emancipation of Africans or African-Americans in this country. Of course the yoke was removed from the necks of the enslaved by the Civil War and Acts of Congress. Nevertheless full emancipation was and still is a work in progress: the freedmen and freedwomen endeavored to earn it the old fashion way. What would be required were successive generations who were willing to do their part, through hard work and commitment, through unrest, dedication and faith, through protest, struggles and determination to make America a better place, a place free of the hypocrisy that has gripped this great nation for over 300 years.

Let us try to imagine the atmosphere and conditions under which this ancestral generation had to operate, perhaps then we will be more capable of fully appreciating Elias' acts and accomplishments.

Our history books state very eloquently that a historic group of Africans were brought forcibly as slaves to America, to Jamestown, Virginia in 1619. An often under-publicized fact is that long before the slave trade industry was established, blacks of African origin, both as slaves and free men, played very significant roles in shaping America through their participation in the many Spanish explorations as well as colony building. Actually the first blacks arrived on the shores of South Carolina in 1526 aboard a Spanish slave vessel. Millions followed during the slavery era at which time the federal government determined property taxes and congressional representation by counting slaves as three-fifths of a human being, essentially downplaying and disregarding their invaluable contributions.

It is yet to be determined whether any Kelly or Bacote ancestors were on any of those early passages. The way official records of the slaves were kept at that time, I wonder if we ever will know. Today many of the official poorly maintained records are difficult to read, scattered, damaged, mildewed, burned, torn or tattered as many Americans did not believe this history merited preservation anyway. However, history has shown us, that the truth somehow has a way of resurfacing.

Over two centuries of bondage ensued, and as mentioned earlier, in 1857 the Supreme Court decreed that blacks had "no rights which any white man had to respect" with its infamous **Dred Scott Decision**.

Dred Scott was an African-American slave. He had moved with his owner, an officer in the U.S. Army from the slave holding state of Missouri to the free state of Illinois and later to the free territory of

Wisconsin. He lived as a free man for many years. When the officer was ordered back to his assignment in Missouri he took Scott back with him, back to a slave holding state. However when the officer died in 1846, Scott with assistance of Abolitionist lawyers had to sue for his freedom. He claimed he should be free since he had lived as a free man for many years in Free states.

The case went all the way to the U.S. Supreme Court and Chief Justice Roger B. Taney penned the court's decision, ruling that no slave or descendant of a slave could be a U.S. citizen, or had ever been a U.S. citizen. As a non-citizen the court also ruled Scott had no rights and must remain a slave.

This historic ruling actually reversed earlier gains of many African Americans, as black men in five of the original states had been full voting citizens dating back to the Declaration of Independence in 1776.

Elias's ego had been shaped by his extraordinary experience of bondage and slavery where his strength, will, and moral character had been exhaustively tested. From this it appears that he developed a stringent concept of personal accountability. One can imagine "the strong" and "the proud" feeling compelled to exemplify the survival of their inner strength and moral fiber, their intestinal fortitude and will to excel, against all odds, within the confines of this new society. We have to understand here that true freedom is not some superficial condition; it is a feeling, a responsibility, which has to be realized from deep within oneself. **Elias** like the iconic "Iron Horse" and many other freedmen was practically unstoppable in his drive to achieve his lofty goals and self-development, to extend responsibility and accountability to un-imaginable heights.

The noted scholar, W.E.B. DuBois, in <u>Souls of Black Folk,</u> touched briefly on the dilemma that black men of **Elias's** era and beyond faced, when he so eloquently wrote about the tug of war of the black soul, about simultaneously being an American and a Black man. He wrote "the American Negro wishes neither to Africanize America, nor bleach the black self in a flood of white American identity. He simply wishes to make it possible for a man to be both a Negro and an American without being cursed and spit upon by his fellows, without losing the opportunity of self-development."

It appears that Elias opted to add the (e) to his surname, many years after he became a free man. Most references found in historical documents, after the 1880 census and an 1888 deed, refer to him as **Elias Bacote.**

For many freedmen and women, freedom meant not only opportunity, but also accountability for the manner in which they would express or utilize their new found freedom. With that accountability in his mindset **Elias**, like many of his peers, not only accepted but also embraced the responsibility of passing on to succeeding generations a more ideal society, a better environment to develop and pursue aspirations, dreams and goals, and an opportunity for a "better life."

The story goes in Bacote family lore, that when the decree came forth that slavery was outlawed, declared illegal, and the slaves were declared free, the plantation owner, Cyrus Bacot, gathered Elias and the others in a large circle and directed them to leave and depart along specific coordinates or directions within the plantation and adjoining Bacot land holdings. In other words, the family land holdings were so vast, he said to one "you go this way," and to another "now you go that way, and find an area you prefer to make a home for yourself and your family. Establish your home along this particular coordinate." That is another fascinating oral story that has traversed generations of this family. It was a generous offer indeed. I have no specifics on the amount of land allotted or any attached stipulations.

The Bacots owned a very large portion of Darlington County as we know it today. A historical marker acknowledging the life and holdings of legendary Samuel Bacot I is located on present-day McKiever Road, approximately two miles northeast of the southern intersection of Route 52 and Route 401 bypass in Darlington. I estimate that it is roughly ten miles from the Mechanicsville area where the Bacots were entrenched. It appears that at one time portions of Bacot holdings were bordered on the north by the McGown area, the southwest by Mckiever Road, and the east by the Pee Dee River. The McGown area is about 15 miles from Roseville Plantation, later managed by Peter Samuel Bacot.

It really was extraordinary. These pioneering land-owners in the South had vast plantations that extended in some cases hundreds of miles. It is written that the Hairston Plantation in Virginia extended through North Carolina all the way into Tennessee. Most of these owners were granted this land directly by the Queen, simply for settling in the new territory, a territory they would eventually just take from the Indians. "Commissions of Equity" were established in the new land to dole out thousands of acres of land to settlers for essentially no financial outlay. All they really had to do was make a financial commitment to develop portions of the property. In many cases the recipients subsequently sold vast parcels of the undeveloped land for huge profits to new settlers, instantly becoming wealthy real estate magnates. An example of this is shown in Figure 8, and will be discussed later.

After enactment of the 13th Amendment, freed slaves had to legally fight for any allotted lands for extended periods. In many cases only oral agreements were made between the landowners and the freedmen and these were not upheld by the courts. In many cases black families would be under the illusion that they owned certain acreage only to find out later they did not even own the land upon which their meager home stood. Sometimes even when transactions were legally recorded, extreme difficulty was experienced by freedmen in terms of receiving the proper legal documentation. An example of this occurred in this Kelly/Bacote family and is discussed in detail within "The Kelly Side" chapter of this treatise where heralded ancestor, **Shadrack Kelly**, fought for decades to obtain deeds for properties he legally purchased from his siblings and also property that he inherited from his father.

When the Civil War ended on April 9, 1865, South Carolina and indeed the entire South were in political, social and economic turmoil. The Union implemented a reconstruction plan to create social and economic order, hence the beginning of the Reconstruction Era and the establishment of the Freedmen's Bureau. To recapitulate and refresh your memory, the 13th Amendment of the U.S. Constitution which was also ratified in 1865 outlawed slavery in America and freed Elias and his compatriots. The Civil Rights Act of 1866 made them full U.S. citizens, repealing the infamous Dred Scott Decision of 1857. The 14th Amendment in 1868 granted full citizenship to all blacks born or naturalized in America. The 15th Amendment ratified in 1870 granted Elias the right to vote.

Years before all of this legal activity, **Elias** had become fascinated by an attractive slave named **Matilda White**. There are inferences from family lore that Elias and Matilda resided at the same plantation before marriage. One question often raised was why did Matilda carry the surname of White rather than Bacot if indeed they were both at a Bacot plantation? It is generally accepted that slaves adopted or at least had the option to adopt a variety of surnames.

Family lore contends that Matilda had a Caucasian father and a Black mother. Actually the 1870 U.S. Census classified her as mulatto (Table 1). Beginning in 1850, the U.S. Census listed individuals in three categories only: Black, White and Mulatto. The mulatto classification inferred that she was a first generation child of black and white parents. Among family, it was said in typical Southern vernacular, that "she looked like a white woman."

Matilda's Death Certificate as recorded at the Bureau of Vital Statistics, State Board of Health, State of South Carolina, File #2285, lists her as colored, born February 10, 1849 and died February 27, 1924 of bronchial asthma and the flu. Her mother is listed as Janie (Jane) Perkins and her father as Cyrus Bacot. This riveting discovery brings some clarity to one of this Bacote family most intriguing controversies, a subject often discussed by family for the last century at least. It is widely acknowledged, while not necessarily widely accepted, that slave owners fathering children with their enslaved women was hardly uncommon.

Cyrus Bacot Sr. (1780-1868), a son of Samuel Bacot II, as outlined earlier, married Elizabeth Hollaway (1789-1922). Cyrus Bacot Sr. is the uncle of Peter Samuel Bacot. This union produced Cyrus Bacot II and six other children. The 1860 Census of Darlington County lists Cyrus Bacot as 80 years old, and a planter with a plantation valued at $25,550. Cyrus II is listed as forty-four years old. Cyrus II married Rosa Taylor and they had two children, Dembo Bacot (b. 1842) and Jessie C. Bacot (1856-1953).

Since there were two Cyrus Bacots living in the Darlington District at the time of Matilda's birth it is difficult to ascertain with 100 percent certainty which one is the actual father of Matilda. However, if the 1860 Census is correct, when Matilda was born in 1849, Cyrus Sr. would have been sixty-nine years old and Cyrus II would have been thirty-three. Although it is not inconceivable that a sixty-nine year old could father a child, their ages alone would make Cyrus Bacot II the more probable candidate for siring Matilda. Cyrus Bacot's original plantation was located in the northern sector of the Darlington District and included the McGown area.

It has always been regarded as factual, according to family lore, that Matilda "was not raised by her blood mother; that her Caucasian father personally carried her as a baby to another plantation to be raised." Since her enslaved surname was White, it has been argued that Cyrus had her transferred to the Roseville Plantation to serve as the personal slave of Anna Jane White, the wife of his cousin Peter Samuel Bacot. Hence she adopted the surname of White and was raised by a black woman for a number of years there at Roseville Plantation.

A careful examination of the 1857 *Schedule of Negro Slaves and other Chattels of Roseville Plantation to be Partitioned and Divided,* presented in Chapter Four as [Table 3] reveals a slave named Matilda. Could it be just fortuitous that there was a Matilda on the roster at Roseville in 1857, or does family lore loom true again?

We can easily perceive Cyrus Sr. or Cyrus II bringing Baby Matilda, according to family lore, to Roseville Plantation, which was essentially being run by their relative. Cyrus could have felt some heat from his spouse and needed to have his illegitimate child grow up at some other location, for a variety of reasons one can conjure. Some kind of arrangement could have easily been consummated by the Bacot family. It is unclear when she was reconnected with her mother at Cyrus' plantation.

Now, as is the case with the "Iron Horse" ancestor Elias Bacote, we have insight into the names of Matilda's father and mother. The death certificate above, from The South Carolina Genealogical Society Inc., Old Darlington Chapter, provided by historian Scott Wilds, documents that Matilda was actually the daughter of the planter Cyrus Bacot, or his son Cyrus Bacot II, and the slave, Janie (Jane) Perkins.

Because of the nature of society at that time with the documented abuse of female slaves by planters, plantation owners, overseers etc., some may ponder the effect that this tryst and the subsequent birth of Matilda had on subsequent Bacote generations. According to family lore, Matilda had a very good relationship with her father and the white side of her family after slavery ended. The positive nature of that bond suggests that the attraction of Cyrus and Jane was not borne out of abuse of will and power. The fact that Matilda harbored no ill-will or disdain suggests that her parents had a respectable alliance, that Cyrus was accountable and did not disavow the product of their actions.

I have not detected any negative fallout on the Bacote family from that event. The offspring of Elias and Matilda were all strong-willed individuals, devoid of race related animosity. Contemporary Bacotes are secure in their skin and also do not appear to harbor resentment.

I am not attempting to condone what transpired in 1849 in the Back Swamp of South Carolina. However in retrospect, Cyrus and Jane were a little ahead of the times. At that time they represented a distinct minority, today inter-racial marriages and alliances represent a norm in our society, in the Bacote family at-large and the author's immediate family as well.

The identification of Matilda's father is a milestone which, with the knowledge we have of Bacot genealogy, allows us to trace one segment of this Bacote family genealogy in America back to the 1600s and ultimately back to France, as Pierre Bacot was born in France around 1647.

After slavery was abolished, the Bacots and other plantation owners had to address the loss of the cheap labor force they were accustomed to, the force they had utilized to generate tremendous return on the dollar from their vast acreage of land. Although Elias and Matilda had eagerly awaited and anticipated their liberation, their apparent freedom was wrought with numerous frightening uncertainties. They, like hundreds of thousands of other freed men and women, were homeless with few possessions, limited skills, and no cash as well as not many alternatives to generate income. This was a crucial situation and some critical decisions had to be made quickly.

As outlined earlier, the Freedmen's Bureau, was established in the War Department in 1865, to supervise affairs related to freedmen/women and refugees including relief and educational activities, issuing of rations, clothing and medicine. It was also instrumental in the implementation of labor contracts between planters and freed individuals. Legal contracts were constructed, whereas for a share of the harvest, land was provided for the former enslaved to live on and farm. This was perceived as a mutually beneficial compromise, but in some cases was corrupt to the core and led to bad blood and a new form of bondage: economic slavery.

Many former slaves were essentially forced to go back to work on their former plantations for a variety of reasons, and it is not surprising that even with governmental support only a small portion of them actually had legal labor contracts. Some worked as paid laborers and for farming the land were paid anywhere from $9 to $15 per month.

Although there was some corruption in the operation of some branches of the Bureau, I along with many historians believe it served a very useful purpose and benefitted many freedmen including my own ancestors in the Back Swamp.

We have evidence that Elias and Matilda et.al. entered into such an official agreement implemented by the Darlington branch. Records of the Freedmen Bureau of Refugees, Freemen and Abandons, South Carolina 1865-1872 [RG 105] refer to a Cyrus Bacot Labor Contract, dated September 23, 1865. This is a legal agreement between the Cyrus Bacot Plantation and Elias, two of Elias' brothers, Lot and Peter, Matilda and Matilda's mother, Jane, to work on his plantation for the remainder of the 1865 calendar year after the Civil War ended.

Excerpts from the Articles of Agreement are shown below;

"This agreement entered into between C. Bacot of this one part, and the Freedmen and Women of his plantation, that the latter agree for the remainder of the present year to reside upon and devote their labor to the cultivation of the plantation of the former ...etc...

In consideration of the forgoing services duly performed the said C. Bacot agrees,

after deducting seventy five bushels of corn for each work animal exclusively used in cultivating crops for the year, Cyrus Bacote agreed to turn over half of the remaining yields of corn, rice, peas, potatoes, and wheat harvested during the year to the said individuals. He further agreed to furnish the usual rations until the contract was performed.

This agreement to continue till the first day of January, 1866. Witness our hand at the plantation of C. Bacot this twenty third day of September, 1865."

It is signed by Cyrus Bacot and fifty freedmen and women, including the ancestors cited above, with their (X) mark.

Essentially the planter, Cyrus Bacot with this contract, was providing housing, land, rations, and work animals required for the project.

The clause in the contract, "This agreement entered into by C. Bacot of this one part, and the Freedmen and Women of his plantation, that the latter agree for the remainder of the present year to reside upon and devote their labor," is very revealing. It suggests that the newly freed were residents of "his" plantation earlier in the year. We are talking here about the fall of the year 1865, after the War ended, when they were free individuals.

This contract offers strong support for the earlier assertion that the bondage home of Elias Bacot was the Cyrus Bacot Plantation. His brothers Lot and Peter, as well as Matilda and Matilda's mother Jane apparently had been housed at the Cyrus Bacot Plantation when the War ended also.

The contract also provides the rationale for the earlier assertion establishing the Cyrus Bacot Plantation as the bondage residence of Benjamin and Sara Bacot. It is entirely reasonable to assume that since three of their sons had been housed at Cyrus Bacot plantation, that they spent their bondage years there also unless we invoke the purchase of their three sons by Cyrus from another Bacot planter.

Shortly after the Civil War officially ended and during the rocky Reconstruction Era several Southern states passed "Black Codes," which generally restricted the rights of freedmen to own property, controlled where they were allowed to live, established curfews, and levied taxes on free blacks who attempted to pursue non-agricultural careers, in an attempt to lock them into a lifetime of employment as agricultural laborers or domestics in the primarily agronomic society.

As outlined earlier, in 1866, the Civil Rights Act returned to **Elias** and **Matilda** and other freed slaves the rights and privileges of full citizenship and some "Black Codes" were rendered unlawful. Radical Republicans fought for ratification of the noted 13th, 14th, and 15th Amendments. The passage of the 15th Amendment, which gave **Elias** and his peers the right to vote, resulted in numerous black politicians being immediately elected into office in the South. As was the case in most of the labor intensive Southern States, blacks outnumbered whites by a large margin in South Carolina. As early as 1720, the slave population in Darlington was double that of whites primarily because the plantations were very large, requiring large labor forces. Actually, until 1922 African-Americans comprised the largest racial group in the entire state of South Carolina.

In 1868, Elias and his peers utilized their political clout to elect a black majority to the South Carolina Legislature. Francis L. Cardoza, a black politician, was elected Secretary of State in South Carolina and in 1870 Joseph Rainey was elected to the United States House of Representatives, making him the first black member of this branch of the government. During this era there were eight black men from South Carolina in Congress, more than any other state in the Union.

In addition, Republican governors used their influence to appoint blacks to many state and federally appointed offices and other power bearing positions. A black man from Charleston was appointed Darlington County Sheriff. Blacks also held important administrative positions such as voter registrar, county clerk, and auditor during this period.

Elias and Matilda were married in January, 1870. An entry in the 1870 United States Federal Census Record, taken from Ancestry. com, dated 2nd day of August, 1870, references the life of Elias Bacote and his young family. They are listed as inhabitants of Whittemore Township in Darlington County. Elias is listed as age 22 and a farm laborer. Matilda is recorded as age 20 and a stay-home mother. The listing includes one child, Phillip, age 8 months.

This is very interesting because in 1870 Cyrus Bacot II's residence is also listed as Whittemore Township, South Carolina. [See Figure 6] It appears that Matilda sought to maintain a presence close to her father. She had a good relationship with Cyrus and it is very likely that this father-daughter relationship resulted in their settling in that neck of the woods. According to a survey on file at the Darlington County Historical Commission an article in the May 9, 1878 issue of the *Darlington News* stated "in 1878 the County Commissioners voted to change the names of the Reconstruction Townships to more familiar names," as shown in Figure 5. Among the changes, Whittemore Township was changed to Darlington Township.

A small tract of land had been carved out of Cyrus Bacot land holdings for **Elias** and **Matilda** in the area which later became known as McGown. McGown was the central location for cotton and corn mills in the Darlington area when cotton was king, and is situated between presently positioned Darlington and Society Hill on Route 52. The McGown mill pond with its array of lily pads is still clearly visible today on Route 52 just before the Route 401/52 intersection, north of Darlington. **Elias** and **Matilda's** original tract of land is still under the ownership of a Bacote descendent.

It became very clear during the investigation of the life of Elias that he was not a freed man that was just sitting around running out the clock. He was young, active, energetic, full of ideas, seeking to exercise his rights and avail himself to all the perks of full citizenship.

However there was tremendous resistance and opposition from Southern whites toward the progress of the freedmen during this period. They initiated an array of illegal tactics to discourage them. It eventually reached the point where the 15th Amendment, which prohibited States from denying citizens the right to vote based on race, color or former status as a slave, had to be enacted.

The Federal Government would pass laws and the Southern States would simply disregard them or find ways to circumvent them. Arguably one of the most favorable proceedings of the rocky Reconstruction Era occurred after the controversial election of President Rutherford B. Hayes to the nation's highest office in 1876. His infamous **Compromise of 1877** allowed for the withdrawal of Federal troops from the South in April 1877, removing vital protection for the rights of the freedmen, essentially forcing them to become more proactive.

It is very interesting to note that Elias was involved at the political level during the turmoil of the Reconstruction Era. I do not desire to misrepresent his role in the Civil Rights Movement, but his actions suggest he was an activist of sorts. The congressional elections of 1876 and 1880, as well as the 1876 presidential election were highly contested. The simmering bad blood between the white "red shirt" population and the powerful coalition of Republicans in Darlington exploded into a near-war as the underdogs made last-ditch efforts to steal the elections by preventing some Republicans from voting. They sought to utilize scare tactics in their effort to suppress the black vote. Having exhausted their illegal tactics they resorted to the strong arm approach of physically barricading the steps to the polls with groups of "red shirts." Elias, who was a Republican, attempted to vote in the 1880 congressional election and was denied access to the polls. He was not allowed to complete the process and exercised his right as a citizen and protested. As a result he was summoned to testify about his experience at a congressional hearing in 1881.

He accepted the invitation, when many of his peers were awe-struck of such exposure. Many probably beseeched him not to appear, asking "why do you wish to stick your neck out by testifying"? He was opening himself and his family up to reprisals by the Ku Klux Klan, "red shirts," disgruntled Democrats and others who sought to impose their immoral will. What the naysayers did not realize was that this man was fearless. It appears that, in Elias' viewpoint, it was about a sense of responsibility, responsibility of the Federal Government to enforce the Constitution and insure the rights of all citizens, as well as the responsibility of individual citizens to communicate, publicize and denounce injustices at the highest possible levels, otherwise why would he adopt such a bold posture.

He was summoned to appear at the Darlington County Courthouse between the 18th and 26th day of February, A.D. 1881, to testify and make affidavit in a case of contested election for member of Congress from the First Congressional District of South Carolina in which Samuel Lee was the contestant and John S. Richardson, contestee. Elias was sworn in and the following questions, answers and statements were taken directly from records of the proceedings:

Q. How old are you? A. Thirty years old.

Q. Where do you reside? A. Darlington County.

Q. How long have you lived in this County? A. Thirty Years.

Q. What poll did you attend on the day of the last general election? A. At Darlington.

Q. Did you vote there? A. No sir.

Q. Why not? A. The Democrats prevented me.

Q. How? A. By crowding the step

Q. Did the crowd of Democrats A. It did.
on the Court House steps
prevent you from reaching the
ballot-box and casting your
ballot?

Q. What ticket you desired? A. The Republican ticket.

For whom you desired and A. Samuel Lee.
intended to vote?

Q. Did you vote anywhere on A. I did not.
the day of the last general
election?

He was then crossed examined by Geo. W. Brown, Esq.:

Q. What time of day did you A. About half after eleven.
leave the Darlington poll?

Q. Did you hear the order of Jack A. I did.
Smith for all Republicans to
go home?

Q. What time was that order A. Between ten and eleven.
given?

Q. Are you a Republican? A. I am.

Sworn to and subscribed before me this 19th day of February, A.D. 1881. Signed E. H. Deas (Notary Public, South Carolina)

As stated in the Preface, one of the goals of this thesis is to gain some insight into the mindset of the iconic ancestors featured herein. What was it about their behavior, and their actions that made their unheralded contributions so significant to American history?

The battle for the right to vote has been an ongoing process for nearly as long as the black man has been in America. Mr. Array Stevens, another participant at the hearing, testified that "the steps were crowded from the bottom to the top from 8am to 3pm and every time he would seek to enter the Democrats would push him back." The voting process today still requires much of our attention and energy. The steps of many polls are still blocked, but this blockage takes place in more sophisticated forms. One only has to re-examine the 2008 and 2012 presidential elections for corroboration of that assertion. As recently as 2013 the U.S. Supreme court ruled that nine states are free to determine their election laws without federal approval. This ruling has evoked major concerns that some states might begin to implement discriminatory voting laws anew, placing obstacles in certain citizens' paths to the polls.

This appearance of Elias and Array before the Congressional Committee, was uncovered by historian Scott Wilds during his survey of the proceedings of the hearings, and graciously brought to the author's attention. The Committee was established to investigate cases of voter intimidation and other voter improprieties and Elias' appearance had significant implications. It demonstrated a strong commitment on his part, as a young man, to fight for human rights and civil rights, i.e. one's right to vote. It revealed three of his very noteworthy traits; his social consciousness, fearlessness and rebellious disposition.

We must not forget that Elias was a rebel of sorts. As a teen/preteen he had put his life on the line demonstrating his disdain for bondage. As outlined earlier, he was tagged a runaway. He could not speak for all blacks or all Republicans, but he realized the coalition had huge stakes invested in America, stakes of too great a magnitude, to sit idly by and observe such shenanigans take precedent.

As such the Bacote family is very enlightened and uplifted by the fact that this man, a legend in the family, is on the roster with thousands of Americans, both black and white, who waged and endured numerous, frontline battles during their individual eras, in their own individual manners, so that all citizens can exercise the precious right to vote, a right that is putatively guaranteed by the United States Constitution. It is the sum total of the large and small individual battles and confrontations of this nature that will eventually lead to ultimate enforcement of this right. This endeavor is a testament to Elias' leadership ability and insight. Obviously he believed and had faith that his individual battle would not be in vain, that ultimately it would help future generations of Americans, over a century removed, elect blacks to leadership positions in the country. Could it be that Elias was that perceptive? Don't forget he had witnessed as a young man in South Carolina the power of the black vote. His legacy was fulfilled on January 20, 2009, when Barack Obama assumed the prestigious office of President of the United States of America.

In addition, one compelling point we must not understate or forget is during that period in American history freedmen like Elias put their family's safety, their own life, and in many cases their ability to earn an honest living in jeopardy when they stood tall and defiant to defend their constitutional right to participate in the electoral process. Even though he did not lose his life like Medgar Evers, Andrew Goodman, John Chaney or Viola Liuzzo, to name a few, he was indeed on the frontline for the cause, never expecting anything in return for his efforts.

This was all occurring while **Elias** and **Matilda** were starting their young family. As mentioned earlier, the 1870 Census lists a son Phillip, age 8 months, as their first offspring. Phillip died as a youngster and is thought to be entombed at the African-American cemetery on Cyrus Bacot plantation lands. It is believed that other Bacote ancestors are also entombed in this historic boneyard located off of Charleston Road in Mechanicsville, south of Route 34. In 1877, another son, Elihu, spelled Elihue in an old Bacote family bible, was a mere five years old.

During a period in history when the former slave and his peers were already seriously challenged, they were also subjected to the emergence of Jim Crow and the Ku Klux Klan with its harassment tactics. **Elias** and **Matilda** and their counterparts in the South were essentially stripped of many of the basic social and political rights they had fought hard for. Although they were reduced to second class citizens again, change had already begun and it was difficult to contain.

It's no wonder that the blues and gospel music developed and prospered in our communities primarily throughout the South. These genres have always been staples in the South as they were the ritual of life on a day by day basis. Blacks sang blues songs expressing a desire for something better, songs to ease the pain of torturous labor, songs of escape to a less grueling existence, songs of faith and hope. They were constantly dealing with life-altering situations. There was no relief, no organizations to turn to, and no governmental support. Young brothers and sisters of today who don't understand and appreciate the blues would benefit by going "retro" and living through those times that **Elias** and **Matilda** endured, when the primary foe was not ourselves, but rather a segment of society that was determined to undermine and wreak havoc on one's existence in South Carolina and indeed throughout many communities in this country.

As stated earlier, after the Civil War, **Elias** and his peers with the assistance of the Federal Government experienced early political success with the election of many black political figures during Reconstruction. This was short-lived as they were subsequently systematically barred from voting by illegal organized tactics, such as blocking the polls, poll taxes, harassment, literacy tests and grandfather clauses as they were left stranded by the Federal Government to fend for themselves. They were essentially silenced, their voices muted and disrespected for many decades. This era is a prime example of the ultimate utilization of politics in controlling the overall scheme of life in America.

In retrospect, it is very clear that the political landscape and the overall culture of the South were counter-productive and essentially served as a deterrent to progress for Elias' generation as well as his children's generation. And the status quo and culture of the South remained relatively constant and consistent until 1954's landmark U.S. Supreme Court decision of *Brown v. Board of Education of Topeka Kansas.* This revolutionary case, argued and won by legendary attorney Thurgood Marshall, resulted in the desegregation of public schools.

We are cognizant enough to realize that every generation has its own set of personal challenges, and that the true measure of their grit is how they handle these challenges, adversity and difficult situations.

Majestically and courageously **Elias** and **Matilda** weathered many storms. It appears that they had been socialized appropriately to handle the rigors of a self-sufficient, family existence. Farming and agriculture was the way of life and cotton was king in Darlington. Farming was the premier vocation.

During Reconstruction blacks held an array of positions in the South Carolina economy. Many eked out decent incomes as tradesmen, bakers, artisans, butchers, tailors and barbers. However the masses of the formerly enslaved could be placed essentially into two categories: the share-croppers and the independent small farmers. As stated earlier, an overwhelmingly large amount of them remained at the plantations, where they originally toiled as an unpaid labor force, working now as paid day laborers. Many were duped into share cropping and many legally opted for it because farming was what they had plenty of experience in, and what they had the most knowledge of.

With all due respect to the members of this family who lived portions or all of their lives as share croppers, I have the highest regard for their decisions and the lives they carved out. Share cropping was indeed a hardworking, honest and proud way for a family to eke out a living as a unit.

Share cropping was a system whereby subsistence and housing would be provided by the landowner or planter, in exchange for labor in the fields by the entire family and a share in the profits if indeed there were any. Of course the landowner kept the records of expenses and revenues and any sharecropper profits were marginal even under the more honorable agreements. The system was essentially just a step away from slavery, but to some newly freed men it seemed like a viable option as many were brainwashed or manipulated to believe they were incapable of surviving beyond the plantation.

Prior to the Civil War, the plantations had a monopoly on farming in the South, with the slave owners at the helm. They possessed money generating machines, like the ATMs of today, based primarily on their free labor force. But now a new day had emerged. Some of that free labor force was now their competition for a lucrative cotton, corn and tobacco market share. They wasted no time putting machinery into place to minimize the impact of this competition.

The business of farming requires large capital outlays on the front end. Items like seed, fertilizer, soil preparation and planting must be paid for in the spring. In addition, harvesting expenses must be expended before any revenue is attained from the sale of crops. Armed with extensive knowledge regarding this aspect of the process, the powerful land owners decided the most efficient approach was to limit the financial resources of their competition; limit their ability to obtain bank loans, subsidies and agricultural technology. Legislation was enacted at the federal and state levels to increase barriers and minimize the impact of the small independent African-American farmers, making it more difficult for them to succeed.

It is said that Elias was a confident, industrious leader and a wonderful provider for his family, the first post-slavery family of this noble clan. Fate had cast him at the head of the family at a very critical juncture in its development. He believed that the future of the newly freed was to a large extent dependent upon actions they themselves undertook, and embraced the idea of uplifting himself and his family by their bootstraps through hard work, integrity and dedication.

In the early 1950s, Isaiah Berlin, a noted British philosopher, discussed two contrasting forms of leadership and leaders that exist in our society: foxes and hedgehogs. They are essentially characterized as follows. The fox appears to know many things and his actions are all over the place, pursuing many small fixes, often unrelated and sometimes even contradictory; a middle of the road safe approach. On the other hand, the hedgehog knows one big thing, has a bold alternate plan, and offers an unwavering, unchanging inner vision to that end.

Elias Bacote was a hedgehog. He was not focused on easing the pain or the unfortunate circumstances of his existence. This was a time that required great vision, a cool head, plus a willingness and aptitude to take risks. He possessed an alternate vision, a passionate inner vision, a bold approach to self-realization, fulfillment, and economic security. While many of his peers were merely seeking to survive, Elias was one step ahead, very conscious of not pigeon-holing himself. He considered himself a universal man, meaning all men are created equal, free to pursue possibilities and to think "out of the box," so to speak. He embarked on paths considered remote to many of the formerly enslaved.

He opted to work for himself, a daring entrepreneurial move indeed during that era. Entrepreneurs don't follow the trends, they create the trends. Entrepreneurs don't seek refuge, they take risks and place their skills and strengths on the line. There were setbacks that were difficult to fathom, but they did not destroy the will of this warrior as he steadfastly proceeded with his business model.

If he and Matilda could successfully steer the family through the turbulent times and along a productive path, it would pay financial as well as psychological dividends for generations to come. It was of paramount importance for this first post-slavery family to create a good modus operandi, a foundation laced with pride, and a strong ethos; their teachings would indeed be passed along for centuries.

It is very important to understand that many of the formerly enslaved had just emerged from a condition where they were not allowed to function as a genuine family unit. The challenge was no longer dealing with the ever perplexing survival at the plantation, but preparing themselves and their prodigy for immersion into the complex county, state and countrywide issues of their times. Elias and Matilda were in unchartered waters. There was no grace period, training period or crash courses available. The way out of their dilemma would require rather radical economic and behavioral policies, the likes of which were not commonplace among newly freedmen in South Carolina.

Many historians and sociologists suggest that during the era of bondage, generally there were limited family or relationship values developed among the enslaved, because of the long arduous working hours and, in many cases, the demands or stringent rules of the owners as well as the constraints of their condition. Hence once freed, there were few innate guidelines for establishing family life and relationships between man and wife, as well as parents and children. This may have been the case in some family situations. However, many former slave families, including Elias and Matilda, appeared to handle the situation impressively and developed strong family ties amongst their offspring setting the tone for the development of a rich Bacote tradition.

It seems that they fully understood the severity of the task they were undertaking and realized they had to be strong on many fronts. Conversations with some elder family members reveal a common thread among all of Elias' offspring. It is apparent that he effectively drilled into all his children the need to not only advance themselves and their family economically but also emotionally, socially and most importantly, spiritually. Much of that well rounded thread still exists in Bacote descendants today.

Elias and Matilda were firmly entrenched in the Baptist Church. With the Supreme Being as their leader they created the spiritual dynamic that has become a credo for succeeding generations. With a keen long-term vision and a no-nonsense ethic shaped in the annals of time, they sculpted the components of a strong foundation, a foundation primed to prosper and endure. History has shown us that a solid foundation and preparation are prerequisites for a productive existence. If you build a house on a weak, fragmented foundation it eventually will crumble; it will not withstand the rigors of time. A classic example is what happened in Haiti during the earthquake of 2010. Thousands of lives were lost because construction requirements were based on short-term goals.

History has also demonstrated that this former runaway slave was a wise man. Rather than walk around depressed, bitter and down-trodden with a chip on his shoulder, he apparently realized that anger is not always productive, and, as a matter of fact, may distract attention and energy away from the problem, delaying the arrival at a solution. If he had allowed himself or his offspring to be controlled or overwhelmed by bitterness and anger of the situation fate had thrust upon him, he would not have been capable of forming the alliances or developing the contacts required to make his dreams a reality.

Elias methodically used his wit and guile to forge relationships that made his life more productive. According to family lore he was a no-nonsense type of man who did not waste his time and energy on relationships that were not positive or productive. He was a man with a plan who stood tall for what he believed. He did not compromise his beliefs and demanded respect across all racial lines. It's an art that all of his offspring learned quite well from this great man as they carefully observed how he operated. There is an art to being strong willed, yet non-confrontational, brave and self-driven, yet not arrogant.

It is very interesting when one revisits the apparent modus operandi of his offspring, not one of them were "angry black" women or men; not even one. In addition, none of them exhibited malice or deceit, hypocrisy or envy, greed or arrogance, all very detrimental traits; not even one. They all possessed a calmness that served to disarm the antagonist while fostering respect and good will from all humanity. They acquired that critical skill from their father.

In the early 1870s, the railroad industry, a very critical early American business, was growing at a remarkable rate. This industry was very important in linking Charles Town and other port cities to the agricultural regions of South Carolina for lucrative import and export opportunities. It served as the primary transportation venue for cotton, coal, corn, freight, etc., and also passenger transportation. This mode was much more reliable than the use of canals and rivers, including the Pee Dee River, which was only available for navigation about six months out of the year because of decreased water levels.

The historic Wilmington & Manchester Line passed ten miles below the Darlington Courthouse, from east to west. [See Figure 4 and Figure 7] It is interesting that this line also passed through the lands of Cyrus Bacot. A second line, the Cheraw and Darlington Railroad which originated in Cheraw and was completed in 1853, was erected to connect with that line. Nearby Florence served as a railroad junction and transfer point for the Northwestern, Cheraw and Darlington Railroads as well as the 162 mile long Wilmington (NC) & Manchester (SC) Railroad. Later another line connecting Hartsville and Darlington was also constructed during the 1880s. This matrix of lines formed a route by which tonnage of products and passengers from central North Carolina, Virginia, West Virginia, and northeastern South Carolina could be transported to the Port of Charles Town and other important commercial centers in the region.

At this important juncture in South Carolina history a reliable transportation system was essential for agricultural and industrial progress in Darlington. Understanding the significance and importance of the railroad industry, Elias recognized a niche, a business opportunity. He identified an opportunity to diversify from total reliance on the traditional South Carolina markets of cotton and tobacco, the two trusted and profitable agricultural sectors of its economy. After a few years farming the McGown tract, with a small bankroll, he purchased a strong mule, a reinforced heavy wagon, heavy duty saws and axes and chose rail splitting and the production of railroad crossties as his primary vocation. He was still a serious farmer, but added railroad entrepreneur to his resume.

He understood the opportunities that the innovative railroad industry offered and utilized his skill and knowledge to embark on a path to economic security.

Elias hewed and sold 7x9 inch x 8½ feet long crossties to the railroad industry, earning twenty-five cents per cross tier. Farming was essentially a spring-fall operation, whereas the production of the crossties represented a year round initiative. During the winter months, rather than he and his crew, including his sons once they were old enough to work with him, sitting around the fireplace getting obese, they were out generating revenue to solidify his business undertaking. There were no chain or power saws available during that time to cut those bountiful red or white Darlington oaks, a.k.a. hardwood specimens; just exceptional arm and leg power. It was demanding, labor intensive work but paid good money at that time.

Life was promising for this family during the early years of their marriage. The farm was producing good crops and the crosstie business was flourishing. Matilda was busy as a housewife and mother giving birth to the large family they desired.

A portion of the 1880 Darlington County Census Report referencing this family is shown in Table 1. Elias was recorded as thirty years old and Matilda as twenty-five. I have not been privy to any birth certificates of Elias', but if the 1880 census taker recorded his age accurately he was born in 1850. The report also shows Matilda and Elias with four children in 1880: Elihu age 8, Boyd age 6, Sarah #1 age 3 and an unnamed daughter age 8 1/2, possibly Phyllis. Note that Elihu was the oldest male sibling and Matilda, Elihu, Sarah, and possibly Phyllis were classified as mulatto, a person clearly of mixed heritage.

Being classified mulatto during that era brought along with it a mixed bag of circumstances. The North American mulatto was the result of a custom which was generally ignored by society: the by-product of forbidden passion and an absolute abuse of power, in most cases. It was the product of the continental colonist's refusal to acknowledge that miscegenation was occurring on a broad scale. The mulatto classification was part of the determination of the establishment to disempower the fruit of these liaisons and regulate all non-white citizens.

The broader continental society tended to compartmentalize mulattos rather than accept them as part European, as was the custom in the West Indies. They were perpetuating the myth of the "pure race" philosophy.

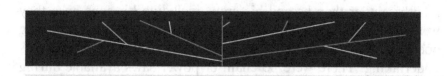

1880 Census - Darlington

No.	Name		Race	Sex	Age	Title	M	Occupation	BP	F	M
		ELIAS	B	M	10	SON	S	FARM LABORER	SC	SC	SC
		JOHNNIE	B	M	9	SON	S		SC	SC	SC
		JAMES	B	M	7	SON	S		SC	SC	SC
		LAYTON	B	M	5	SON	S		SC	SC	SC
		MARIA	B	F	3	DAU	S		SC	SC	SC
		BANNY	B	F	1	DAU	S		SC	SC	SC
269	McCOWN	JOHN M	W	M	23	HEAD	S	FARMER	SC	SC	SC
		BOWEN	W	M	17	BROTHER	S	ATTEND SCHOOL	SC	SC	SC
	PACKER	JOHN	W	M	36	BROTHER	S	MILLER	SC	NC	NC
270	BOSEMAN	SANDY	M	M	24	HEAD	M	FARM LABORER	SC	SC	SC
		ROWENA	M	F	21	WIFE	M	SERVANT	SC	SC	SC
271	GARDNER	THOMAS	B	M	23	HEAD	M	FARM LABORER	SC	SC	SC
		DIANA	B	F	20	WIFE	M	FARM LABORER	SC	SC	SC
		ELLEN	B	F	1	DAU	S		SC	SC	SC
	KING	EVANS	B	M	4	STEPSON	S		SC	SC	SC
272	BACOT	ELIAS	B	M	30	HEAD	M	FARMER	SC	SC	SC
		MATILDA	M	F	25	WIFE	M	FARM LABORER	SC	SC	SC
		ELIHU	M	M	8	SON	S		SC	SC	SC
		BOYD	B	M	6	SON	S		SC	SC	SC
		SARAH	M	F	3	DAU	S		SC	SC	SC
		UNNAMED	M	F	8-1/2	DAU	S		SC	SC	SC
273	HEARON	SAM	B	M	35	HEAD	M	FARMER	SC	SC	SC
		HANNAH	M	F	29	WIFE	M	FARM LABORER	SC	SC	SC
		PRESTON	M	M	13	SON	S		SC	SC	SC
	WILLIAMS	JENNIE	B	F	20	SIS-IN-LAW	M	FARM LABORER	SC	SC	SC
	RHODES	LYDIA	B	F	60	M-I-LAW	W		SC	SC	SC
274	COOK	EZIKIEL	W	M	65	HEAD	M	FARMER	SC	SC	SC
		MARTHA	W	F	55	WIFE	M	KEEPING HOUSE	SC	SC	SC
		JACOB	W	M	16	SON	S	FARM LABORER	SC	SC	SC
		JUDSON	W	M	12	SON	S	FARM LABORER	SC	SC	SC
275	REDDICK	JOHN J	W	M	42	HEAD	M	FARMER	SC	SC	SC
		SARAH	W	F	38	WIFE	M	KEEPING HOUSE	NC	NC	NC

KEYS
Race key: B=Black W=White M=Mixed
Sex key: M=Male F=Female

Table 1. 1880 Census Darlington

However, while the law rarely differentiated between a black person and a mulatto, there is evidence that the broader society often did. Some sources indicate that during slavery mulattos were preferred over blacks as house servants or concubines. It also seems clear that mulatto slaves were more likely to be taught a craft or skill or receive a formal education versus being relegated to brutal field work. Records also show a remarkably high proportion of mulattos among the list of emancipated slaves.

History reveals that the black community also held mulatto status in relatively high esteem after slavery. Some mulattos migrated north, and posed as Caucasians (passed for white) in order to receive a legitimate opportunity at an equitable existence, a level playing field, while many remained in the South. In some cases, psychologists report symptoms of extreme inner turmoil and duress as mulattos also received some denunciation from both communities. In some instances mulattos felt superior to their darker skinned contemporaries, because they often received preferential treatment from whites. Psychological damage is known to have occurred in many cases.

A major blow to the continuity of Elias' family was encountered when a catastrophic diphtheria epidemic descended upon America wreaking havoc not only in South Carolina but throughout the nation.

It appears that every generation, more or less, has their bout with viral or bacterial diseases of one form or another. From the black plague, to the diphtheria epidemic, to polio, to tuberculosis, to avian "bird" flu, to SARS and the dreaded AIDS and Ebola viruses of today, with every generation there is a relentless effort to find a cause, a vaccine and ultimately a cure for their scourge. New bacteria and viruses are constantly evolving via events such as mutations, genetic shifts and horizontal gene transfers. It is a phenomenon of nature.

Diphtheria is a highly contagious illness caused by the corynebacterium which attacks the upper respiratory system or the skin. In addition, the bacteria release a toxin that circulates within the body causing inflammation of the heart and paralysis in the throat, lungs, eyes, and breathing muscles.

From 1876 to 1905 this disease occurred either sporadically or in widespread proportions in this country, reaching epidemic status in 1880. Technology did not exist in 1876 to treat or save children who were infected. One's only hope was directly related to the strength of their immune system. Once infected the victims went to the Golden Shore in four to seven days. By the mid-1880s it was almost non-existent with later cases appearing very infrequently and rarely spread to epidemic proportions.

Family lore has it that Matilda and Elias produced a total of nineteen children during their lifetime and that nine of them died during this tragic epidemic. However, family records only indicate that offspring Phyllis, Ida, and Raney died in 1882, at the ages of 9, 7, and 5, respectively, and Sarah in 1883 at the age of 5, as a result of the epidemic. Their first son Phillip died between 1870 and 1880 of unknown causes.

Elias and Matilda dealt with a tremendous amount of adversity during their lifetime. Losing a child is tragic under any circumstances. When the loss is due to something like a national tragedy, never ending referrals to the tragedy creates additional, unbearable, long-term anguish on an ongoing basis. The loss of their cherished children, one after another, in a situation where there was absolutely nothing they could do, had to be very devastating. It is life-altering circumstances like this which brings families to the table, at least once during their lifetime, as one, in quest of help, strength and peace. How they endured those fitful years is a tribute to their faith, inner strength and resiliency.

This scenario prompted me to ponder; is it possible that having experienced and endured the era of bondage, their brains were pre-conditioned to tolerate such sudden, unexpected tragedies, fostering the development of better skills for coping with adversity?

Their plan moving forward was bold and ambitious. Family lore has it that they counter-acted immediately, setting out to replace all of the deceased by giving birth to an entirely new group of offspring. Not surprisingly, this lore is supported by the fact that census and birth records, shown on the following page, indicate that Matilda gave birth to not one, but two children in 1883, exactly one year after the epidemic claimed the lives of three of her children. It is also espoused by family lore that they gave some of the later offspring the same names as the ones that perished. To a degree, that served to keep them emotionally connected to the lost ones. The beloved Sarah Bacote #2, a family icon in her own right, appears to be an example of that. The first Sarah died in 1883 and Mayo High School records indicate a second Sarah Bacote was in the 2nd grade in 1891. That would have made her seven years old, hence born in 1884, one year after the death of her deceased namesake. I have not been able to account for all nineteen offspring; four deaths of their young children remain to be documented if indeed family lore is correct in that regard.

This tragedy was a very difficult obstacle for Elias and Matilda to deal with. Although they responded bravely and courageously, it is said they never fully recovered from the shock of losing their young children.

The 1880 Census Report is very interesting in that it shows that as late as 1880 Elias was still spelling his last name as Bacot without an (e) at the end. The precise date that he made the change is unknown, although documents after 1890 show that he signed his name as Bacote. It was a bold, defiant statement to make during that period in history in a small town where the Bacots were still very powerful players. Elias wanted to make it very clear that he was his own man now. Ala World B. Free, Muhammad Ali, Kareem Abdul Jabbar and Metta World Peace, he sought to dispel any notion of his connection to the wealthy, land owning, Bacots of the bondage era.

The names and years of birth/death of the known children of Matilda and Elias Bacote, son of Benjamin and Sara Bacot are:

i.	Phillip	b. 1870
ii.	Elihu	b. 1872- d. 1929
iii.	Phyllis	b. 1873- d. 1882
iv.	Boyd	b. 1874
v.	Ida	b. 1875- d. 1882
vi.	Rainey	b. 1877- d, 1882
vii.	Sarah #1	b. 1878- d. 1883
viii.	Junious	b. 1881- d. 1980
ix.	Minnie	b. 1883- d. 1945
x.	Bennie	b. 1883- d. 1957
xi.	Sarah #2	b. 1884- d. 1966
xii.	Brock	b. 1885- d. 1951

xiii. Harry   b. 1891- d. 1927
xiv. Sammie
xv.   Leo   b. 1892- d. 1979

Each of the surviving siblings attended elementary school in Darlington County, mostly at Lee Bell and Pleasant Grove, schools that no longer exist.

This generation of Bacotes was a God-fearing lot, like their parents. An old adage states that "the fruit never falls far from the tree." Sometimes when people examine their family history and the things that were passed down, they fail to include family behavioral patterns, which may also be passed on.

It is said that Elias systematically passed his talent for farming to his sons. However, it is apparent that he passed down a lot more than that. It certainly appears that he and Matilda had a basic appreciation of how good parenting can affect an offspring's future behavior and how it can influence how succeeding generations parent their children. Sociology clearly states that positive as well as negative family behavioral patterns can be passed down through generations. From what I observed and was told, all of their children displayed a cadre of ideal traits, such as a strong work ethic, honesty, character, courage, tolerance of others, curiosity, patriotism and family loyalty. None of them was ever charged or convicted of any capital offense, or even lesser offenses involving moral turpitude or character degradation. That is an astounding parenting achievement. It is much more difficult to be successful building character versus building farming aptitude.

It appears that **Elias** and **Matilda** had an appreciation and understanding of their role and responsibility as parents. Their children were not perfect individuals by any criteria, but there is no evidence of destructive activity in any of their behavior, they earned everything the old fashion, law abiding way and they supported one another with utmost unanimity. It appears that early on they chose family unity over family conflict and discord, and made it a reality. That is important because even today, with vicious negative attitudes so pervasive in America's culture, this nation is blessed by the absence of a criminal element in this family at large.

Thirty-one years after the end of slavery, when Elias was in his mid-forties, the historic *Plessy v. Ferguson* Supreme Court decision established the "separate but equal" doctrine. This law had an extremely negative effect on life in the South. In June 1892, a thirty year old black shoemaker named Homer Plessy was jailed for sitting in the "white" car of the East Louisiana Railroad. Plessy went to court in Louisiana and the judge in the case was John Howard Ferguson. Plessy lost, but appealed the decision all the way to the U.S. Supreme Court. Separate but equal was fine, except that equal was never equal. Equal was a relative term that was distorted by the establishment to achieve its unfair and unjust goals, especially in the areas of education, housing and employment for decades.

Other Bacote ancestors, who will be formally introduced later in the text, during the next sixty years, bravely endured an essentially separate existence-harassed, terrorized and controlled by Jim Crow tactics, the Ku Klux Klan and racial segregation, in a noble, unprecedented manner. They always espoused a keen faith in God, while striving to minimize their losses until the posse arrived. Deep in their hearts they knew that "we shall overcome some day."

It is also very interesting that Matilda and Elias had eight boys and all of them pursued farming as their profession. They are the first post-slavery generation of this family, a generation not unlike its predecessor, which sacrificed, endured and stood courageously to ensure the survival of the clan. They were all excellent farmers, diligently schooled by their father, and always had large, state of the art, farms that produced vast crops of tobacco, cotton and corn. None of them were sharecroppers. They were pioneers and trendsetters in Darlington. For example Leo, who had the largest farm, was in the forefront when the change from plowing with a mule to plowing with a tractor occurred. He was one of the first farmers in the area to purchase a new tractor for his large farm.

Records show that **Elias** was industrious as well as independent in his approach to life. He produced most of the nutritional items consumed by his family, items like tomatoes, watermelons, sweet potatoes, beans, cabbage, okra and collard greens. Hogs, cows, oxen and other livestock were also raised there.

Macedonia Baptist Church history indicates that this was a Christian family, that he was very active in the church. He even participated in the construction of the original, community oriented, church which was founded in 1866 under the dynamic leadership of Reverend Isaac P. Brockington, an ex-slave of Lee County, South Carolina. This sanctuary was formed after a group of black members withdrew from the primarily white Darlington Baptist Church on February 11, 1866. Mr. Brockington served as the pastor there until his death in 1908.

Even before the separation from Darlington Baptist Church, the need for black churches in America had become apparent. As early as 1789, Reverend Richard Allen helped established the precursor to the present African Methodist Episcopal Church (A.M.E.) in America due to ideological clashes with white Quaker, Episcopalian and Methodist officials.

The first trustees at Macedonia Baptist Church were Evans Bell, Peter Dargan, Lazarus Ervin, Antrum McIver, Samuel McIver, Samuel Orr, and Samuel Parnell.

The original sanctuary was located at the intersection of what is presently Hampton/Russell Streets, across the street from where the old Greyhound Bus Station was located in Darlington, on land purchased between 1866 and 1874. It is said that Elias played an important role in the construction of the foundation, utilizing his expertise to provide perfectly hewed logs, ensuring a firm foundation for the church. Elias' early association with Macedonia led to it being the religious sanctuary of choice for many of his siblings and their families as well. The present site of the church was acquired in 1922 and the building was occupied on February 3, 1935. Many family members are still actively associated with Macedonia Baptist Church, presently located on South Main Street in Darlington, including Norris Bacote and Gladys Bacote Hunter. Waddell Bacote and Evelyn Kelly Brown also were members there until their deaths in 2007.

The question is often asked, "how did the Bacotes amass so much property?" It appears to have been due primarily to the courage, ingenuity, guts, and long term vision of **Elias Bacote.** Although detailed data about his operation is unavailable, key features of his business model appear to have been relatively straightforward, with some important prerequisites. These prerequisites added a degree of difficulty to its implementation.

The concept was basic: as a farmer, acquire as much rich, fertile land that you can afford, and efficiently manage. The key point here is the more land you possess the greater the volume of crops you can plant. If you're proficient, the higher the bottom line profit. Of course, expenses are going to be greater, more equipment may be needed and more manpower will be required as you increase the amount of acreage you utilize. You will need some cash since this model requires large capitol layouts on the front end. If you are an astute business person with good management skills and an ability to convert a profitable small scale operation to a profitable large scale operation you have a winner. Elias's primary source of cash was undoubtedly his railroad tie business, which afforded him leverage to execute the expansion of his farm lands.

It was a great model which initially required him to carefully select land that met two rigorous criteria. It had to be richly endowed with stands of mature native hardwood oaks from which to produce the highly marketable crossties. After utilization of the selected oaks he would sell the remaining timber to lumber yards. Secondly the soil had to be fertile enough to support diverse agricultural endeavors. The next step was to clear away debris and stumps, generating rich agricultural farm land that he either rented or farmed himself. During this period in Darlington County, with its never ending forests, forest land could be purchased for as little as fifty cents to one dollar per acre.

Many businessmen are reluctant or incapable of making large sacrifices on the front end to reap a harvest later, maybe years later, maybe even generations later. It appears that some people are born with an aptitude for self-enrichment and long range foresight. They visualize beyond merely a simple day-to-day survival mentality. These prototypes also seem to be propelled by an immense inner drive.

A survey conducted on March 20, 1925 indicates that **Elias Bacote** once owned a large tract of 107 acres, more or less, in a prominent section of Darlington County, on Cashua Ferry Road. The property was subsequently deeded to Bennie Bacote, Sarah Bacote Williams, Leo Bacote, and Elihu Bacote as shown in Figure 9. It is very interesting that a portion of this tract was inherited by him from the estate lands of Benjamin and Sara Bacot. In addition, a portion was purchased from certain of his brothers and sisters who were also heirs of Benjamin and Sara.

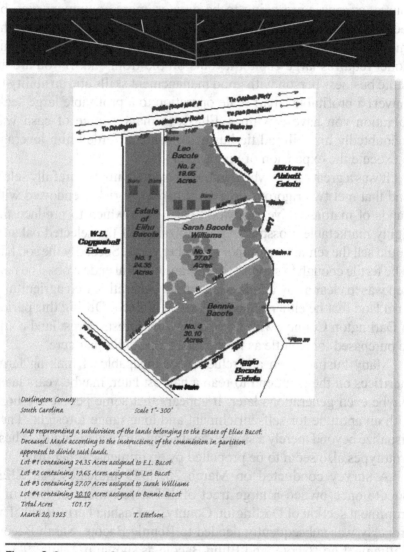

Darlington County
South Carolina   Scale 1"- 300'

Map respresenting a subdivision of the lands belonging to the Estate of Elias Bacot.
Deceased. Made according to the instructions of the commission in partition
appointed to divide said lands.
Lot #1 containing 24.35 Acres assigned to E.L. Bacot
Lot #2 containing 19.65 Acres assigned to Leo Bacot
Lot #3 containing 27.07 Acres assigned to Sarah Williams
Lot #4 containing 30.10 Acres assigned to Bennie Bacot
Total Acres   101.17
March 20, 1925   T. Ettelson

Figure 9. Survey and Subdivison of Elias Bacote Estate on Cashua Ferry Road

Another interesting conclusion we can draw from the above historical survey is that the heretofore unknown post-bondage home site of Benjamin Bacot, the newly documented early Bacote ancestor, was there on Cashua Ferry Road near the old Elihu Bacote/Sarah Bacote home site. The reasoning being; the 107 acre tract included some land from the original Benjamin/Sara home site, as well as additional acreage. The final piece of this puzzle is the fact that we know from current maps that the old Sarah Bacote home site abuts Elihu Bacote estate lands; hence the site of Benjamin and Sara's property has to be contiguous.

Many indicators suggest that the 107 acre tract was one of Elias' initial purchases. It was there that he secured and expanded the original family acreage with some adjoining acreage after Benjamin went to the Golden Shore in 1870. As was the scenario in many families during that era, some of his siblings were not interested in farming so he purchased the rights to their land also.

When Cyrus Bacot issued the decree to his freed slaves at the Cyrus Bacot Plantation in 1865, "to select an axis and proceed along that axis to select the location of your home," Benjamin proceeded due southeast, about five miles away from the McGown area.

Elias always had his eyes peeled for a real estate deal that offered potential and fit his business model. It appears that he understood that economic inequality is one of the barriers to community visibility as well as civil and equal rights. He understood that overcoming that barrier can begin with ownership initiatives. In 1888, he identified a tract of 130 acres of forest in the Mechanicsville section of Darlington County which included a stretch of Alligator Branch that impressed him. He made an offer that was accepted. Same being the tract of land conveyed by J.M. Lide to Elias Bacot, by deed dated November 19, 1888, and recorded in the office of the Clerk of Court for Darlington County in Deed Book 6, on page 488.

Being the entrepreneur that he obviously was, he later purchased another large tract in the Springville section of Darlington County. This tract was located between Darlington and Mont Clare on Old Society Hill Road.

Elias exhibited impressive acumen with his choice of locations for his various real estate purchases. Pundits say location is everything in real estate. Careful analysis reveals that all were located in close proximity to the major thoroughfares of that time. This was important for a variety of reasons, the more significant being ready access to major shipping and marketing venues for your products. If one studies a map of Darlington County, Figure 4 and Figure 7, it is clear that these three properties afforded him quick access to Cashua Ferry and Pocket Landing, major county shipping ports.

It is my belief that the purchase of the property in Springville was made for two primary reasons. The first was the need for a new source of hardwood oak tree specimens to fuel his railroad crosstie business. The soil in Springville probably favored the growth of the tougher, decay resistant white oaks which prefer a soil pH of 6.5-7.0 and a deep loamy soil. Post oaks and white oaks were preferred over red oaks for use as the highly prized railroad crossties. Secondly, the properties in Springville and McGown offered easy accessibility for the utilization of the railroad in exporting ventures. The Cheraw & Darlington Railroad had a depot in the Springville section of Darlington.

The 8½-9½ foot crossties could weigh up to four hundred pounds each and presented transportation problems during the horse and wagon era. Hence the closer the sources of his products were to the railroad the stronger his position, from a business standpoint. As discussed earlier, the railroad replaced the rivers as the faster, more reliable and major mode of transportation of exportable goods through South Carolina and North Carolina during that era. Utilizing this resource he was poised to export his perfectly hewed railroad tiers as well as cotton to many areas, possibly free or at a reduced rate because the railroad after all, was his client.

It was his desire that the 130 acre tract in Mechanicsville, off of Buddy Lane and Bull Road, be subdivided into seven tracts after his death. These sections based on a survey carried out in 1935 and again as recently as 1968, were carved out for **Brock, Boyd, Sammie, Junius, and Minnie**. [See Figure 10] Alligator Branch majestically flowed between **Minnie's** acreage and that of **Junius** and **Sammie,** and still does today. Minnie's tract #5 is referred to in family circles as "across the branch," because one has to traverse Alligator Branch to get there.

There was once a functional, free flowing, spring very near this beautiful tract that produced endless gallons of pure, ice cold spring water on a daily basis, even during the summer months. This gem was actually located on Junius' tract about twenty to thirty yards from the bridge which spans Alligator Branch, just after the bend in the road on the left side as you approach the branch. One had to be wary of snakes near the spring. One day it should be resurrected and restored to its original beauty and functionality.

The March 20, 1935 survey, conducted by T. E. Wilson, designated Minnie's section as Tract #5, bounded now or formerly as follows: on the northeast by lands of A.C. Coggeshall; on the southeast by Alligator Branch, which separates this land from Tract #3 owned by Sammie Bacote, and from Tract #4 owned by Junius Bacote; on the southwest by Tract #7 owned by Junius Bacote; on the west by Tract #6 owned by Boyd Bacote; and on the northwest by lands of A.C. Coggeshall. The 1968 survey designated Tracts #1 and #2 to Brock Bacote and Boyd Bacote respectively, and bounded the entire 130 acre tract on the east by lands of the Charles Estate as shown in Figure 10.

Over the years Tract #5 which was relatively isolated off Bull Road, had its moments in the spotlight and was the source of many joyous occasions when Bacote relatives gathered there to perform farm work or to hunt game. For some reason it always seemed a little cooler across the branch, even in the woods. Perhaps one of its more interesting occasions in the spotlight was when federal authorities discovered a whiskey still fully operating, distilling pure grain ethanol into a large vat, near the branch on Minnie's Tract #5. The still did not belong to Minnie and she was not aware of its operation. According to family lore, her cousins Colon, Handy and Buddy were known for their ability to brew excellent corn liquor back in the day. The spring was conveniently located, perfectly situated for utilization of the spring water in their still which was situated on higher ground. No one was arrested but the still was dismantled by the Feds.

Tract #5, due to its relative lack of traffic was, and still is, an outdoorsman's paradise with its large contingent of deer, wild turkey, wild boar, quail, rabbits and squirrels. The layout itself contributes greatly to its hunters appeal with an open clearing of about ten acres,

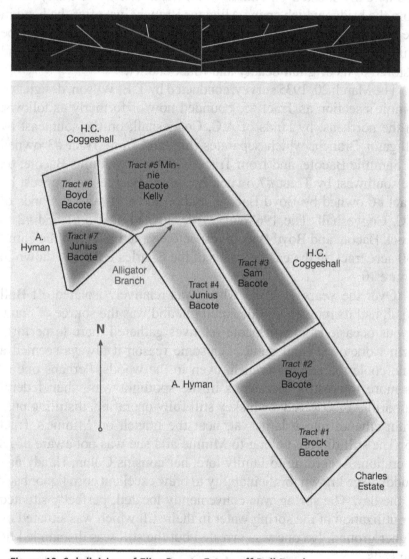

Figure 10. Subdivision of Elias Bacote Estate off Bull Road

surrounded by seventeen acres of forest teeming with billowing oaks and long leaf pines. Years of unharvested pine straw provides a barrier for undesired undergrowth and vines. This particular forest region contains numerous muscadine grape vines and blueberry bushes. My guess is the soil content favors their growth and productivity. Nevertheless, their presence and aroma along with the free flowing Alligator Branch serve as an allure to attract wild animals across the clearing. A perfectly placed, hunter's stand, located downwind in the forest area, overlooking the clearing, places the hunter in an ideal position to observe the quarry.

This tract, for decades, has also been noted for its large colony of exotic snakes. It is home to many of the most poisonous snakes found in South Carolina. The distinct presence of the shiny copper toned copperhead, the enormous, tan, diamondback rattlesnake, and the rare yellow/black/coral red, highly lethal eastern coral snake, needless to say, promote a unique aura in the area. One can readily view these beautiful creatures sunning in the open field, on the road/bridge that traverses Alligator Branch or the copperheads in the chilled branch water especially during the summer months. The copperheads were often referred to as water moccasins. For decades the Bacotes, like many other families in the South, have respectfully co-existed with these deadly predators. I know of no family member who has been bitten, as the snake's right to a peaceful existence has been respected on Tract #5.

The general message among snake enthusiasts is "if you leave snakes alone, they'll leave you alone." If given the opportunity most snakes will retreat or escape to a hole, into the forest, under a ledge or into the water. When they are approached most rattlesnakes vibrate their tails, making a rattling sound, a warning sound. When one hears a rattling sound, across the branch, vamoose!

There is indeed something surreal and enchanting about this beautiful area that both frees the spirit and re-connects the family to its rich heritage, to Elias, Junius and Minnie. The trek across the bridge that traverses Alligator Branch evokes a joyous experience for many family members. You can see it in their faces as their gaits quicken, and their eyes intently focus for any surprises.

A few hundred feet from the bridge, perilously close to the free flowing branch, is an iconic symbol of a bygone era: an old, weathered, twenty by thirty foot, tobacco barn. Once the venue of many fun-filled, hard-working days, it was used to cure the cropped tobacco leaves from that tract, leaves strung securely on tobacco sticks by competent stringers. Stringing was an art form which only certain individuals were allowed to practice. It required years of practice to become a skilled stringer.

While in surprisingly decent shape, the barn is in disrepair and beginning to crumble. Father time has taken its toll on its outer structure.

The interior, on the other hand, constructed of hard oak specimens remains relatively intact. The symmetrically located tiers that supported the strung sticks could still support a full barn today. Remnants of the well-constructed, flue-cured, heating system and numerous intact sticks are strewn along the dirt floor.

Barns of this nature are tangible reminders of the rich agricultural history of South Carolina. More and more, as time and technology progresses, they are becoming an endangered species. In the 1890s tobacco exploded as a cash crop in this section of the state. Although its use has declined sharply in the country due primarily to health concerns; today, only eighteen per cent of American adults smoke, down from forty-two per cent in 1965, according to figures released by the Federal Government, it remains a very significant part of the history and culture of this segment of the state. As such, these barns deserve to be remembered, respected and preserved by contemporary generations of historic preservationists as well as owners.

The entire 130 acre tract is considered to be the treasured old homestead of Elias and Matilda after they relocated from McGown. The original home that was constructed there was destroyed by fire.

After the devastating fire, rather than rebuild there on Bull Road, Elias elected to build a beautiful stately house on his land on Cashua Ferry Road. That elegant home that everyone adores, where his son, Leo, raised his family and where the following generation, Gladys Bacote Hunter raised her family, is still standing today, with a few modifications and updates. The original home had a large detached kitchen that ironically was also destroyed by fire. The current edition contains a smaller kitchen attached to the house. When Elias and Matilda went to the Golden Shore the house became heir property.

Leo bought out all the other heirs for sole rights and possession of that majestic place.

This home is located on the one hundred and four acre tract of Elias's portfolio, not far from the city limit on Cashua Ferry Road in Darlington County. Figure 9 represents a schematic depiction of this portion of his real estate portfolio and shows how it was subdivided into tracts for his heirs, Leo, Sarah, Bennie and Elihu during the probate of his will.

Cashua Ferry Road is also known as Rt. 34 or Mechanicsville Highway, and extends ten to fifteen miles east across the Pee Dee River into Marlboro County, South Carolina. In the late 1800s there was a ferry at the river, hence the name Cashua Ferry Road.

There is an interesting story associated with this home that has been a matter of contention for many decades within the Bacote family. According to family lore, after the fire, Elias is said to have stated "I am going to build a house on Cashua Ferry Road for Matilda and the children to live in," implying to some individuals from later generations that Matilda and Elias may have been living apart. Of course no one wants to believe that because these iconic ancestors were always honored and hoisted on a pedestal for all they endured and ultimately provided. Everyone simply wants to believe they had an ideal relationship and were happy.

Having performed a vast amount of research on the Mechanicsville area during the Antebellum Period, and interviewing numerous Bacote family members I have an informed viewpoint regarding Elias' statement. There have been no indications from my conversations with any descendants or from documents that I have reviewed, that Elias and Matilda had an unconventional relationship. It appears very clear that they were happily married. Secondly, it is a fact that the Back Swamp was indeed what it was called, a swampy region, hot, disease ridden, and practically unlivable during the difficult summer months and Indian Summer. It is written that many wealthy land owners from that historic region shipped their spouses, women, and children to higher ground during these periods to protect them from the dreaded malaria and other maladies imported by mosquitoes and other swamp insects.

In my viewpoint, I believe that was Elias' motive, especially in light of the fact that they had already lost many of their children during the afore-mentioned, catastrophic, diphtheria epidemic of the 1880s. I strongly believe Elias was saying "I want you all out of this area, especially during the summer, while I continue to work on the development of the acreage."

A portion of the tract, 24.35 acres, more or less, that Elias willed to his son Elihu Bacote, is now categorized as heir property because of the large number of heirs involved in its ownership. Figure 11 shows the location and subdivision of the tract into eight divisions mandated for Elihu's original eight heirs.

The status of the Elihu Bacote Estate in terms of heirs involved in 1955 is shown in Table 2. Today its status is much more complex with more than one-hundred heirs involved, a testament to the prolific nature of the Bacotes. Over the years Minnie Bacote's share passed through her son Harold Kelly, then through her daughter, Evelyn Kelly Brown, and ultimately to her grandson, and the present generation in 2010.

In retrospect, Elias' understanding of the inherent value of location in the real estate market is astounding. As of 2010, many of his initial purchases, which are still owned by Bacote descendants, are still highly valued in the real estate marketplace, as they are all primely situated.

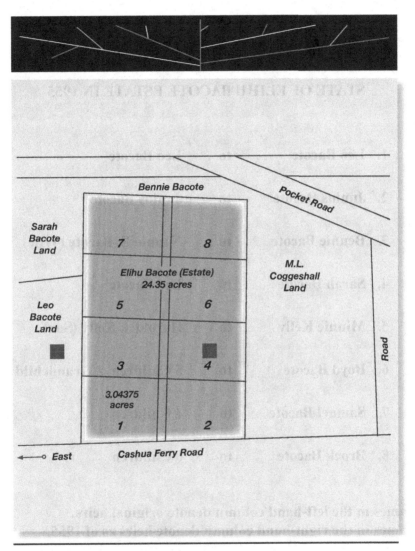

Figure 11. Subdivision of Elihu Bacote Estate

TABLE 2

STATE OF ELIHU BACOTE ESTATE IN 1955

1. Leo Bacote   to   Leo Bacote

2. Junius Bacote   to   Junius Bacote

3. Bennie Bacote   to   Nannie E. Bacote (Wife)

4. Sarah Bacote   to   Leo Bacote

5. Minnie Kelly   to   Harold J. Kelly (Son)

6. Boyd Bacote   to   5 Children, 1 Grandchild

7. Samuel Bacote   to   4 Children

8. Brock Bacote   to   6 Children

Names in the left-hand column denote original heirs.
Names in the right-hand column denote heirs as of 1955.

Can you imagine during that era, stepping up and making financial moves of those magnitudes? Yet the true measure of **Elias's** visionary expertise and fortitude was not simply his accumulation of huge expanses of real estate in Darlington County, but his exceptional work ethic and the consistency, against all odds, with which he repeatedly managed to get himself in position to expand his portfolio. His insight set the stage for many new business ventures undertaken by the family after he had gone to the Golden Shore, and clearly for many years to come.

From my vantage point it appears that the Bacotes in general, like this predecessor, exhibit a phenomenal work ethic. I was particularly fascinated when I discovered a distinct correlation between Elias' work ethic, which he passed on to all of his offspring, and that of the Bacotes that are alive today. Descendants of Elias Bacote, to an extraordinary degree, are not afraid of hard work or a difficult, challenging problem. Bacotes step up to the plate. They have no problem being seen "plowing the fields." They are a proud people, but not too proud to accept a lower level position or work temporarily in a low profile capacity to achieve their goal. There are numerous examples of this in the family history. They accept the challenge of adapting or remaking themselves to get from point A to point B in a positive manner. This is very important, because what it suggests is that these people possess a built-in resilience to overcome adversity or rebound from losses that would devastate many individuals. This is a mindset that has been nourished and developed over centuries and generations, it is not merely some haphazard behavioral occurrence that just appeared out of the blue.

Only the historian can truly make accurate judgment of the effect of prior activity in a family. That's why it's good to take a backward perspective sometimes. Satchel Paige the great baseball player once said "don't look back someone may be gaining on you." However, I say "look back sometimes, maybe you'll be fortunate to re-discover a model that really works."

History will reflect that among the most significant achievements of the Bacote ancestors has been the amassment and preservation of large chunks of real estate in Darlington, South Carolina. I repeat: amassment and preservation. **Will somebody please say amen!**

What is it about Elias' attainment of this real estate that merits accolades? Many will contend that his achievement as a real estate magnate pales when compared to some of the primary white landowners and planters in Darlington like the Coggeshalls, Dargans and Howards, and on the surface that may be true. However, we must not forget that many white landowning families in the South made their initial foray into the land owning business with minimal investments, obtaining grants of massive tracts of real estate from England for settling in the colonies during the era of colonization. I am not denying that many of the early white settlers in Darlington earned what they attained with their insight, courage and bravery. They were indeed courageous individuals.

The English Government established companies to manage and oversee settlement of the colonies. In order to encourage settlements in the virgin lands they offered headrights, up to 1,000 acres tracts of land, to any individual willing to cross the Atlantic and help populate and develop the colonies. Additional headrights, of fifty acres, were awarded for each family member who made the passage. In addition, for paying transportation costs for laborers, indentured servants or slaves, additional fifty acre headrights per individual were awarded to the head of household. This process allowed cash-rich families to increase their net worth and statue immensely, while accruing huge tracts of land and developing large plantations.

Around 1730, the State of South Carolina also launched an initiative to encourage more white immigration and more densely populated settlements. According to the *South Carolina Department of Archives and History: Township Grants, 1735-1761,* township grants of fifty acres per household member were issued to such petitioners.

However, what sets Elias' achievement apart and makes it special is that none of his land was donated, giving him an advantageous jumpstart in the real estate industry. A portion of one tract was attained by the purchase of the rights of his brothers in the heir property of their parents, Benjamin and Sara Bacot. Of course he possessed a share in that property also. But the bulk of his real estate was amassed by audacity, imagination, insight, blood, sweat and hard work, especially when one takes into account the nature of the

Reconstruction Era and the prevailing culture of South Carolina at that time.

When we attempt to evaluate an individual's performance during their lifetime from a historical perspective, I think one of the requirements is to factor in the restraints and conditions under which they lived and operated. If you are measuring their success and the magnitude of their contributions or their productivity, then variables like the degree of difficulty of the ventures and the degree of probability of attaining the desired result must also be inserted into the equation. Both are critical variables when we talk about performance, as they position one to put observations in the proper perspective. That being said, when we examine the background and history of the large scale land owners in Darlington County and compare it with the history and conditions under which Elias conducted business, history will ultimately reflect that their accomplishments are less dramatic in many regards and actually pale in comparison to those of this former slave. With a workforce of eight sons, he achieved a measure of overall success uncommon among freedmen in Mechanicsville and indeed America in toto.

Elias Bacote was a skilled craftsman and an accomplished woodsman who capitalized on his ability and skills he acquired and honed during his years on the unpaid labor force. The business of the production of railroad ties required the availability of large amounts of specific, raw, hardwood specimens. The trees had to meet specific specifications in terms of type, size and shape in order to qualify as a potential source of durable weight bearing railroad tiers. This requirement probably induced or led him to the decision to purchase his first large tract of forest, a decision which solidified and optimized his business model. It broadened his pool of specimens to select from, specimens which would eventually be carved into railroad tiers.

Another driving force behind his acquisition of relatively large amounts of real estate was his insightfulness. According to family lore one of Elias' favorite sayings was "I am going to amass enough land so that none of my children or their offspring will ever have to work for anyone else." His assumption was that farming would always be the #1 occupation in South Carolina and he was preparing a place for his descendants. That is the type of insight that begets legends. It is a position that most heads of families during the course of their careers dream of attaining.

What is also outstanding about his approach, as we rehash his existence, was the tremendous discipline he exhibited in maintaining his intended path; discipline to stay the course, discipline to resist the common temptations and distractions that befall most mere mortals, and last, but not least, the discipline to display and demand from others a compelling, un-compromising work ethic. Utilizing his skills as a woodsman, he hewed and molded 7x9 inch x 8 1/2 feet long railroad ties from giant hardwood trees, one at a time, utilizing only hand saws and hatchets. Let us not forget that each tie had to meet rigid specs otherwise it would be rejected. Each tie had to be a perfectly straight and symmetrical creation to handle the extreme tonnage of railroad cars. One at a time, at twenty-five cents a shot, with his eye on a much larger prize he toiled on a daily basis, with his crew and later his sons, in the hot, humid forests of Mechanicsville, banking his earnings until he was positioned to delve in the real estate market again. With each of these processes requiring years of labor and saving, to not waver or divert from the plan required the ultimate discipline; to not generate another idea, another reason to dip into the account required tremendous discipline; to transport the heavy finished products to the railroad sites using horse drawn carts on rutty crude paths was a challenge that also required discipline, I am certain. There were no paved roads or cell phones to call for assistance if you got stuck or your transportation vehicle broke down in Mechanicsville during that era.

That discipline speaks volumes about the man, as over a century later the family still embraces his values, while making a strong commitment to maintain ownership. His model was excellent and although to a large degree farming eventually lost its appeal to the masses, his holdings have accrued in value much more than Elias could have ever imagined. Today, Bacote descendants reside on almost all of his original holdings, with the agricultural areas being leased to mega-farmers in Darlington County.

This real estate has provided a base from which the family can operate; it has provided leverage for the family to expand, to branch out, to get educated, to be great tradesmen and to pursue dreams. Through faith in God and the desire for a better life, this family has branched out from primarily agrarians to a plethora of careers and occupations. They are ministers, missionaries, painters, high school and college educators, counselors, scholars, engineers, truckers, airline pilots, plumbers, mechanics, doctors, nurses, lawyers, accountants, bankers, scientists, pharmaceutical reps, computer specialists, military personnel, performing artists, barbers, fashion consultants, local, state, and federal government officials, entrepreneurs, businessmen and businesswomen to name a few. There is no doubt that these accomplishments can be traced to the efforts of **Elias** and other ancestors who made the sacrifices and fought the courageous battles that set the stage. The Bacotes must never forget from whence they came and how they arrived at where they are today.

The preservation segment is also very significant because so many black families have lost valuable inherited real estate over the years, not only in Darlington County, but over the entire state of South Carolina due to poor management and indifference. One classic example is Hilton Head, South Carolina. At one stage of American history blacks owned almost that entire beautiful tract of "undesirable" real estate.

It is said that **Elias** presented each of his children with a beautiful, manually operated, reclining chair, as a wedding gift, when they married. The one he gave to Minnie, around the turn of the century, is still in the possession of one of her descendants. In 2008, it was restored, stabilized and the cushions re-covered with a beautiful stately fabric. This revered 100 year old chair is placed in his bedroom for comfort and joy. It also serves to keep his family connected with the past. One of Elias' grandchildren also still has the chair presented to Leo when he married her mom. They quite possibly are the only two of these classic heirlooms remaining in the family.

As **Elias Bacote's** historic efforts are revisited and weighed, it becomes very clear to me that his accomplishments represent a classic Negro, a classic American achievement, a la W.E.B. DuBois. It is estimated that during his lifetime this former slave owned nearly five hundred acres of prime real estate in Darlington County. He fully grasped the importance of the concept of ownership of acreage in America and demonstrated how it can be parlayed to success through generations and generations.

Bacote family members must endeavor to celebrate the history of the early beginnings of the family and this courageous, inspirational man. As it was then so it is today. However, please don't be misled here. As demonstrated in his life story, the Bacotes arrival at their present posture was by no means a simple, straight-forward process. There were countless numbers of events, large and small, that contributed, countless deaths, countless sacrifices, countless laws, countless failures and countless successful forays by other unheralded individuals also.

Elias went to the Golden Shore at sixty-three years of age. The inscription on his tombstone in the Darlington Cemetery cites him as Elias Bacoat, b. 1847, d. August 22, 1910. Matilda followed at the ripe old age of seventy-five in 1924. The epitaph on her adjacent tombstone lists her existence from 1849 to 1924. They are very important forbears of the **Bacote** side of this Bacote/Kelly family.

Other cemeteries where ancestral Bacotes are buried are the New Providence Church Cemetery off of Cashua Ferry Road, the Hood Cemetery off of Abbot Road, the Darlington Cemetery, and the Pleasant Grove Cemetery at Pleasant Grove Baptist Church. There is also a black Bacot graveyard on Cyrus Bacot original plantation lands in Mechanicsville and one in Dovesville on property that is still in the capable hands of Bacote descendants.

The Hood Cemetery includes:

Rosa Bacote
Elijah Bacote (Mar 20, 1920-Oct 13, 1976)
Marie Bacote (Aug 1, 1923-April 3, 2007)
Boyd Bacote Jr. (Sept 8, 1931-Sept 8, 1991)
Handy Bacote (May 14, 1920-Sept 1, 1990)

Darlington Memorial Cemetery includes:

Harry Bacote (1891-1927)
Matilda Bacote (1849-1924)

Elias Bacote	(1847-Aug 22, 1910)
Minnie Kelly	(Dec 24, 1883-Sept 29, 1945)
Gladys J. Bacote	(Died May 11, 1938)
Ernest Brown	(Oct 31, 1913-July 12, 1978)
Evelyn Kelly Brown	(May 23, 1909-Nov 18, 2007)
Chester H. Bolden	(1905—1943)
Chester L. Bolden	(Aug 13, 1941-Apr 1, 2005)
Archie Bacote	(Jan 12, 1934-Mar 3, 1959)
Archie Bacote	(April 8, 1959-Nov 15, 1987)
Sarah Bacote	(1870-June 17, 1966)
Leo Bacote	(Oct 6, 1892-Jul 1, 1979)
Waddell Bacote	(1931-2007)
Ernest Griffin	(1921-2003)
Junius Bacote	(Jul 6, 1881-Nov 4, 1980)
Josephine Bacote	(Died Dec 6, 1952)
Columbus Jones Jr.	(Sept 2, 1918-Dec 23, 2012)

Many Bacotes are interred at the Pleasant Grove cemetery which is located on the Pocket Road in front of historic Pleasant Grove Baptist Church. Among them are:

Bennie Bacote	(Aug 1, 1883-Oct 13, 1957)
Nannie Bacote	(Feb 27, 1887-Feb 29, 1972)
Willie Bacote	
Brock Bacote	(Aug 1885-Jan 3, 1951)
Coker Tagus Bacote	(June 9, 1915-Dec-22, 1962)
Annie O. Bacote	(Oct 23, 1916-June 11, 1996)
Alvernie Bacote	Died May 3, 1993
Juanita Bacote	
Gladys Mockabee	(Sept 24, 1922-Aug 30, 1995)

Unfortunately Elias and Matilda did not live long enough to witness the landmark decision of the United States Supreme Court,

99

Brown v. Board of Education of Topeka Kansas which overturned earlier rulings going back to *Plessy v. Ferguson* of 1896, by declaring that state laws that established separate public schools for black and white students denied blacks equal educational opportunities. The decision handed down by the Warren Court ruled that separate educational facilities are inherently unequal. This ruling helped pave the way for integration and the Civil Rights Movement as we know it today.

I have presented in this chapter a few examples of Elias' legendary acts of defiance, for example demonstrating his opposition to being enslaved by non-violently fleeing the plantation, and years later taking the stand to protest the denial of his right to vote by members of the rival Democratic Party. This spirit of social activism, the fight for justice and equality that profiled Elias and was a significant part of the temperament of his immediate descendants, is still alive today in the Bacote family. Today's issues present themselves in different manners and the methods and tools of confrontation are more diverse, but the goal is essentially the same; to spark social change.

Behavioral scientists contend that "the fruit never falls far from the tree," and that some behavioral traits may be gene-linked; or as blues singer Muddy Waters melodically asserts in one of his ballads, "it's in you and it got to come out." To translate, these clichés denote that one's behavior is ultimately influenced by the modus operandi of his/her ancestors, the souls who cleared the paths for us to follow. I am a descendant of Elias and my history clearly demonstrates the continuity of the passage of his trait of fighting for justice and equal rights across generations of Bacotes. To substantiate and drive home this point, I offer a few incidents personally endured over fifty years ago as they relate to the pursuit of equality, justice and freedom. As far as I am concerned, these acts confirm that his legacy is still alive, and as his deeds were deemed legendary, his great-grandson's actions, a century removed, are laid in your lap for judgment.

If you question me today as to why I participated in two of these defiant incidents I would have to honestly answer, "I don't have any idea why." As you will see, it seems as if they were born out of the blue with lives of their own; that I was simply a conduit, not the conductor. Were they merely haphazard occurrences or were there forces at work that we cannot comprehend? I cannot answer that either, but I do know they were real. Occasionally I replay, and might I add not very often, three unmitigated acts, that still on occasion illuminate in my consciousness as clear as the rising sun. Each transpired without fanfare and all except the latter were basically unplanned.

The first was having the unacceptable gall to drink from the "white only" water fountain at the Sears and Roebuck store on Irby Street in Florence, South Carolina, as a twelve or thirteen year old in the early 1950s, as some white shoppers stared at me in apparent disbelief. In the eyes of many that was taboo, an act of defiance that could have caused a lot of pain. It upset my mother so greatly that after promptly whisking my brother and me from the store she broke down and wept profusely. She was overwhelmed by my audacity and apparent lack of understanding of the possible repercussions of such an act. I knew better but for some unknown reason took the plunge. I think for many years thereafter she did not trust how I would respond to the Jim Crow tactics we were subjected to in South Carolina at that time. Nevertheless, a statement had been submitted.

A few years later I was a student at the afore-mentioned Morehouse College. Atlanta, Georgia during that period was considered a relatively liberal southern city, sometimes referred to, in certain circles, as the New York City of the South. The black community was upscale and more respected when compared to some other southern cities due in part to the presence of four black colleges, the noted Atlanta University and the diverse array of black businesses and black professionals. Protesting and black activism was on the rise as citizens and students in Atlanta began to mount increasing acts of defiance during the late 1950s. Most of these protests did not receive national exposure or even extensive local coverage. Of course there were the two highly publicized incidents in 1957, when six black ministers were arrested for sitting in "white seats" on a city bus, followed by members of Spelman College Social Club "sitting-in" the audience "white section" of the Georgia Legislature.

The second incident occurred in late November 1956. Theron Goodson, also student at Morehouse, and I boarded a Greyhound bus at the bus depot in Atlanta, to travel to Darlington to celebrate

Thanksgiving with our families and friends. Having resided in that progressive environment for over a year and adopting a relatively confident posture, without prior discussion, we sat in the two front seats directly behind the white bus driver without giving it a second thought. It was in the twilight of the evening and not quite dark yet as the bus idled quietly at the gate. We never deemed our action as being overly aggressive or confrontational. In retrospect, it is clear now that there were forces at work that were beyond our control. We were simply proud Morehouse men exercising our right to ride the bus under the new guidelines. Segregation on public transportation had just been declared unconstitutional by the high court earlier that month, a ruling that had been vigorously celebrated on campus. The driver never said a thing, never asked us to move, never even blinked an eye, as he masked his feelings and muted himself. Eventually the bus was semi-filled and we departed Atlanta.

After about two hours of full speed ahead in the rural backwoods of Georgia, somewhere between Atlanta and the city of Augusta, in a darken woody area he abruptly stopped the bus in the middle of the two-lane highway, turned on the interior lights and opened the bus door. The sudden stoppage and tumultuous clanging of the heavy doors alarmed the passengers. Everyone thought a regular passenger was being picked up. In a stone-faced manner he turned to us and uttered in a deep southern drawl, "you nigras got to move to the back of the bus where you belong or get off." Some passengers were asleep, some were awake, however no one, black or white said a word. We were caught by surprise and shocked beyond belief, because we were not in a conscious, formal, testing mode but it was perceived that way. The older blacks on the bus looked at the college boys in disbelief as they were apprehensive about our safety. It was very clear that the driver was serious; what was not clear was how far he was prepared to push with his Jim Crow mindset to achieve his goal. For some unknown reason we stayed calm and remained in our seats for a minute or two and ultimately surmised that if we de-boarded the bus in that area, at that time of night, we would probably never be seen alive again. Only God knows how close we were to a violent confrontation that was not uncommon in the South during that period even though it was our constitutional right to sit anywhere we chose.

I remember thinking, what the heck have we gotten ourselves into? He was not visibly brandishing a gun but we had to assume he was armed. His body language, demeanor, tone of voice and the remote location of the bus forced us to conclude that our position was not strong and maybe it was smart to move to another seat and live to fight another battle another day. It was the Reconstruction Era revisited in 1956, where constitutional guarantees were frail bases upon which blacks could not rely, when such guarantees, which are contrary to popular prejudice, are not rigorously enforced.

My vivid anticipation was that upon arrival in Augusta, or possibly even before, a mob of klansmen or their counterparts were going to board the bus and attempt to take us away, or we would be detained in Augusta on some fabricated charges. Well despite the odds neither of those scenarios materialized; we not only survived but seized the opportunity and matured as black men. Elias was pleased as he cast his shadow of protection upon my compatriot and me. Our presence had been felt, our rights were denied but we made a statement.

I find it extremely interesting that over the ensuing years Theron and I never revisited or rehashed what occurred that dark night in Georgia. We were together many times thereafter and never found a reason to discuss what transpired. Except for my immediate family, I cannot ever recall discussing it with others or revisiting it with our peers in Darlington, Joshua Pearson and Roland Davis, once we arrived. They were students at South Carolina State at that time and were abuzz, ranting and raving during the entire holiday about the student protest movement on their campus in 1956 that garnered national press. Theron and I never countered with our experience.

It was truly a difficult experience. In retrospect, I guess we were simply overwhelmed by the reality that we came face to face with the devil that night in the rural back-woods of Georgia and walked away intact. Nothing else had to be said. We were like the Vietnam War veterans who never find a need to reexamine what happened on those rainy nights in the jungles of Vietnam.

Oh how times have changed, today most Americans don't even ride the Greyhound bus, they utilize Delta, Jet Blue, American

Airlines etc., and make their seat reservations in advance, via the internet.

The third defiant act occurred a few years later, in 1963 or 1964. One day while employed at the National Institute of Health I had a serious conversation during lunch with the wife of my Department Head in the Institute of Arthritis and Metabolic Disease. There is a high probability that she is deceased, so I will call her Claire to protect her identity. Claire, a liberal Jewish woman, iterated she had never seen a person of color in the public swimming pool she frequented with her young children near the Maryland state line on Connecticut Avenue in Washington, DC. She doubted that the pool was in compliance with the statute that ruled segregation in places of public accommodation as illegal and unconstitutional.

Shortly thereafter with the support of our spouses, we decided to test the situation with no planned strategy except to confront the establishment and the people in charge. Here was Elias' influence again getting me involved in the struggle, in Washington, DC no less, the capital of our great country. We stood in line for over an hour awaiting the opportunity to be admitted to the pool. Upon reaching the entrance, Claire was allowed entry without any questions and I was denied. I protested vehemently, to no avail, and was instructed to apply for membership which could take weeks to process. They presumed we would relent and go away quietly to some obscure corner. I patiently completed the bogus application form and was informed that they would notify me of the result of my application in due time. We knew it was bogus because Claire and her family had never been asked to submit any application for membership. The situation was playing out exactly as we expected.

After almost two months and with no response from the pool our findings were delivered to the American Civil Liberties Union (ACLU) for review and to battle in the courts. The pool was desegregated in 1965 without further fanfare.

As it has been in many human rights and civil rights efforts in this land, Claire and I never sought nor received adulation or acknowledgement that I can recall, for our action. As stated earlier, it is the sum total of the individual, small initiatives of this nature that facilitate change at all levels. We were very pleased with the result, and our reward was passing the crowded facility on a hot summer day and noting the diversity of the swimmers. It was years later after I departed Washington before I fully appreciated the magnitude of what we accomplished.

These ventures which went under the radar and were non-splashy or headline grabbing, underscore the challenges many of Elias' descendants encountered during the pre and modern Civil Rights Eras in the Jim Crow South. They confirm that his legacy, a central part of Bacote culture is still alive today. I know because that legacy is in me and in quite a few of my relatives.

Elias Bacote 1847-1910

Minnie Bacote

Norris Bacote, Gladys Bacote
Sarah Bacote, Arthur Bolden

Norris Bacote, Arthur Bolden

Leo Bacote   Nanny and Benny Bacote

Mae Ruth Bacote   Ezekiel, Chaney and Royal Bacote

CHAPTER THREE

THE BACOTE SIDE

All of **Elias's** surviving offspring remained or settled in Darlington County on land purchased by this great man. His real estate purchases still provide residence for the family, three to four generations removed. Today, one hundred years later, contemporary generations still reside at the original home sites of his children, **Leo, Boyd, Brock,** and **Sammy.**

They have retained these lands purchased by Elias not merely because of residential implications but, to a large degree, because of the historical significance they represent to the family. The mass migration of nearly 90 per cent of earlier Bacote generations altered the mind-set when it came to farming, but not the firmly engrained Bacote culture. Elias and Matilda established an endearing presence and tradition in Mechanicsville that is still being honored. He was very adamant about what he expected from his massive purchases and for over fifty years, after he went to the Golden Shore, Bacotes utilized the land as farmers. However, today there are no Bacote farmers that I am aware of in Darlington County. Nevertheless, most of his tracts are still in the possession of Bacote descendants.

The enclave of Bacote residences off of Rt. 180 (Bull Road) and its counterpart off Rt. 34 and the Pocket Road, from the early 1900s to the 1970s, were bustling self-contained mini communities, like Bacote-Town, USA. [See Figure 7 and Figure 10] The Bacotes were perfectly situated to assist, nurture, protect and care for each other when circumstances required it. From a farming standpoint this was very advantageous, because the large individual families insured a communal type of labor force to work the land and harvest the crops. This was not a free labor force but a reliable, dependable one. For example if Sammy, his wife and children assisted Junius in "putting in tobacco," each worker received the going rate of pay at the end of the day and vice versa. It is important to note here that sometimes the parents of the children received the wages due their children, not the children themselves. In 1950, that was about $3 per day per worker. This system was very beneficial because as the farmer whose land was being worked that day, the boss of the day, you knew what you were getting in terms of ability, workmanship and reliability; you knew the workforce would be there and on time.

The families worked well together and eagerly anticipated the opportunity to network. The work day was filled with joy, laughter, and camaraderie and, might I add, rigorous work.

Some of the men were serious hunters; some had expert gardening abilities with their own specialties, so to speak. Some families grew pecan trees; some liked an array of fruit. More significantly however, from a family communal standpoint, everyone shared the fruits of their labor.

As one examines the legacy of this generation of Bacotes it is very clear that they possessed longevity. Many of the old timers lived well into their eighties and nineties during a period when you were fortunate if you made it to sixty years of age. Longevity can be attributed to numerous factors, among which are DNA composition, environment, lifestyle and diet.

It has been clearly demonstrated by the scientific community that what we consume is extremely critical to our well-being. Now in retrospect when we look back and examine the old homesteads and what was occurring there, it appears that early on the Bacotes were onto something special in terms of diet. Contemporary nutritionists rant and rave about the importance of nuts, fruit and fresh vegetables in our daily consumption.

There is one item that stands out when we talk about the old Bacote homesteads, and that is the numerous nut trees, fruit trees and large gardens of vegetables, potatoes, tomatoes and other essentials. Ancestral generations of Bacotes consumed a lot of nuts and fruit. Everyone had pecan trees on their property except Benny. Leo had five or six pecan trees between the house and the barn. Buddy Bacote had fifteen pecan trees leading up to his home. Brock, in addition to his pecan trees, adorned his property with numerous hardy peach, pear and fig trees. Although Benny had no pecan trees, he planted numerous Black Angus walnut trees at his homestead that produced delicious walnuts for decades. Sarah and Minnie had walnut trees also. Brock's diverse assortment of fruit trees provided ample fruit for the entire Bacote clan off of Bull Road and kept the women busy canning fruit for weeks on end, to be consumed during the winter months and the remainder of the year. In addition, the forests were teeming with wild blueberry bushes, nestled below the bellowing longleaf pine trees, whose fruit were easily and readily harvested.

It is very obvious that the Bacotes complimented their meals with a healthy diet of nuts and fruit. They obtained their supplements of vitamins, antioxidants, pulp, tannins and minerals the old fashion way. They grew them and as postulated they experienced longevity.

As mentioned often in this treatise, farming during that era was very labor intensive and at the end of the day you had a lot of muscle aches and pains. Let it be emphasized, you had to be healthy and fit to perform farming duties, and one of the events that our Bacote ancestors on Bull Road eagerly anticipated was the weekly visit of the traveling "Watkins Man." The Watkins man played an essential role in the subsistence and survival of many rural Southern Americans during that era, as he delivered vital homeopathic remedies to the front door, eliminating the need to make that trip into town to visit the drug store.

First and foremost the Watkins man was known for his cache of liniments which provided much needed relief and comfort from rheumatic aches and pains, soreness, muscle strains and aches due to over-exertion. The renowned Red Watkins Liniment was the first product made and sold by J.R. Watkins as early as 1868.

Another of the mainstays of his arsenal was the bright yellow Three Sixes or "666," a cold remedy and anti-malarial agent which contained quinine, and an iron supplement. Three Sixes also provided relief from body aches and pains. He also sold Cocoa Quinine which was a mixture of one part quinine and three parts cocoa, and Juniper Tar, a chest congestion expectorant that was utilized to provide relief from chest colds. Let's not forget Black Draught, a laxative, which implemented an important step in the treatment of colds.

A decade or two after the appearance of the Watkins man a new entrepreneurial venture, called the "Rolling Store," emerged that also benefited that generation of agrarian Bacote ancestors. This venture differed from the Watkins man in terms of products offered as well as place, frequency and time of delivery. Basically their marketing strategy revolved around the fact that rural communities had transportation difficulties, so they delivered very basic goods to them, on an on-going basis, a smart, ambitious, marketing concept. It was called the Rolling Store because it really was a store installed on a truck. It carried simple items like milk, rice, flower, sodas, chips, candy, bread, potatoes, a few can goods, pork skins, cigarettes, fresh vegetables etc., to name a few.

The Rolling Store was a truncated version of today's 7 Eleven store providing convenience store-like products. It had a regular schedule, servicing specific routes. You knew when to expect it and on those dark rural nights one could see the lights of the store from one to two miles away. Its operating hours in Mechanicsville were usually around sunset or early night. It also differed from the Watkins Man concept, in that delivery was made at the intersection of your promenade/driveway and the main road, not at your doorsteps. The convenience was worth any surcharge that was added to the final cost of each item.

The first post-bondage generation of Bacotes was essentially the last to remain in Darlington in large numbers. They capitalized on the opportunity at their disposal and provided future generations with options, with opportunities to branch out, to live anywhere desirable; these generations migrated to New York, Philadelphia, Detroit, Ohio, Mexico, Denver, New Haven, Connecticut, New Jersey, Washington, D.C., Europe, etc. They explored the planet. Many youngsters take those opportunities for granted, but it didn't have to be that way. Hard work, insight, discipline and faith by these early Americans reaped dividends for future generations.

For the purpose of discussion I will assign a number to each of the ten children, eight boys and two girls, which survived the diphtheria epidemic. For example Harry will be designated #1, Junius #2, Leo #3, etc.

Harry Bacote, #1, died at a young age, around twenty years old. It is said that he died in an automobile accident. His car overturned and he suffered a broken neck. Sometimes also called Pat, Harry had two sons and was married to Ms. Rosa Hunter. He was also a WWI veteran. Some family members felt that a feud with another family could be related to the accident. In other words the accident could have been induced.

Junius Bacote, #2, was married to Ms. Josephine Martha Tate on May 1, 1912. Reverend E. Ham of Timmonsville, South Carolina performed the ceremony. This union produced six children. The names of the children of Josephine Tate and Junius Bacote, grandson of Benjamin and Sara Bacot are:

    i.   Royal Bacote
    ii.   Joseph Bacote
    iii. Colon Bacote
    iv. Rosebud Bacote
    v.   Beatrice Bacote
    vi. Chaney Bacote

It is said that **Junius** also contracted diphtheria during the 1880s epidemic that killed nine of his siblings, but he survived to live over 99 years. His spouse, **Josephine,** was a distinguished Darlington County educator. She taught K1-8 at the old, renowned, one room, St. Paul School on Georgetown Road in Mechanicsville and New Providence Elementary School during the 1930s and 1940s until her death in 1952. Almost all the older African-Americans from that area of the county express fond memories and respect for her. She was the only teacher in the historic, one room St. Paul School for years. Josephine did not own a car, so she faced the same perils of the journey to school as her young students. She walked two to three miles daily to these schools, at least two miles through the woods (the back way) to New Providence Elementary School with no one to possibly stop by and give her a ride. History will show that this strong, courageous woman played a vital role in the educational venue of Darlington County during some crucial years and positively impacted the lives of hundreds, maybe thousands of young brothers and sisters. Her commitment and contribution will never be forgotten.

Junius, also called "Junebug" by elder members of the family, was a tall, gregarious, smart, outgoing, jovial, kind man. From my viewpoint he was unique among all his brothers, although I admit

I did not get to know many of them really well. Heck, I was only a kid. Junius always had time for me; he would hug me and my young cousins and always exuded love, affection, and genuine support.

During an interview with his daughter Beatrice when I inquired what it was like growing up in Junius' household she revealed that life was very straight-forward and strict at their large farm. She said "we had three mules, a large garden where we grew many of our essentials, a large barn and a great warm house." She reiterated a couple of times, "we went to school, went to church, came home and went to work," that their upbringing was very labor intensive, that they knew there had to be a better way.

This crafty codger had his own unique way of teaching young family members life lessons. He had a habit of chewing Bloodhound Chewing Tobacco, a famous brand of that era that had an image of a red dog on the package, and always kept a small pocket knife in his pocket to slice off a small parcel. One day his young niece Pat asked for a piece. Being the accommodating uncle he was, he gave her a small slice and the next thing we knew she was sick as a dog, having swallowed some of the juice. Needless to say, that experience taught Pat an invaluable lesson. She never smoked cigarettes or chewed tobacco, thereafter.

There was always good food at his house. He had the reputation for being the sharp shooting hunter in the family and hunted everything from deer, to rabbits, squirrels, coons and possums. Although he did not eat possum meat he still hunted them. The legend goes in the family, that according to Junius, the reason he would not eat possum meat is because he once saw one coming out of a grave. He kicked the possum and the possum grinned at him and fell over like he was dead (played possum). When he returned the next day the possum was gone.

In addition to his uniqueness and outstanding traits, Junius was also quite a character. A few years after his wife passed he was diagnosed with tuberculosis. For those of you that don't know about tuberculosis, it is an infectious disease caused by the rod shaped bacillus bacterium, and is characterized by nodular lesions of the lungs, pulmonary decay and consumption. Before the discovery of antibiotics like erythromycin, streptomycin and tyrothricin, tuberculosis was a very serious medical problem in America. TB, as it was called, would kill you. Streptomycin, discovered in America in 1944, was the first anti-tuberculosis drug. Its use in conjunction with para-aminosalycilic acid proved a very successful early combination in the treatment of this dreaded disease. Isoniazid, which remains a very effective drug in killing tubercle bacilli was discovered later, and used clinically in 1952. In the 1960s, rifampicin, perhaps the most effective drug in the treatment regimen was discovered.

During those days the patient had to be isolated from the general public and **Junius** was confined to the Tuberculosis Infirmary on Rt. 52 between Darlington and Florence. Being the maverick that he was, at night he would slip out of the infirmary via his room window, visit with his girlfriend in Florence and return before dawn before the authorities knew he was missing. He also refused to take the medication the doctors prescribed for treatment of this deadly disease. Well wouldn't you know it, as God would have it, this cunning old timer beat tuberculosis. After a few months he no longer exhibited his initial symptoms. He was a character indeed, an inspiration to everyone. He overcame diphtheria and tuberculosis, two legendary, dreaded diseases of his time.

Later in life he happily resided at his brother, Elihu's, original home on Cashua Ferry Road, the same house that Elihu's sister Sarah lived in after Elihu's death in 1929. I remember visiting him one very hot day in August, when he was well into his nineties, and he was on top of the house repairing the old tin roof. Have you ever been on a hot tin roof in August in South Carolina? It is a venue that separates the men from the boys. Well it was then as a young man, that I realized there is longevity and durability in the Bacote family genes.

Royal wed Charlotte, an educator, and begot Roy Jr. of Winston Salem, North Carolina.

Joe wed Queen, a beautician, and begot Shirley. **Joe** also had a son, Pete Bacote, who lived in Darlington until his death in December 2008 at age seventy-five. Pete was a decorated U.S. Army veteran, having served in Korea and Guam. Pete wed Vivian Gillard. The names of the children of Vivian and Pete Bacote, the great-great grandson of Sara and Benjamin Bacot are:

    i.   Janice Bacote
    ii. Patricia Bacote
    iii. Stephanie Bacote

Chaney attended Shaw University and later wed Leroy Walker. They begot no children. Cheney had a successful career in the Detroit, Michigan corporate community before relocating to Florence, South Carolina later in life. Chaney suffered from diabetes and congestive heart failure, two disorders that have a high incidence of occurrence among Bacote females. She went to the Golden Shore in July 2014 at age eighty-five.

Beatrice attended Paine College in Augusta, Georgia before moving to Washington, DC. where she had a distinguished career with the US Civil Service Commission and the National Weather Service. She had two sons, Larry and Mark. Mark is deceased.

Rosebud wed Ezekiel Bacote, begot no children, and adopted Linda.

Colon wed Sarah Law and begot Laverne. Sarah, who grew up on the West End of Darlington, resided at Junius' old homestead until her death in 2010. Her parents Daisy Rouse and Hezekiah Law are buried at the old Shiloh Church cemetery.

Laverne begot Roger at an early age. Later he wed Clemmie and begot Deidre who has a son and resides in Florence, South Carolina. Laverne attended Mayo High School, Class of 1955. He went to the Golden Shore in 2007.

Leo Bacote, #3, born 1892, wed Gladys Johnson, who died giving birth to their daughter, Gladys. The names of the children of Gladys Johnson and Leo Bacote, the grandson of Benjamin and Sara Bacot are:

    i.   Waddell Bacote   2/13/1931-2007
    ii. Norris Bacote   b. 1933
    iii. Archie Bacote   1/12/1934-3/3/1959
    iv. Gladys Bacote   b. 5/13/1938

The old timers did not talk much about the past. I guess they spent most of their energy dealing with the present and the perils of their times. When asked about his father Elias, Leo's favorite reply was "Elias was a very serious man, a hard worker and when he came home from work he had rigorous expectations. One of them was he expected a tub of warm water to be ready for him to soak his aching muscles." I had to laugh when Leo's daughter related that to me because when I was working and returned home from the lab, one of the things that really relaxed me was fifteen to twenty minutes in the jacuzzi. It was yet another classic example of Elias exerting influence on my behavior. Anyway back to the story. Leo related that his job as the youngest man in the house was to prepare the water for his dad's old school jacuzzi. First the water had to be drawn from the well. During the warm months the water was strategically placed in the sun during the day, and relocated when the angle was no longer optimum, to maximize the warming process. Moments before Elias would immerse himself, Leo would add a pot of boiling water to raise the water to the desired temperature. As a youngster Leo was very proud that he was able to do that for his dad, as he was too young to cut crossties and plow.

In many regards, some family members cite Leo as the unofficial leader of the family during his generation, although he was the youngest sibling. He was very outspoken and influential in family matters, was always there for everyone and had the cash to back it up. He was a very caring man as witnessed by the fact that he welcomed into his family Richard and Ernest Griffin, two young orphaned relatives who needed assistance at a very young age. He essentially adopted, nourished and taught them to be respectable, productive citizens.

Although Leo had a reputation for not being too generous with his cash, when his brother Elihu went to the Golden Shore in 1929, he came up with the cash to pay for the funeral. For the record, he was subsequently reimbursed by the Elihu Bacote estate, not that he needed it. From a religious standpoint, Leo was also a very well respected deacon and trustee at the afore-mentioned Macedonia Baptist Church in Darlington.

Patriotism is a very important facet of American life. It was and still is an essential ingredient of our culture. Many Americans, from the founding fathers to the disenfranchised, from the enslaved to the formerly enslaved, even descendants of former slaves, have demonstrated this trait during pivotal periods in the history of this country. Leo, like some other Kelly and Bacote ancestors cited in this treatise, was no different. He has the distinction of being the second male of this Bacote family to serve in the United States Armed Forces.

Some historians contend that since the Armed Forces were not integrated during World War 1, African Americans did not contribute significantly to the success of the Allies. It will surprise many to learn that Leo Bacote and other blacks fought on the combat front lines during World War 1, fighting for freedom world-wide at a time when Jim Crowism was in full bloom in America denying them their own freedom at home. Although they were no longer subject to barter and sale and although a movement was adrift encouraging blacks to consider leaving America, Leo served. According to family lore, Leo said "he saw it as an opportunity to fight for his own freedom, to show that he was willing to put his own life on the line to demonstrate his patriotism and entitlement as an American citizen."

His primary duty was as a cook (not uncommon during that era of Armed Forces history) but he was also called upon to do combat duty. He talked a lot about his experiences in the Army. One of his most compelling recollections was about an unsuccessful reconnaissance mission, where all of his platoon except he and one other soldier were killed. He said that after a long hard-fought gun fight which spilled over into the darkness of night, upon daybreak he looked around and saw that they were the only ones alive. Somehow they managed to escape before being discovered, and reconnected with their company. Many veterans who have experienced combat of that nature and survived, feel they have been granted a second chance at life.

He probably suffered post-traumatic stress disorder (PTSD)-then referred to as "shell shock." Kneeling in a foxhole in the midst of his dead platoon mates, in danger of being killed or captured himself and placed in a prisoner of war camp on foreign soil was a heavy load to recall. After that demanding encounter Leo would later declare "his heart was never the same," leading to his premature medical discharge from the Army. He returned to Darlington a national hero.

In retrospect this probably explains the relatively passive attitude exhibited by Leo later in life, when I knew him. One can imagine that after casting your eyes on a scene of that nature, there is not too much that could excite you or even make you smile. Leo was never abusive, always very calm, never raised his voice or got overly excited.

History should not overlook the fact that decades later, all of his sons as well as his adopted sons also served honorably in various branches of the military, having drawn their inspiration from his heroic service during World War I.

All of Elias's siblings had nice homes, but Leo's with its two stories and expansive, wrap around porch was breathtaking and exciting and served on numerous occasions as a focal point for family gatherings. Sometimes during the school year, because of the three to four mile shorter distance, some of Junius', Sammy's, Brock's and Boyd's children lived with Leo or Sarah during the week to get an education at Mayo High School in Darlington. Colon, Willie, Rosalee, Bunche, Leola, and Herbert all used this plan, which was primarily for convenience. They would then walk from there, approximately three miles, to school. On the weekend Leo would take them home, presumably in the elegant 1938 Chevrolet that he owned. I don't think Junius or Boyd drove a car. Junius was once involved in a bad automobile accident and refused to get under the wheel again. Both Leo and Brock had driver's licenses.

Sometimes the young students in the family at-large would gather at their Aunt Minnie Bacote Kelly's home if they were too early for school, or the weather was bad, and wait in the warmth of her home there at 501 Chestnut Street for the first bell to ring at Mayo High School. Minnie's residence was just across the street from the school. Rosa Lee (Brock's daughter) stayed there during the week for an entire year to attend high school. Colon, once he became of age to obtain a driver's license, would drive her home on Fridays in his truck.

This convenience-driven establishment of temporary residences demonstrates that there was a concerted effort by that minimally educated generation of Bacotes to insure greater education of the next generation. These ancestors set the precedent and that attitude toward education carried over into later generations with even greater intensity and dedication. Shortly thereafter young Bacote women and men were headed off to college and graduate schools.

Leo also had the largest farm of his siblings. He was a very intelligent farmer, with an abundance of business savvy. He learned from his dad, Elias, the value of land in the agriculture arena, having also purchased over one hundred acres of additional farm land himself, to maximize his earnings. Some people would say he was "tight with his money," but they did not comprehend the financial role he played in the family. This shrewd businessman was always there for the Bacotes when it involved business and financial matters. His sisters, Sarah and Minnie, as well as his niece, Evelyn K.B. Brown relied heavily on Leo for advice in business matters even though they were all self-proficient women.

All of the brothers also had large gardens where they grew most of their families' daily meals. I have first-hand knowledge of Leo's substantial garden, having spent a great amount of time at his home. Everything he grew such as, collard greens, peas, string beans, onions, cucumbers, okra, watermelon, cantaloupes, cabbage, sweet potatoes and tomatoes was grown without the use of pesticides, or chemical fertilizers. He produced his foods in a holistic manner even back then. One of the greatest thrills was to go into the garden early in the morning before the sun had fully emerged over the horizon, while the dew was still on the vines and in the fresh air, and the blooms of the honeysuckles were still unfurled, pull a ripe, fire red tomato from the bush, clean it with the moisture of the dew and eat it right there on the spot. The taste was so unlike the tomatoes purchased from the local A&P grocery store in town.

Waddell wed Everline Carraway and this union produced five children. The names of the children of Everline Carraway and Waddell Bacote, the great grandson of Sara and Benjamin Bacot are:

    i.   Archie Bacote
   ii.   Linda Bacote
  iii.   Wayne Bacote
  iv.   Demetrius Bacote
   v.   Jackie Bacote

Wayne wed Wanda Davis and they have three children. The names of the children of Wanda Davis and Wayne Bacote, great-great-grandson of Sara and Benjamin Bacot are:

    i.   Jermaine Davis
   ii.   Ryan Davis
  iii.   Tovierre Bacote

Demetrius wed Jean and they have five children. Jackie had two offspring. The names of the children of Jackie Bacote, great-great granddaughter of Sara and Benjamin Bacot are:

   i.   Tonya Caldwell
   ii. LaMorris Bacote

LaMorris wed Tara, whom he met while a student at South Carolina State College. He is one of the few scholar-athletes of this Bacote family at large. His family now resides in Rock Hill, South Carolina. The names of the children of Tara and LaMorris Bacote, great-great grandson of Sara and Benjamin Bacot are:

   i.   Janelle Bacote
   ii. La'ryn Bacote

Leo's daughter, **Gladys**, wed A.J. Hunter of Darlington. This union produced two children. The names of the children of A.J. Hunter and Gladys Bacote, great granddaughter of Sara and Benjamin Bacot are:

   i.   Morris Hunter   b. 12/9/1962
   ii. Leo Hunter   b. 5/19/1964

Gladys also raised LaMorris, Jackie's son, from a little tot to adulthood.

Norris wed Blanche McRaven. They had no children.

Archie died in the Navy. He had no children.

Boyd Bacote, #4, wed Anna Jane Brockington. The names of the children of Anna and Boyd Bacote, grandson of Sara and Benjamin Bacot are:

   i.   Mary Ida Bacote
   ii. Annie Mae Bacote
   iii. Handy Bacote
   iv. Maxine Bacote
   v. Rosalee Bacote

     vi. Boyd Bacote Jr.
    vii. Matilda Bacote

Boyd and **Elihu** were the oldest surviving offspring of Elias and Matilda. Both of them possessed a light, smoky-brown complexion and curly hair. **Boyd's** arm of the family was probably the most religious, due to Anna's influence. Her maiden family produced numerous deacons and trustees. They were very instrumental in the construction and establishment of New Providence Baptist Church as a major institution in Mechanicsville, SC. Boyd was a kind, meticulous man who thrived on neatness. He always kept his plows neatly arranged and, his barn always stood out because he kept it trimmed with fresh paint.

After attaining adulthood, most of Boyd's offspring sought a livelihood away from the soil and migrated to cities near and far. Only Handy decided to remain in Mechanicsville.

Mary Ida lived in Detroit, Michigan.

Annie Mae wed William Chestnut and lived in Wilmington, NC.

Maxine wed William Martin and lived in Washington, DC.

Boyd Jr. had a son in Detroit and a daughter Veronica, who lived in Silver Spring, Maryland. As a youngster Boyd was known for his devilish, mischievous pranks. He was the life of his clan and was also a Korean War veteran.

Matilda, aka Doll Baby, died young.

Rosalee wed **Rev. A.D. James,** former pastor of Spring Street Baptist Church in Toledo, Ohio. On February 5, 2013, she was the last of her siblings to pass on to the Golden Shore. She lived in Toledo.

Handy wed Zilthia and begot five children, while residing at the old homestead on Bull Road. The names of the children of Zilthia and Handy Bacote, great grandson of Sara and Benjamin Bacot are:

     i.   Handy Bacote Jr.
    ii.   Edith Bacote
    iii. Mary Bacote
    iv. Jeanette Bacote
    v.   Maxine Bacote

Handy Jr. wed Bertha and they reside on the old family homestead. The names of the children of Bertha and Handy Bacote Jr., great-great grandson of Sara and Benjamin Bacot are:

    i.   Benita Bacote
    ii. Tico Nicole Bacote

Edith has no children.

Mary wed Maurice Norkhird, a Jamaican national who grew up in England. Mary graduated from the College of New Rochelle and earned a master's degree in public administration from New York University. They lived in Queens, New York before relocating to Tamarac, Florida. Maurice went to the Golden Shore in 2013.

Jeanette wed Ernest Shaw. This brave women retired from the US Army after spending over thirty years defending this great country. The name of the children of Ernest Shaw and Jeanette Bacote, great-great granddaughter of Sara and Benjamin Bacot are:

    i.   Matilda Shaw
    ii. Jenise Shaw
    iii. Stephanie Shaw

Matilda is a professor at Voorhees College and Stephanie a LPN in Columbus, Georgia.

Jenise resides in Darlington and has four children. The names of the children of Jenise Shaw, great-great-great granddaughter of Sara and Benjamin Bacot are;

    i.   Kristein Monique
    ii. Eddie Lee Robinson
    iii. Brigette Robinson
    iv. Kirby Samuel

Kirby attended Morris College in Sumter South Carolina.

Maxine Bacote wed Robert Cooper and begot Earnestine Deborah Cooper of Darlington.

Minnie Bacote, #5, wed **Shedrack Kelly** whose heritage is shown in Figure 2. The names of the children of Shadrack Kelly and Minnie Bacote, granddaughter of Sara and Benjamin Bacot are:

    i. Esau Kelly
    ii. Montessa Kelly
    iii. McIver Kelly
    iv. Evelyn Kelly   5/23/1909-10/18/2007
    v. Harold Jacob Kelly   7/19/1913-1/4/1985

McIver and Esau died as babies and Montessa at age 13 from infantile paralysis.

Evelyn married Chester Harcourt Bolden from Barbados, British West Indies. The names of the children of Chester Harcourt Bolden and Evelyn Kelly, great granddaughter of Sara and Benjamin Bacot are:

    i. Arthur H. Bolden   b. 7/21/1938
    ii. Chester L. Bolden   8/13/1941-3/1/2004

Arthur, a retired biochemist with degrees from Morehouse College, Howard University and Fairleigh Dickinson University spent thirty-five years as a research scientist at the National Institute of Health and the Roche Institute of Molecular Biology. The latter institute, where he spent the bulk of his career, was dedicated to fundamental research in biochemistry, biophysics, genetics and other areas in the domain of molecular biology. Some of his work led to the development of a drug currently utilized in the treatment of the dreaded AIDS virus.

Arthur wed Evelyn Jacquelyn Matthews. Jackie, as she is affectionately called, in addition to being a great mother and spouse, served over thirty years as a devoted educator and administrator in the Washington, DC and New Jersey school systems. She was born in Martinsville, Virginia and has degrees from Hampton and Columbia Universities. They currently reside in Coral Springs, Florida.

The names of the children of Evelyn Matthews and Arthur H. Bolden, great-great grandson of Sara and Benjamin Bacot are:

    i.   Sydne Bolden Long b. 11/25/1966

    ii.   Arthur H. Bolden II b. 6/22/1968

    iii. Troy Bolden   b. 7/7/1971

Arthur II, a New York City banker, and Troy, a real estate specialist and entrepreneur in Mexico, are businessmen. Both are Hampton University graduates.

Arthur II served on the Securities and Exchange Commission's Credit Ratings Roundtable, in 2013, in support of reforms by the Dodd Frank Wall Street Reform Act. His product expertise includes municipal bonds, mortgage backed securities, rates derivatives et al.

Sydne, a former fashion editor for some of the major fashion magazines in the country, including *Vogue* and *In Style*, wed Lewis Long, a corporate executive with an MBA from Harvard Business School. Both are Howard University graduates and they reside in Florida and New York City. She is currently with a luxury online retailer.

Chester, a Hampton University graduate with a master's degree from Iowa State University was an emerging, expressionist artist and art professor. He served on the faculties of Elizabeth City State, Fort Valley State and Bennett Colleges where he was Professor of Art History and Painting. Many of his works hang in private collections in the United States and Europe. Chester went to the Golden Shore on March 1, 2004.

Harold Jacob Kelly married Viola Antrum who was originally from Hartsville, South Carolina. Viola was the sister of Annie Ophelia Antrum who also married into the Bacote family, having wed Coker Bacote, as discussed later. After Harold's divorce from Viola he begat Linda Wormly.

Throughout this treatise Minnie's husband's name will be spelled many ways, Shadrack, Shedrick and Shedrack, as found in the numerous sources cited. The union with **Minnie** was his third marriage. He had offspring from his other two marriages. It is important to mention that at this point, because his children from the earlier marriages became integral parts of his marriage family with Minnie.

Josephine, born in March 1895, was the product of his first marriage to Josephine Backus. Ms. Backus passed away a couple of years later due to complications from an attempted childbirth.

Almeta, a daughter, born in November 1898 was from his 2ⁿᵈ marriage to Lougenia Richardson. She went to the Golden Shore at the tender age of twenty-three. It appears that a son, **Horace,** was also a product of that union. It was not that Shedrack could not stay with one woman, unfortunately God decided to take his first two wives at an early age. It seems rather tragic that he, as a young man, had to survive the deaths of two young wives and four of his children at very young ages. His faith was severely tested as a young man, but he pushed on being the warrior he was.

Josephine wed Andrew Graham of Hartsville, SC and they begat Elizabeth Graham. Elizabeth resided in Hartsville on her father's original family homestead almost her entire life.

Elizabeth was born April 27, 1929, nearly a month before Shadrack went on to the Golden Shore. Very shortly after her birth, Andrew and Josephine moved to Winston Salem, NC, where both gained employment at R.J. Reynolds Tobacco Company. They returned to their roots in Hartsville in 1939 to become farmers, to work the land they so dearly loved.

In the mid-1940s Elizabeth lived with her Aunt Evelyn's family on Chestnut Street in Darlington, to complete her 9ᵗʰ and 10ᵗʰ grade years at Mayo High School. It was not the first time a member of the Bacote family resided at that residence while pursuing a high school diploma at Mayo. Situated across the street from the school, it eliminated the demanding, arduous five to six mile early morning trek to high school that she would otherwise have had to endure in Hartsville. Since Evelyn was an educator it also provided a very critical educational environment. In return, Elizabeth was the source of invaluable assistance to Evelyn with her young children, as well as their ailing grandmother Minnie who was suffering from dementia. After two years Elizabeth returned to Hartsville, to the comfort of her own home, family and friends and ultimately received her high school diploma from Butler High School in Hartsville. She went to the Golden Shore in 2013.

Horace and Viola Brockington begat Annie Ruth. Horace later migrated to Richmond, Virginia, and Annie Ruth grew up with her mom on Celia Hyman's place in the Back Swamp. Annie Ruth currently resides in Florence, SC and at nearly ninety years old is still healthy and hearty. Annie Ruth Hankins begat Ulysses Brockington, career, retired U.S. Army who now resides near Savannah, Georgia. Ulysses was very active during the famous Berlin and Cuban Crises and the more recent Iran Hostage Crisis. He wed Mildred McKever of Effingham, South Carolina. The children of Mildred McKever and Ulysses Brockington, great-great grandson of Carolina Kelly are:

    i.   Deterrell Brockington
   ii.   Garry Brockington

Garry, a firefighter and converted Muslim is now known as Abdul-Rasheed Kilal. Abdul wed Asma and the family currently resides in Dumfries, Virginia. The names of the children of Asma and Abdul- Rasheed Kilal, great-great-great grandson of Carolina Kelly are:

     i.   Jasmine
    ii.   Ashley
   iii.   Faizah
   iv.   Juwairiyah
    v.   Zakariya
   vi.   Sumaya
  vii.   Saffiyah
 viii. Abrahem
   ix.   Hamza

Benny Bacote, #6, wed Nannie E. Woods, a registered midwife from the highly respected Woods family of Timmonsville, South Carolina.

It is said that Nannie's father, Theodore Luther Woods, who had the ability to read and write, was a "free" black man during the era of bondage. The details of his attainment of this noteworthy status are unclear at this time. However, it is very clear, according to family lore, that after attaining his "free" status he earned and accumulated enough cash as a farmer to purchase his mother's freedom. This ancestral son financially bought his mother out of slavery. She was able to live her remaining years in his household as a free woman, free of the yoke, free of the stigma of being an enslaved black woman at that point in history, free. Do you comprehend what it means to be free?

The full impact of this heralded ancestor's actions may not be readily apparent to many outsiders; however his progeny and succeeding generations continually benefit from the positive impact of his efforts. Theodore's status to a degree separated him from many of his peers. He had the personal freedom to choose his field of endeavor, to be gainfully employed, to own property, to vote and to travel wherever he wished. It afforded him the opportunity to economically, spiritually, mentally and physically adopt and pursue an aggressive positive mindset that would spill over into succeeding generations. I am astonished today at how contemporary members of this sub-clan of Bacotes speak with beaming pride and respect of this man, as he has boosted their level of expectation and confidence to great heights, even though he lived over a century ago. It is another classic example of how one's ongoing actions as a family member can impact a family, generations removed from the lands of their forefather.

Benny, who is named after his grandfather, like siblings Sarah and Boyd, had a very fair complexion and straight hair, traits inherited from their mom Matilda. He and Nannie appeared to be a model couple. She was a Sunday school teacher at Pleasant Grove Baptist Church and was well known for her stylish wardrobe. There have been references to a beautiful black coat and tall black hat embellished with a feather that she was seen in over fifty years ago. Obviously it must have been a fashion statement because that person still remembers it today. Benny played a very active, significant role as a deacon at Pleasant Grove.

Like most of his brothers, who were skilled woodsmen and carpenters, he built his home himself on the Pocket Road in Darlington County, a home that is still very beautiful in this year 2014. The home had a functional attic or 2nd floor area that his grandchildren would gather in when visiting. It was an enjoyable frolicking area that Ronald, Donald, Posey, Sylvia, Earl, Margaret and Benjamin recall with glee on occasions when they would visit from out of town. It took him about five years to construct that masterpiece. It is said, he cut some of his own trees to generate lumber for the project.

Among his many talents Benny was also an accomplished molasses maker. He had a bonafide molasses mill operation on his property that ground and crushed sugar cane. It was powered by three to four old mules walking around in a circular fashion, rotating the plungers that crushed the cane, generating a syrupy solution. The syrupy solution was then cooked for a specific amount of time to produce an excellent tasting molasses that was then stored in wooden kegs or colored jars to avoid exposure to sunlight and prevent breakdown of the molasses. He was well known locally for his homemade molasses, which was marketed commercially. There was nothing tastier than hot, buttered, flaky biscuits or flower bread laden with some of Benny's molasses.

Much like Brock, Benny with his alert eyes and thick, mixed grey hair was a very serious man, but he also had a gregarious, outgoing, fun loving side. In an effort to offset the mental and physical rigors of farming he became an avid fisherman and loved to fish the many fresh water streams in Mechanicsville. His favorite fishing spot was "the Bonnet Hole" located in the beautiful, serene Black Creek which runs through Darlington County and meanders within a mile of his home on the historic Pocket Road. He was known for returning home in the evening with a string of sweet tasting bream and large-mouth bass.

He loved to share his knowledge and give life lessons to youngsters who would listen. One of his favorites related the effect of the wind direction on how fish would attack the lure. He would say, "if the wind blows from the North the fish will bite like a horse, if the wind is from the east they bite the least, if it blows from the South they bite like a mouse, if from the West they bite the best." I have no idea of the validity of his assertion, however if Benny said something there was a very good chance it was true.

Another of his adages which he often iterated was, "you can tell whether a prolonged rainy period is on the horizon if you see certain ants moving their nest/eggs to higher ground," like up a tree, for example. The weather was and still is very important in agriculture in determining when to place young plants or seeds in the ground to start a crop or a garden and Benny according to legend utilized that maxim in his decision making process when determining when to plant certain crops.

To the union of **Benny Bacote** and Nannie E. Woods, eight children were born; five girls and three boys. The names of the children of Nanny and Benny Bacote, grandson of Sara and Benjamin Bacot are:

    i.   Mae Ruth Bacote
    ii. Theodore Bacote
    iii. David Bacote
    iv. Sammy Bacote
    v. Benzena Bacote
    vi. Gladys Bacote
    vii. Alberta Bacote
    viii.Cleo Bacote

This branch of the family vigorously stressed education, due primarily to the efforts of the matriarch, Nannie and her oldest son, Theodore. Within this group of Bacotes, Theodore is credited with establishing the education trend, becoming the second Bacote to enroll in college. He attended South Carolina State College. The education trend encompassed many of his younger siblings and exhibited itself even more extensively in subsequent generations.

Mae Ruth wed Zetty Brown. They had no children.

Gladys wed Walter Mockabee and they had no children. Gladys is a South Carolina State College graduate and taught in the South Carolina and New York school systems for many years. Her field of interest was Home Economics. Gladys went to the Golden Shore on August 30, 1995.

David wed Bannie Jackson and they begot one daughter. The name of the child of Bannie and David Bacote, great grandson of Sara and Benjamin Bacot is:

    i.   Margaret Bacote

Theodore wed Octavia Jones from South Boston, Virginia and they begat one son. The name of the child of Octavia and Theodore Bacote, great grandson of Sara and Benjamin Bacot is:

    i.   Benjamin Earl Bacote

Theodore went to the Golden Shore in 2003 and Octavia in 2010. Benjamin Earl who also attended South Carolina State College, wed Patricia Ancum in 1957. The name of the child of Patricia and Benjamin Earl Bacote, great-great grandson of Sara and Benjamin Bacot is:

    i.   Benjamin Earl Bacote Jr.

Benjamin Earl Bacote Jr. is deceased.

Sammy Bacote left Darlington at age eighteen and went to New York City to establish himself. He resided with Theodore, but after one year of hard work at an ice plant and prodding from Theodore he decided to return to South Carolina and attend South Carolina State College where he graduated. Around 1937, he pledged Kappa Alpha Psi fraternity becoming the first member of the family at large to become a member of this noble clan. The Bacotes boasts of a number of its men in the ranks of Kappa Alpha Psi. Sammy is a past Polemarch [president] of the chapter at South Carolina State, a distinguished honor indeed, as well as a charter brother of the Kingstree, South Carolina Alumni Chapter.

He served in the United States Navy during WW II. Sammy married Fanny Wright, whom he met at South Carolina State, and proceeded to have two daughters and an illustrious career with the South Carolina branch of the Federal Home Administration. This devoted father and avid golfer went to the Golden Shore on November 24, 2010. The names of the daughters of Fannie Wright and Sammy Bacote, great grandson of Sara and Benjamin Bacote are:

    i.   Sylvia Bacote
    ii. Rose (Posey) Bacote

Sylvia, a Hampton University graduate, married Lorenzo Archer. The names of the children of Lorenzo Archer and Sylvia Bacote, the great-great granddaughter of Sara and Benjamin Bacot are:

    i.   Alexis Archer
    ii. Lorenzo Archer Jr.

Alexis is a guidance counselor at a high school in Norfolk, VA and Lorenzo Jr. a physical education teacher in Washington, DC.

Rose Bacote, also a Hampton University graduate, married Willie W. Mattison of Williamston, SC. The names of the children of Willie Mattison and Rose Bacote, the great-great granddaughter of Sara and Benjamin Bacot are:

    i.   Stacey Mattison
    ii. Sonja Mattison

Stacey attended UC Berkeley and Emory University attaining a master's degree in public health. Sonja graduated from Norfolk State University and works in computer software marketing. They reside in the Atlanta, GA area.

Benzena wed Terry Hodges. The names of the children of Terry Hodges and Benzena Bacote, great granddaughter of Sara and Benjamin Bacot are:

    i.   Allan Hodges
    ii. Ruby Hodges

Ruby had four daughters and they all reside in the Washington, DC-Maryland area. Unfortunately Ruby went to the Golden Shore suddenly, as a young mother. The current names of the children of Ruby Hodges, great-great granddaughter of Sara and Benjamin Bacot are:

    i.   Joyce Steel
    ii. Sharon E. Jones
    iii. Anglia Ellis
    iv. Shandra E. Eull

After Terry Hodges' death Benzena married Floyd Tyner and they begat Perry Tyner. Perry attended Howard University and married Georgia. He is currently a retired New York state trooper. They have one son named Jordan Tyner.

Allan attended Morehouse College and wed Amril, a very smart woman of Caribbean descent. Both of them enjoyed successful careers as medical doctors in the Pittsburg, Pennsylvania area. She was an internist, and Allan is a pediatrician. Unfortunately, Amril went to the Golden Shore unexpectedly in the prime of her career. They had two sons.

The names of the sons of Amril and Allan Hodges, great-great grandson of Sara and Benjamin Bacot are:

    i.   Damian Hodges
    ii. Marcus Hodges

Cleo Bacote wed Benjamin Ruff from Macon, GA. They were blessed with twin sons. The names of the sons of Benjamin Ruff and Cleo Bacote, great granddaughter of Sara and Benjamin Bacot are:

    i.   Donald Ruff   b. 1/25/1938
    ii. Ronald Ruff   b. 1/25/1938

Ronald and Donald Ruff currently reside in the Bronx and New Rochelle, New York, respectively.

Ronald has two girls. The names of the children of Ronald Ruff, great-great grandson of Sara and Benjamin Bacot are:

    i.   Rhonda Ruff
    ii. Ronelle Ruff

Alberta, aka Bert to family, was the youngest of her clan. She attended Johnson C. Smith University and North Carolina Central University, attaining two bachelor degrees in library science. Alberta had an illustrious career as an educator in the New York City School system, and was married to Winfred Lewis, a career military man. They adopted Michael Lewis, an orphan of Japanese descent, who also attended Johnson C. Smith University and now resides in

Virginia Beach, Virginia. For many years Alberta resided in the famous Dorie Miller Co-ops near Shea Stadium in Queens, NY. The grand lady went to the Golden Shore in December 2011 while this treatise was being penned.

Michael Lewis was married twice, first to Carlotta Lynnette Ellis with whom he had one son. His second bride was Roxanne Richardson and they produced one daughter. The names of the children of Michael Lewis are:

    i.   Brian Lewis
    ii. Simone Lewis

Brock Bacote, #7, whose farm was across the road from Boyd's farm on Bull Road, wed Drucilla Lee. The names of the children of Drucilla and Brock Bacote, grandson of Sara and Benjamin Bacot are:

    i.   Jael Bacote
    ii.   Herbert Bacote
    iii. Coker (Tagus) Bacote
    iv. Leola (Lee) Bacote
    v.   Prince Bacote
    vi. Alvernie (Bunch) Bacote
    vii. Juanita Bacote

Brock, like his brothers, was a kind and gentle man. But in addition, he possessed a special type of sensitivity. In his effort to provide meat for his family he preferred to ensnare wild animals in traps versus hunting them down like his sharp shooting brother Junius. This special sensitivity manifested itself in other ways also. Many Bacotes admired him for the manner in which he treated his children. In seems that during that era many patriarchs were so heavily laden with earning a living, providing for their family and surviving that they did not outwardly show a lot of love and affection to their children. But Brock was different. It is said that when he came in from the fields, although tired and exhausted, before he fulfilled his own needs, he found quality time for his children. He was known for exhibiting interest and concern, talking with them about their problems, about school, about how they were doing on an ongoing basis. Among family he had a reputation as a father extraordinaire.

Leola wed Eugene Johnson. The names of the children of Eugene Johnson and Leola Bacote, great granddaughter of Sara and Benjamin Bacot are:

    i.   Ronnie Johnson
    ii. Alfreda Johnson

Up until March 16, 2013, **Leola** was the last sibling alive from this group. She was residing near her roots in Florence, SC.

Alfreda has two offspring. The names of the children of Alfreda Johnson, great-great granddaughter of Sara and Benjamin Bacot are:

    i.   Juanita Nicole Morning
    ii. Aisha Vashanda Harrison

Both reside in the Atlanta, Georgia area.

Ronnie lives in Panama City, FL and has two children. The names of the children of Ronnie Johnson, great-great grandson of Sara and Benjamin Bacote are:

    i.   Ronnie Jr.
    ii. Veronica

Veronica the great-great-great granddaughter of Sara and Benjamin Bacot has two children who represent the seventh generation of Bacotes.

Jael wed twice, first to Richard Johnson and the second time to Wilson Sligh. The names of the children of Jael Bacote, great granddaughter of Sara and Benjamin Bacot are:

    i.   Cynthia Johnson
    ii. Elaine Johnson
    iii. Joel Sligh
    iv. Gwen Sligh

Cynthia, who resides in New Haven, Connecticut wed Ed Bynum and they begot four children. The names of the children of Ed Bynum and Cynthia, great-great granddaughter of Sara and Benjamin Bacot are:

i. Eric Bynum
ii. Yolanda Bynum
iii. Cedric Bynum
iv. Monique Bynum

Eric, Cedric and Monique reside in New Haven. Monique is a graduate of Marist College.

Yolanda wed Daniel Barnes and they live in Baltimore, MD with two children. The names of the children of Daniel Barnes and Yolanda Bynum, great-great-great granddaughter of Sara and Benjamin Bacot are:

i. Ananda Barnes
ii. Daniel Barnes II

Ananda and Daniel are seventh generation Bacotes.

Elaine, who is deceased, wed Harvey Lewis. The names of the children of Harvey Lewis and Elaine Bacote, great granddaughter of Sara and Benjamin Bacot are:

i. Michelle Lewis
ii. Tonya Lewis
iii. Derrick Lewis
iv. Kim Lewis
v. Okima Lewis

Michelle and Tonya are deceased, and Kim and Okima reside in Lakeland, Florida.

Gwen still lives in Darlington.

Bunch never married and had no offspring.

Herbert wed Sadie Dupree and they lived in New Haven, Connecticut. They begot eight children. The names of the children of Sadie and Herbert Bacote, great grandson of Sara and Benjamin Bacot are:

    i.   Janice Bacote
    ii. Lynwood Bacote
    iii. Ricky Bacote
    iv. Hazel Bacote
    v.   Roger Bacote
    vi. Herbert Bacote Jr.
    vii. Calvin Bacote
    viii.Terry Bacote

Janice and Lynwood went to the Golden Shore in 1970, and Ricky and Hazel in 2004.

Coker (Tagus) wed Annie Ophelia Antrum from Hartsville, South Carolina and they begot eight beautiful children, all whose first names begin with the letter "C." The names of the children of Ophelia and Coker Bacote, great grandson of Sara and Benjamin Bacot are:

    i.   Constance Bacote
    ii. Carolyn Bacote
    iii. Clarin "Bunny" Bacote
    iv. Cecelia Bacote
    v.   Charles "Bobby" Bacote
    vi. Carl Bacote
    vii. Clarice Bacote
    viii.Claudette "Dixie" Bacote

Constance wed Robert McCain.
Carolyn has one daughter, Teshi.
Clarin wed Lizzie Lucky. The names of the children of Lizzie Lucky and Clarin Bacote, great-great grandson of Sara and Benjamin Bacot are:

    i.   Sonya Bacote
    ii. Kimberly Bacote

Sonya and Kimberly, great-great-great-granddaughters of Sara and Benjamin Bacot, begot Brittany and Candace, respectively. These two generations live in New Haven, Connecticut. Clarin currently resides in Darlington.

Cecelia wed Odell Cohens and they begot five offspring. The family resides in New Haven, Connecticut. The names of the children of Odell Cohens and Cecelia Bacote, great-great granddaughter of Sara and Benjamin Bacot are:

    i.   Odell Cohens Jr.
    ii.   Linda Cohens
    iii.   Lynn Cohens
    iv.   Michael Cohens
    v.   Debra Cohens

Debra wed Bradley Taylor. The names of the children of Bradley Taylor and Debra Cohens, great-great-great granddaughter of Sara and Benjamin Bacot are:

    i.   Christopher Taylor
    ii.   Chandler Taylor

Charles wed Helen Brown and they have no children. Charles, also referred to as Bobby, has one son, Cedric Moses, by a previous alliance, who is a sixth generation Bacote.

Carl, aka Reginald, wed Josephine Scott from Darlington. They reside in Hartsville and have three children. The names of the children of Josephine and Carl Bacote, great-great grandson of Sara and Benjamin Bacot are:

    i.   Reba Bacote
    ii.   Chante Bacote
    iii.   Rod Bacote

Clarice wed George McPhail and they begot three sons. The names of the sons of George McPhail and Clarice Bacote, great-great granddaughter of Sara and Benjamin Bacot are:

    i.   Darrell
   ii.   Selwyn
  iii.   Terrence

Clarice also had a son, Charon Ricks via another alliance. Clarice went to the Golden Shore in 1985.

Claudette wed Samuel Toney. The names of the children of Samuel Toney and Claudette Bacote, great-great granddaughter of Sara and Benjamin Bacot are:

    i.   Patris
   ii.   T.J.

Patris, a sixth generation Bacote, is a podiatrist in Chicago, Illinois.

Prince died at age eighteen, he had no children.

Juanita wed Henry Sligh, brother of her sister's husband Wilson Sligh. They lived in Detroit and had no children. She attended South Carolina State College and taught for a short period at Butler High school, located in Hartsville, South Carolina.

Sammy Bacote, # 8 wed **Evelyn Brockington**. The names of the children of Evelyn Brockington and Sammy Bacote, grandson of Sara and Benjamin Bacote are:

    i.   Calperta Bacote
   ii.   Roceda Bacote
  iii.   Robert Bacote
  iv.   Willie Bacote
   v.   Elijah "Buddy" Bacote

Calperta wed Robert Witherspoon, a union that produced no children.

Roceda had a son, Randolph Bacote. Both are deceased.

Robert lived in New York, married Virginia, they had no children.

Willie lived in New York and married Annie. The names of the children of Annie and Willie Bacote, great grandson of Sara and Benjamin Bacot are:

    i.   Cheryl Bacote
   ii.   Tara Bacote

Elijah Bacote wed Marie Pierce, daughter of Johnny and Sarah Richardson Pierce. The Pierce family are longtime residents of old Georgetown Road in Mechanicsville. This union produced fifteen children. The names of the children of Marie and Elijah Bacote, great grandson of Sara and Benjamin Bacot are:

      i.   Roceda Bacote
     ii.   Patricia Bacote
    iii.   Sammie Bacote
    iv.   Elijah Bacote Jr.
     v.   Henry Bacote
    vi.   Curtis Bacote
   vii.   Baby X
  viii. Calperta Bacote
    ix.   Everlina Bacote
     x.   Marilyn Bacote
    xi.   Nathaniel Bacote
   xii.   Elvira Bacote
  xiii. Marjorie Bacote
  xiv. Marshall Bacote
   xv. Warren Bacote

Discussions of family history conjure up images from the past. Our minds often default to the old homesteads, which often evoke pleasant images and memories. Buddy and Marie's homestead was one of those iconic spots. The large family resided in a modest, quaint abode on Sammy Bacote's original Tract #3 [shown in Figure 10] off of Bull Road, also known as SC Rt. 180 as shown in Figure 7. To get there, you made the turn off of Bull Road, drove past Junius and Josephine's house, past the stable, past the hog pen, and made the right turn at the tobacco barn. After proceeding about 100 yards you veered right onto a promenade. The revered residence evokes scenic memories as the promenade and the yard leading to the home was adorned with fifteen gigantic Stuart pecan trees, planted in 1923, that still produce hundreds of pounds of pecans every other year. It is indeed a sight to be remembered. In the early autumn, the house appeared to be symmetrically situated, amongst a sea of puffy, white, cotton plants with the large pecan trees looming grandly in the foreground.

Roceda wed Melvin Dawson. They have two children. The names of the children of Melvin Dawson and Roceda Bacote, great-great granddaughter of Sara and Benjamin Bacot are:

    i. Natashia Dawson
    ii. Nigel Dawson

Patricia wed Moise James, a distinguished Viet Nam veteran. The names of the children of Moise James and Patricia Bacote, great-great granddaughter of Sara and Benjamin Bacot are:

    i. Mario James
    ii. Monica James

Patricia and Evelyn Brown, featured later in this treatise, were 2nd cousins. She took care of Evelyn during many of her later years, serving as confidante, nurse and caretaker. Pat is the prototype of an angel, a special person, like a Barack Obama, sent from heaven above, to do special things. All of Buddy and Marie's offspring are really special people, but Pat is the pearl. From my viewpoint, she is the most sincere, compassionate, caring, God-loving cousin that I have and I have the ultimate respect for her.

Mario, a Virgin America Airlines pilot, married Lee Ann and they have two children. The names of the children of Lee Ann and Mario James, great-great-great grandson of Sara and Benjamin Bacot are:

    i. Lilianna James
    ii. Nathanial James

Monica has three children. The names of the children of Monica James, great-great-great granddaughter of Sara and Benjamin Bacot are:

    i.   Nyasia James
    ii. DeAngelo James
    iii. Jamesey James

They represent seventh generation Bacotes and live in Darlington.

Sammie "E..J." wed Georgia Berry, and they have five children. The names of the children of Georgia and Sammie Bacote, great-great grandson of Sara and Benjamin Bacot are:

    i.   Angela Bacote
    ii. Melissa Bacote
    iii. Teresa Bacote
    iv. Gregory Bacote
    v. Michelle Bacote

Elijah Jr. died at eleven months of age of pneumonia.
Henry died as a baby.
Curtis wed Betty McIver and they had one son, Eric.
Baby X died at birth.
Calperta never married.
Everlina has one son, Brandon Bacote.
Marilyn wed Gilbert Bostick. They have one son, Adrian Cage.
Nathanial wed Diane; a marriage that produced one daughter, Kelsey.
Elvira wed Elvis Johnson, they have one child, Chantae.
Marjorie has two children. The names of the children of Marjorie Bacote, great-great granddaughter of Sara and Benjamin Bacot are:

    i.   Stacy Bacote
    ii. Chad Bacote

Chad, a graduate of Clemson University, has distinguished himself as a MEP (mechanical, electrical, plumbing) engineer in

Atlanta, Georgia. He has an eight year old son, Chad Bacote II, a great-great-great-great grandson of Sara and Benjamin Bacote.

Marshall wed Cora Jones and they produced three beautiful children. The names of the children of Cora Jones and Marshall Bacote, great-great grandson of Sara and Benjamin Bacot are:

    i.   Octavia Bacote
   ii.   Destiny Bacote
  iii.   Jessica Bacote

Warren wed Andrena, and as of 2014 they have no children. Warren served in the secret service for two South Carolina governors, was a South Carolina Highway patrolman and possessed the rank of Lieutenant Colonel in the US Army reserves as of 2008.

Elihu Bacote, #9, shared the home with his sister, Sarah, on Cashua Ferry Road for a long time before going to the Golden Shore in 1929. He left no wife, but one son named Moses, who lived in Florence, SC. The real estate portion of Elihu's estate consists of 24.35 acres of what is now termed "heir property." It is located east of Darlington on Cashua Ferry Road. Table 2 also shows how ownership in the estate evolved from 1929 to 1955. It is much more complex today, nearly sixty years later, with greater than 100 heirs. The intricacies of heir property demonstrate a classic example of the importance of estate planning in the management of real estate portfolios.

The land is bounded by Cashua Ferry Road on the north, lands of Leo and Sarah Bacote on the east, M.L. Coggeshall land containing a stand of large pine trees on the west, with Benny Bacote's land on the south. [See Figure 9] The stand of large old pines on W.D. Coggeshall's tract was cut in 2008 for what seemed like redevelopment of that property.

This is a very significant tract of real estate that requires the attention of the present broader Bacote family at this time. **Sammie Bacote** was the family appointed representative for many decades, living well into his 90s while performing that arduous task in an extremely efficient and professional manner. Consistent with Bacote family history the next generation has stepped up and taken control here. New legislation is now enacted in South Carolina that provides assistance in "heir property" issues that families can take advantage of. The least desired scenario is the loss of this valuable property that the noble ancestors fought so hard to acquire and maintain for over a century. Descendants of Benny Bacote have volunteered and grasped the reins in the forefront of the efforts to unify and optimize the management of the estate for the united Bacote family.

Sarah Bacote, #10, wed Frank Williamson. After a very short unhappy marriage, she never remarried and lived the remainder of her years at her home on Cashua Ferry Road, on a tract of land adjacent to her brother Leo. **Sarah** did not have any children of her own, but she happily nourished and cared for most of her siblings' offspring. She was a quiet, kind woman whom everyone loved, and loved to be around. Almost everyone in the broader Bacote family during her era spent some serious time at her place. She loved to get dressed up and ride the children around in her pretty buggy with her smart, pink horse named Joe. Sarah, like her brother Boyd, had a profound love of horses. With all of her daintiness and love for laces, she was also an astute business woman having purchased several real estate properties as well as stocks in various companies during her lifetime. Sarah loved her family dearly and remained in contact with all, especially those who ventured from the homes of their fathers to other states and countries, using some of the addresses and telephone numbers shown below.

David Bacote	Annie Jenie Kelly	Roy Bacote
14 W. 98th Street	RFD 1 Box 357	PO Box 2855
New York City	Florence, S.C.	Winston Salem, N.C.

Leola Bacote Johnson	Ernest Griffin	Evelyn Kelly
663 N. Frazier Street	1400 Clinton Ave #9	203 W. 118th Street
Florence, S.C.	Bronx 56, New York	New York City

Mary Bacote Harris
615 E. Canfield Apt 1
Detroit 1, Michigan
Temple 2-7966

Herbert Bacote
28 Gill Street
New Haven, Conn.

Rubin Kelly
1823 N. 25th Street
Philadelphia, PA
Stev 2-4308

Josephine Graham
Rte 1 Box 152
Hartsville, S.C.

Dorsey Kelly
220 Sheas Terrace
Ardmore, PA

Chester Bolden
1793 Riverside
New York, NY

Archie Bacote
223 E. 11th Street
Richmond, Virginia

Sarah Kelly
613 Coit Street
Florence, S.C.

George Kelly
Mullins S.C.

Harold Jacob Kelly
1915 N. Judson Street
Philadelphia, PA
ST 4-7801

Gladys Bacote
554 Eastern Parkway
Brooklyn 25, NY
PR 2-2124

Mae Ruth Bacote
3432 Park Ave
Bronx, NY
Melrose 5-5610

Maude Sargent
158 Jefferson Street
Brooklyn, New York

Beulah Holloman
303 W. 114th Street
New York, NY

Rosa Lee Bacote
615 E. Canfield
Detroit 1, MI

Gladys B. Marcabee
825 Morrison Avenue
Bronx 72, New York
Tivoli 2-4021

Richard Griffin
2915 8th Avenue
New York, NY
Audobon 6-9088

Cleo Ruff
667 E.164th St.
Bronx, NY
Lu 9-6219

Mary Bacote Harris
4420 St. Antoine
Detroit 1, Michigan

Maxine B. Warfield
Rte 3
Rockville, Maryland

Sammie Bacote
411 Eastland
Kingstree, S.C.

Chaney Bacote Walker
2747 W. Eight Mile Rd.
Detroit, Michigan

The above list is some early addresses and telephone numbers, courtesy of Evelyn Brown's chest, of some Bacote family members, cited at the beginning of this chapter, interspersed with some Kelly family members, who left Darlington to pursue their dreams away from the farm. Like their predecessors and parents they were pioneers also. This listing is a virtual historical time capsule, taking us back decades into the storied past.

Shadrack Kelly

Evelyn K.B. Brown in 2005

George Paris Kelly Sr

James Kelly Sr. and Mary Pierce Kelly

Rosa Kelly Robinson

Eugenia Russell Kelly

Mary Gregg

James Kelly Jr.

Franklin and Vivian Kelly Wilds

Roseville Plantation House

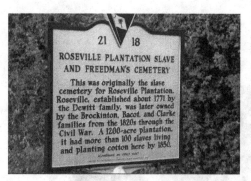

Freedman Cemetery Marker

Bolden Family in
Barbados, 1935
Gwendolyn, Carl, Ethylene,
Melville, Ermine

Wesley and Lanie Bailey McPhail, 1951

Frank J. Kelley & Family

Participants in 1979 Kelly Reunion

CHAPTER FOUR

THE KELLY SIDE

What is it about this Kelly family that merits the attention given herein? What distinguishes it from other families that we know? Why is there a need to bring the history of this Kelly family to the public forum?

From a historical perspective, a careful examination of the behavioral patterns and modus operandi of these Kellys, originally of the Back Swamp, Colfax or Riverdale sections of Darlington, South Carolina, reveals succeeding generations of family-oriented, community-oriented, gregarious, God-fearing, proud individuals. From its earliest ancestors in America, through the post-bondage generations, a clear pattern emerges: one of perseverance, dedication to excellence, dependability and the honoring of God's word.

After the Civil War ended many freed slaves adopted the moniker, Kelly or Kelley, as their surname based on a variety of reasons. Various census reports reflect this, listing this family as Kelly or Kelley. This simple difference in the spelling is a very critical input not only for the numerous search engines that crank out family history but also the tomes that house this history. It can serve as a screening device in identifying the origins of specific Kelly/Kelley families.

It seems very evident from most early family documents that I have been privileged to review, that Kelly is the original spelling of this family's surname. Although there are isolated examples of documents signed as Kelley and a few individual sub-clans adopting the Kelley version, I opine it is very significant that John Kelly Sr., possibly the most important forbear of this family, who simultaneously as you will see later utilized three surnames during his lifetime, is listed as John Kelly on page 386 of the 1870 Census of Colfax Township. Ensuing generations overwhelmingly are cited as Kelly.

A key underlying operative word in Kelly parlance is perseverance. It is one of the family's core values. Members have demonstrated this value for generations and continue to live it on a daily basis. Their stories included herein are a reminder of what the forbears sought to promulgate-that no matter how difficult the journey becomes or how unfair a situation may appear, it is important to resist conceding and throwing in the towel.

When this project began there was no doubt that the primary focus was family history for the reasons outlined in the Preface. As more and more information was amassed, I was impressed by the massive respect contemporary Kellys have garnered in their respective communities across this nation. As thought-provoking information from ancestral generations was discovered, perused and decoded, I made the conscious decision to present the story not in a popular conventional format, i.e. focusing primarily on genealogy, but focusing on some achievements of a few selected ancestors in a diverse array of arenas and circumstances. I sought a fresh perspective which addressed not merely personal achievement, but achievement (against all odds) that benefitted the general populace as well. This family has demonstrated a will to excel when the deck was pre-stacked against them, when the game is on the line and you're facing a three foot putt for eagle and ten skins.

Individual family members have distinguished themselves in many fields of human endeavor including religion, the trades, technology, education, the military, science, government service, the arts, agriculture, social work, public service, banking and the legal system, to name a few.

It is revealing that a scholarship fund administered by the Kelly family has provided a multitude of scholarships for over a quarter of a century for young students in the Pee Dee Region of South Carolina, providing much needed financial assistance in the attainment of college educations; that a member of this family was in the forefront of the ground-breaking research leading to the development of a drug currently utilized in a cocktail for the treatment of AIDS; that a young Kelly descendant, an Opera singer, is currently wooing audiences nationally as well as internationally on the operatic stage; that a member of this family leads a noted ministry, national in scope, that is shaping the lives of thousands of Americans.

The Kellys produce positive results. They were and essentially still are low-keyed operators, constantly striving to make a difference and a contribution to the betterment of America, and their legacy merits distinction.

Each generation has unique histories, special stories, and adventures about the family, early ancestors, their contributions and their accomplishments. Just as the construction of a strong bridge serves a locale for decades, the construction of a strong family tradition and mindset serves its members for generations. The careful installation of one unit at a time occurs over the course of generations. It does not occur in one grand swoop, it is a slow, deliberant process. Barriers have to be dismantled, obstacles negotiated, ideals established, nurtured and developed. It is unfortunate that over long periods of construction many of the early contributors fall into obscurity, their files and journeys lost in the sands of time.

As a young lad establishing my identity in Darlington and observing the remains of some old, decaying, plantation houses, as well as the preserved historic ones, I often wondered what plantation(s) had housed early Kelly ancestors, ones that I had no knowledge of, as well as oft-celebrated **John Kelly Sr.** who was well known via Kelly family lore. When traveling through Mechanicsville, deep inside of me, it always seemed it had to be somewhere in that area, not Society Hill, not Palmetto, but Mechanicsville. For some strange reason, unbeknownst at the time, I always experienced an abundance of spiritual energy when traveling Old Georgetown Road, a feeling even stronger than that experienced when in the presence of my relatives on their farms off of Bull Road. It was not a compelling drastic difference, but there was clearly a difference. Now I comprehend, now I understand, that it was my very active subconscious, natural, spiritual energy diligently at work even as a very young man.

The journey that led me to Roseville Plantation was like a miracle, like the parting of the Red Sea when Moses was leading his people out of Egypt to the Promise Land. During the course of the rigorous research and gathering of information for this treatise I spent many hours and days browsing and perusing old, interesting, historical documents at the Darlington County Historical Commission, documents not necessarily related to Kelly/Bacote early beginnings. One day miraculously and mysteriously, I stumbled upon an account of an ambitious researcher, Vivian H. Guyton, discovering her Brockington roots at the famed Roseville Plantation. It was like "ask and ye shall receive," and I immediately became thoroughly engrossed. The work was a classic short story, extremely exciting reading. I recall thinking it must be very satisfying and exciting to be able to make such a significant discovery and contribution. The author's email address was on the document so I contacted her and we communicated numerous times. We talked about the process, about how she went about it, about people and institutions that assisted her and about how much the newly found information meant to her surviving family members and the history of Darlington.

In a later email Ms. Guyton mentioned that she believed some Kellys, possibly several of my ancestors had also been housed at Roseville, but she was not certain. She graciously suggested I get in contact with South Carolina genealogy researcher and historian Scott Wilds, who assisted her in her quest for history of the Mechanicsville region. Much of the information in this chapter is the result of Mr. Wild's relentless foray into historical internet sources for data, and serves as a testament to his skill and expertise. Upon contacting Mr. Wilds, an expert on the bondage and post bondage history of the Darlington District, an entirely new world opened up to me. A wealth of information emerged from the depths of obscurity. He knew immediately, and revealed to me that one of the Kelly family iconic ancestors, **John Kelly Sr.**, had indeed been domiciled at Roseville and outlined where I could attain official documentation.

Quite amazingly, Mechanicsville Baptist Church tax documents indicate that early Kelly ancestors resided at Roseville. These documents show **John Kelly Sr.** [father of **Shadrack Kelly, John Kelly Jr., Meshach Kelly** et al, Figure 2] on the list of the enslaved owned by the planters Richard Brockinton, as well as Peter Samuel Bacot later when he inherited the plantation. **John Kelly Sr.** was born there in 1804, and lived all of his life at Roseville until he became a free man in 1865. His oldest children who were born into slavery accordingly were also born there.

This is a very significant discovery because three to four centuries after African slaves arrived in America, Kelly descendants, many like myself who were not fortunate enough to have experienced life even with their grandfathers, can finally identify a site where historical, pre-dated, generations of specific, cherished, courageous ancestors toiled, flourished and eventually went to the Golden Shore.

It is difficult to determine the precise number of these individuals that matriculated at Roseville Plantation, or how they were actually treated by the Brockintons and Bacots or the bulk of what happened to them before death. As a result we are forced to analyze the barest clues with the realization that at best they may represent only a fragment of reality. For example there is a documented slave graveyard on the plantation grounds but there are only a few markers therein. There is a very strong probability that there are many Kelly ancestors entombed there, a reality that possibly could be eventually confirmed by DNA analysis of bone fragments, in the future. It is known that John Kelly Sr. is entombed in the family graveyard at Kelly Place, but some of his offspring who passed to the Golden Shore before slavery subsided are very probably entombed at the Roseville Plantation Slave Cemetery.

This remarkable discovery provided the proof I had been so diligently searching for and marked the beginning of the accumulation of much surprising information regarding the domicile location of many of the courageous ancestors cited in this treatise. It affirmed and kindled my belief that "hidden, Kelly, family history" was not destined to remain obscure, that its exposure was at my fingertips. Much of this family history had been oral in nature. What happened here is a tool was graciously provided that allowed me to document and support many oral assertions and also uncover novel facts regarding what transpired with some ancestors cited herein.

Richard Brockinton was at the helm of the Brockinton family holdings in the early 1800s when the noted Roseville Plantation was purchased and when John was born on April 10, 1804.

Richard, a planter and former State Representative was married to Mary Hart, of the Hart Family, of Hartsville, SC. They had no children of their own but adopted the children of Mary's half-sister who had been married to Peter Hannibal Bacot (See Chapter Two). The adoption occurred because the two young parents died tragically at an early age. The children were Richard Brockinton Bacot, Mary Allston Bacot, and Peter Samuel Bacot (1814-1864), the latter who would play a major role in the history of Roseville Plantation.

Darlington County land maps show that the expansive Bacot family land holdings adjoined the equally prominent Brockinton family land in Darlington and Florence Counties in the heart of the Back Swamp.

Peter inherited Roseville Plantation after Richard's death in 1843 and Mary's subsequent death shortly thereafter. The inheritance included many of the enslaved Africans, African-Americans and American Indians housed there. The 1860 Darlington County Census lists Peter Samuel Bacot as a planter, age forty-nine, with a plantation valued at $38,400. Roseville was one of more highly valued plantations in the county.

When Florence, South Carolina was incorporated in 1888 it took a portion of the original Back Swamp lands away from Darlington County, including the area that contained the historic Roseville Plantation.

Historical documentation of **John Kelly Sr.** is found on the *Schedule of Negro Slaves and Other Chattels to be Partitioned and Divided,* a document utilized in the Darlington District, in 1857, during the official execution of the wills of Richard Brockinton and his wife Mary Brockinton. [Table 3]

Table 3 is the presentation of a very critical document in the annals of early Kelly history because, it confirms the names (shown in bold print) and location of numerous ancestors cited in the 19th century genealogy of these families. It is a very powerful, illuminating, historical source of information which, drafted in 1857, contains the names of slaves originally owned by the Brockintons at the time of Richard Brockinton's death in 1843. In addition, many of the slaves purchased or born at Roseville Plantation after his wife's death years later are also included. It also shows that in 1857 there were 132 slaves, 143 hogs, forty-eight heads of cattle, four mules and two yokes of oxen at Roseville Plantation, one of the larger plantations in that region of the Back Swamp.

The original Table 3 is a hand written document. Due to the uncertainty of the spelling of some names and the translation of some abbreviations a new table was constructed. This table (as shown) contains clarifications and considerations deemed appropriate by the author based on the spelling of names in a similar earlier

Table 3

#	Name	#	Name	#	Name	#	Name
1	Jack	34	Tembe	67	Cloe	100	Lena
2	Abram	35	Ned	68	Daphney	101	Dorean
3	Daniel	36	Cato	69	Richard	102	Ben
4	Adam	37	Phillis	70	Frank	103	Lusannah
5	Phillip	38	Peggy	71	Dinah	104	Oliver
6	Esau	39	Delila	72	Glasgow	105	Simon
7	Jerry	40	Lambert	73	Martilla	106	Miranda
8	Dave	41	Tim	74	William	107	Jane
9	**Harry**	42	January	75	Albert	108	Jane
10	Victoria	43	**Carolina**	76	Charlotte	109	April
11	Elizabeth	44	Mapey	77	Ada	110	Isabelle
12	**Mary**	45	Lousinda	78	Venus	111	Katty
13	Anson	46	Keyiah	79	Lucy	112	Sylvia
14	Rose	47	Dick	80	**Sarah**	113	Patience
15	**John, Carp**	48	Julius	81	Polly	114	Henry
16	**Nancy**	49	Rose	82	Horace	115	Auin
17	**Lewis**	50	Isaac	83	Lizette	116	Nathan
18	**Tom**	51	Doctor	84	George	117	Mary
19	**Jonas**	52	Betty	85	Bitty	118	Cow Daniel
20	**John**	53	Patty	86	Franky	119	Joseph
21	**Billow**	54	Peggy	87	Dinah	120	Betsy
22	**Leah**	55	Katy	88	Betsy	121	Birdy
23	Bob	56	Ned	89	Linda	122	Isabel John
24	Cornelius	57	Louisa	90	**Carolina**	123	Washington
25	**Hannah**	58	Masiah	91	Margaret	124	Little Sam
26	**Matilda**	59	Bob	92	Esau	125	Toby
27	Lydia	60	Amy	93	Toney	126	Alfred
28	Peter	61	Jackson	94	Susy	127	P. Moses
29	Lud	62	Judy	95	Alexander	128	Moses
30	Ann	63	Rachael	96	Aunie	129	O. Adam
31	Hetty	64	Charles	97	Lisbon		
32	Mapey	65	Joe	98	Hopkins		
33	Daphney	66	Lot	99	Lucy		

Together with the negro slaves born since the making of the inventory of Mary H. Brockington deceased.

Mules named Rock, Frank, Joe, Blue, 48 head of cattle, 2 yoke of oxen, 143 Hogs, sideboard, rocking chair, misscow fan, ox cart

1857

Schedule of Negro Slaves and other Chattels to be Partitioned and Divided

document, entitled *Schedule P, Appointment of Negroes of Estate of R. Brockington*, filed 12 February 1854, where the recorder or writer exhibited more readable writing skills. Fortunately the names and abbreviations in question do not affect or impact the intended usage of the information therein. A copy of the original Table 3 is presented in the Appendix.

In addition to the actual listing of assets, there are other aspects of this document that merit consideration and discussion. First and most importantly it documents the domicile location of many of the Kelly ancestors cited in this treatise, as Roseville Plantation, during the era of bondage. Secondly, if you carefully observe, you detect that it touches on a very subliminal point. The enslaved individuals represented in this document have no surname. It is a point that after years of extracting pertinent data therefrom, finally blind-sided me squarely on my frontal lobe.

From all that has been written, it is very clear that the culture of bondage, the slave owners, plantation owners etc. sought to preclude any markers of lineage of the enslaved in the eyes of America and indeed in worldwide society. The listing of merely a first name was a subtle tool which created an aura of invisibility and anonymity, perpetuating that "less than a human being scenario." It was essentially a cover-up by omission, because the plantation record books, in many cases, contained surnames for these individuals. In general, newborns were given the surname of the mother, but numerous entries were made with the offspring possessing the surname of the father. An example is presented later in this chapter. That was the culture during that era.

Nevertheless, from a historical point of view, I find it very enthralling that many of the relocated proud Africans would not allow such disenfranchisement to occur, as they upheld their innate concept of family and maintained the official continuity within their collective brain cells, sometimes in clandestine or fugitive manners via the very important African-American oral tradition.

If you search for Mechanicsville on any current map larger than a Darlington County map, you will be hard pressed to find this beautiful, historic area (Figure 4, Figure 5). Cashua Ferry Road, aka Route 34, dissects the heart of Mechanicsville which now features a few stores at the crossroads, three old churches, a deer processing center and farmland that is probably being leased to one of the mega farmers in Mechanicsville. The road enters the Pee Dee River basin via a sloping incline and a large bridge spans the Great Pee Dee River. The river as it did in earlier times serves as the eastern border for a large portion of Mechanicsville (Figures 4, 5, 6, 7).

Let us take a closer look at this important residence that appears to have played a very prominent role in Kelly family history. The historic Roseville Plantation house, which dates back to 1771, was situated in the "Back Swamp" on 1,200 acres of beautiful river front land, bordered on the east by the Pee Dee River. The classic two-story, colonial, antebellum manor had all the trappings of the prototypical southern plantation home, a porch that wrapped around three sides of the home, a long entrance hall, a parlor, large kitchen and pantry, five fireplaces, a large cooking stove, two small heating stoves, and numerous bedrooms on the upper level. The organized grounds contained a chicken house, breeder house, smoke house, buggy house, tobacco pack house, fertilizer house, livestock barn and lot, woodshed, shop, ironing house, outhouse, water tank, pump house, wind mill, a large farm bell which had coded signals for the slaves and residents of the plantation to respond to specific situations like an emergency, fire, illness, mealtime etc. The grounds also contained six one-room, "shotgun-cabin" type slave quarters.

Between 1840 and 1860 the enslaved Blacks and American Indians there, including many Kelly ancestors, numbered well over one-hundred, the number constantly changing from year to year due to sales, purchases of new slaves, deaths and the encouraged births of valuable newborns. Newborns instantly became the valuable property of the landowner. If for any year we assume there were 100-120 slaves on site, occupying six, one room, shotgun type cabins; that calculates to an astonishing sixteen-to twenty people per cabin. With all the grandeur of the "Big House" looming in the foreground, with all your wildest imagination can you even visualize twenty people residing in one of these one room, shotgun cabins for their entire lives?

Roseville extended eastward through a swampy region all the way to the river. Above the bluff were upland fields dispersed between natural stands of pines that served as buffer regions and erosion controllers. This land was not very fertile when compared to river bottom land. The fields extended westward toward Old Georgetown Road.

Old Georgetown Road barreled through the plantation. This old historic road was a stagecoach lane before the days of the railroad and modern automobile transportation. Many of the old timers shown in Figure 2 were privy to the visualization of many gallant carriages as they meandered bouncingly along the winding lane to Charles Town, or The City by the Sea as it was also called during those days.

The plantation also contained river bottom land that was cleared, developed, and worked by these ancestors. This was a strip of an astonishingly fertile alluvial plain that extended to the river. Normally each spring the river would overflow, depositing a fresh layer of fine soil that contained all of the vital nutrients of natural plant food. When the water level subsided and the soil dried sufficiently, **John Kelly Sr.,** his sons and other ancestors later shown to also have been housed at Roseville, would plough, prepare the soil, and plant major crops of cotton, tobacco and corn. The yields were prodigious, as you can imagine, from these naturally fertilized fields.

The overflows or freshets as they were also commonly called, with their huge upside also came with a downside. They did not consistently occur during the spring. Occasionally they would happen after crops were planted, or in the late summer before harvesting had taken place. The flooding could be enormous, in addition to crop loss, sometimes livestock, property and human life was also endangered. This was an on-going issue for planters and farmers who worked that portion of the Back Swamp's farmland. In addition, the health conditions in these areas were very perilous, particularly during the hot summer months. Dreaded diseases such as malaria and yellow fever were commonplace on the swampy, mosquito laden plantations such as Roseville. It was so dangerous that many planters and/or some of their families would flee to Springville or other less treacherous locations during the summer months. Unfortunately our ancestors were not afforded that luxury; they had to persevere, endure and produce against all odds.

In 1850, early Kelly ancestors at the Roseville Plantation, under the helm of Peter Samuel Bacot, assisted in the production of 173 bales of cotton (400 pounds per bale), 6,500 pounds of corn, 4,500 pounds of rice, 500 bushels of peas and beans, and 250 bushels of sweet potato yams on the large plantation. I would say 1850 was a very good year. There were a total of 132 slaves on site including the "Iron Horse," (46 year old John Kelly Sr.) and other Kellys who are discussed later.

Roseville was primarily an agricultural center whose rich fields produced a surplus of foodstuffs and durables which could be sold or traded for manufactured goods. The bulk of the surplus grains and foodstuffs not utilized by the plantation were shipped by barges to Charles Town via rivers, canals and waterways. Many goods were sold at ports or plantations along the shipping route, while ultimately most cotton and other important durable products were exported to Europe, coastal colonies and the Caribbean. The gentle Pee Dee River was of paramount importance for the ultimate success of the venture at Roseville Plantation. The river's strategic location afforded the plantation the ability to easily utilize this primary mode of transportation for large amounts of goods during that era.

The grand home, modest by today's standards, is still standing majestically at its original location in the Bank Swamp. It was a very upscale house for its period. The dramatic entrance consisted of a long, straight, avenue about an eighth of a mile in length, lined with huge old oak, longleaf pine and sycamore trees draped in mounds of "low country" swamp moss. The plantation house was a well-known stopping place for travelers who were always accorded "good ole" southern hospitality. Tradition has it that Mary Brockinton had 365 hams cooked each year. Some say this was done primarily to be prepared for visitors, in the tradition of the old South.

Church records show that residents of the plantation, whites as well as blacks, attended the Mechanicsville Baptist Church (currently located at the crossroads) in the village of Colfax/Mechanicsville. That church is still a thriving institution.

Roseville Plantation, now a national historic landmark, is currently listed on the National Register of Historic Places in South Carolina and was recently restored by the Carl and Eleanor Tucker family to much of its original architectural design before the Antebellum Period.

There are presently two historical roadside markers on Georgetown Road, between Louthers Lake and Interstate 95, in Florence County, that pay homage to the plantation. The first marker which was unveiled November 13, 2004 commemorates the Roseville Plantation Slave and Freedman's Cemetery. It reads as follows; "This was originally the slave cemetery for Roseville Plantation. Roseville established about 1771 by the Dewitt family, was later owned by the Brockinton, Bacot, and Clarke families from the 1820s through the turn of the century. A 1200 acre plantation, it had more than 100 slaves living and planting cotton here by 1850."

The cemetery, sometimes referred to as the Clarke Cemetery, about 150 square feet in area, is located approximately 500 feet from a swampy section of the plantation and is bounded by two large ravines. Some gravesites are located in the area between the ravines and some in the ravines. Some are found along the slope of the easternmost ravine very close to the swampy region. It contains a minimum of 148 graves and it is speculated that it could contain as many as 250. This historic burial site dates from before the War Between the States and was used originally as a burial ground for Roseville Plantation slaves. The noted Cato Brockington, as discussed later, is reportedly entombed there. There are undoubtedly ancestral Kelly slaves, freedmen and descendants, as discussed later, buried in that boneyard alongside two century's worth of other forgotten souls, awaiting discovery. It was last surveyed by John L. Andrews, Jr. on June 01, 1997, under the name of the Clarke Cemetery.

The historical marker recognizes the historic significance of these individuals and contributes to the preservation of the cemetery while helping prevent additional destruction to the site. Already many of the gravesites have been claimed by the elements.

The plantation site was nearly dismantled in 1997 when the International Honda Corporation with its powerful lobby sought to acquire the land for construction of the Honda automobile assembly plant currently located off of Interstate 95 near the Timmonsville exit. But as fate would have it Carl Tucker stood up and refused to sell his land and the old manor due primarily to his respect for its historical relevance and out of reverence to the brave souls entombed there. My thanks are extended to Mr. Tucker's estate, otherwise I probably would have never discovered the plantation, and never embarked on this remarkable journey.

That corridor of Florence County is rapidly evolving, progress is in the works, and it behooves all families with interests there to become more vigilant and proactive in the attention and protection of this historical site.

A vast amount of Kelly history occurred at Roseville Plantation. Many of our early ancestors were born there, many died there, and many lived through the Civil War as residents there. Some of their history has been preserved and registered at The South Carolina Department of Archives and History, various Universities and the Darlington County Historical Commission. In addition, much has been preserved through the efforts of the African-American Brockington and Kelly families as well as the Caucasian Bacot and Clarke families. Ada Bacot Clarke wrote in her diary, "The Confederate Nurse," a very expressive sentence. Clarke stated, "African Americans living on the plantation were respected and treated as part of the family at Roseville."

Traversing the grounds of Roseville Plantation, exploring the old house and the slave cemetery was an especially powerful experience for me. I did not shed tears or feel weak in the knees, but I realized something special was happening. The profusely widespread chirping of numerous avian species in the ageless, undisturbed, swamp-like huge pine and oak trees as well as the absence of vehicular sounds of civilization made it very serene and tranquil there. My consciousness, focus, and imagination soared to another level. Somehow I emerged from the visit with an appreciation of the magnitude of Roseville Plantation life and a greater sense of respect for those heroic individuals. It afforded me a renewed appreciation of their resiliency and a greater respect for their courage. It also revealed the depth of the feelings I have for history. The eerie amount of spiritual and sentimental energy I experienced was much like what most African-Americans sense when they visit noted slave trading sites such as Bights of Benin and Biafra, Calabar in Cameroon, Lagos, Nigeria, the House of Slaves in Senegal, Jamestown, Virginia and Charlestown, South Carolina. I envisioned the apparent strength and courage of the enslaved individuals who matriculated there on a daily basis during the days of lore, fulfilling their destiny and place in history.

It is my most fervent desire that Kelly descendants outlined herein, as well as those not listed, get to experience the walk down the avenue leading to the restored manor. The spiritual energy, simply put, is off the charts, resonating decibels above normal encounters and has to be experienced to believe. Those who possess the innate ability to operate at the spiritual level can appreciate what I am trying to relay here.

Discovering Roseville Plantation was like finding a flash drive in an enormous haystack, a flash drive that contained gigabytes of data about everything I sought knowledge of. It was indeed a miracle.

Many times on the grounds, I physically hesitated and asked myself what is the meaning of this symbolic revelation, not just to me but to all descendants who would follow, including my own offspring? I am not just talking about logistically, but philosophically and spiritually. There was no answer then and I don't have one now. Suffice it to say, some of my more perceptive contemporaries contend it was simply divine intervention. That forces greater than we mere mortals were at work.

It must be similar to the intense feeling of reverence and awe that Jews experience when they visit some of the Holocaust's preserved, Annihilation and Forced Labor Camps like Auschwitz, Belzec and Buchenwald to name a few. It was similar to riding a time capsule back into the storied past. My own will to excel in my endeavors was expanded by magnitudes I cannot fully express. I became energized. If my forebears could survive, flourish and claw their way back to a real sense of respected humanity and normalcy in such an extraordinary manner, with so little, then surely the sky is indeed the limit for me and their many descendants.

Needless to say the debt has not been fully erased; the account has not been settled. We as humans have been psychologically and emotionally impacted by the era of slavery much more intensely than many can even imagine. The connection between those generations and contemporary generations is eternal and must never be forgotten or taken for granted.

The second marker, entitled Roseville Plantation, reads; "in the 1850s the plantation passed to the Brockinton's nephew, Peter Samuel Bacot (1810-1889), a planter, whose daughter Ada White Bacot Clarke (1832-1911) was born here and was later a confederate nurse and diarist. The Clarkes remodeled the house in 1885 and again in 1910. Roseville was more recently restored by the Tucker family and listed in the National Register of Historic Places in 1997."

Before the above outlined facts were uncovered, regarding early Kelly family history, documentation relating the history of Roseville Plantation meant little to contemporary Kelly families in Darlington or those far away from the homes of their fathers. Now, from a historical perspective, the words embellished on those historic markers along Georgetown Road in Mechanicsville will have special meaning, providing documented proof that early Kelly individuals played a primary role in the establishment, survival and contributions of this old landmark and indeed Darlington, South Carolina.

When I laid eyes on the second marker and saw that the Bacot family owned the Plantation during the bondage era, my heart fluttered briefly and I began to sweat. I knew I was onto something special. To locate and traverse the grounds where my early ancestors lived, toiled and survived was a moment I never even dreamed of experiencing.

From my vantage point and with the resources at my disposal, I have attempted to revisit some of the subtle dynamics of Antebellum and pre-Civil War plantation life via the lives of early iconic Kelly ancestors. As such I have chronicled some of their achievements and their roles in the development of early Darlington, South Carolina history. This re-visitation is continued through the Reconstruction, Jim Crow, Mass Migration and Civil Rights eras via post-bondage generations of Kellys and highlights the roles the family played in developing the county's agricultural industry, and the bravery a few family members displayed on the battlefields for America. It is a snapshot of both individual struggles that this family endured, as well as accomplishments and achievements attained in the quest for equality, excellence, personal development and a strong Kelly culture.

During the course of researching, documenting and amassing family information I discovered that the identity of many ancestral matriarchs was lost or undisclosed over the course of time. There is a very straight forward explanation for this disturbing, unfortunate phenomenon. First of all, the surname of a patriarch's male descendants remains unchanged over generations simplifying the identification of paternal ancestry. Whereas to the contrary, a few generations of females adopting the surname of their spouses renders the original, matriarchal, maiden name hidden in the paperwork, essentially lost for all eternity; not only from a record keeping standpoint but also from a historical perspective. For example, even today on Ancestor. com it is much easier to access data on a male ancestor versus a female ancestor because the surname is a critical element for the search engine. This loss of matriarchal surname visibility can result in the loss of family identity as it relates to female ancestors. Because of this societal nuance, I have consciously attempted to highlight the genealogy of numerous female offspring of clans presented herein and included maiden names when appropriate.

From the beginning, whether they, as an enslaved family, were allowed the simple courtesy of communication or not, much of the rich family history of the nineteenth and twentieth century Colfax/ Back Swamp/Riverdale/Mechanicsville African-American Kelly generations was rigorously maintained and accurately transmitted through the very important oral channel tradition.

I submit this statement with ultimate respect for the oral channel cast members, young and old, who for whatever motives stored the nuances of this history in the mega-bytes of their brain cells. They must be acknowledged as visionaries for having the discipline to accurately process and retain pertinent data, when many others failed to recognize its importance. Were it not for these cast members, over the course of our history in America, much of our earlier existence, particularly as it pertains to matriarchal ancestors, would be much more obscure.

It has long been considered that this large, robust, diverse family consisted of three primary wings, with each wing representing descendants of the slaves **Dublin and Nancy Robinson Kelly**, **Carolina and Sarah Jackson Kelly**, and **John Sr. and Hannah Harrison Kelly**.

Reverend James W. Kelly, currently regarded as the family historian, is credited with being the founder and organizer of the first modern day Kelly reunion in Darlington in August 1979. Early that year Reverend Kelly, descendant of Dublin and Nancy; Evelyn Kelly Bolden Brown, descendant of John and Hannah; and Hattie Kelly Wayne and Elvira Kelly Warren, descendants of Carolina and Sarah; the four primary members of the reunion organizing committee, embarked on the momentous task of amassing, documenting and publicly discussing some of this oral history. Their efforts were not in vain as they accomplished their mission of getting the family re-united and back on a cohesive tract. With the emergence of the rapidly expanding "new world order" they recognized the necessity for the family to get re-organized for a productive run into the 21st century. The historic gathering took place in Darlington at Friendship Baptist Church where a small amount of history and genealogy was presented to the family members assembled.

A tremendous amount of Kelly genealogy has also been presented in the very informative and detailed 2003 Kelly Reunion Booklet generated by Ms. Rene Peterson, Ms. Catherine Kelly, Bishop Jerry Kelly, Dr. Brenda Kelly, et al. Much of the Kelly genealogy presented in this thesis was taken directly from that thoroughly researched and important historical document.

The story of the Kelly family is very informative indeed, not only to descendants of the many courageous ancestors, but to the general public as well. It is an intriguing story of trust, faith, hard work, respect, family unity and cohesion, and above all the will to excel against all odds. It is a classic American story about the detainment of an extended family structure during the years of bondage. It is a classic American story about families dealing with the horrendous issues of their era and ultimately moving forward in a grand fashion. It is a story about a family's devotion to God and the ultimate effect of faith.

Let us take a closer look at some of the early Kelly personalities and Kelly lineage. Then we can better comprehend and appreciate how this family has evolved.

Family lore, United States Census Reports, and court and church records document the early family presence in the Back Swamp/ Colfax/ Riverdale/ Palmetto/ Mechanicsville sections depending on the period in South Carolina history. [See Figures 4, 5, 6] It is widely accepted among family members that the three men referred to above, John Sr., Dublin, and Carolina were not brothers, nor were the latter two John's sons. The exact nature of their relationship is uncertain, although John Sr.'s son, Shadrack Kelly, and Dublin's son, George Paris Kelly Sr., referred to themselves as cousins later in their lives. These two men visited each other often during the early 1900s, although they lived about eight miles apart. Obviously they knew something, something that occurred decades earlier, something that unfortunately has gotten obscured with the passing of time. One of the goals of this thesis is to present findings that will allow us to gain more insight into the actual relationship of these men. The prevailing mantra among the three Kelly wings is that the three men were related as cousins; hence all succeeding generations are cousins. Some new groundbreaking observations and speculations are presented on the following pages regarding their relationship.

As outlined in the Preface, it is not my goal to generate a complete lineage of this large Kelly family by including all the kinsfolks that we have knowledge of. A semi-random, skeletal, selection process has been implemented and I would like to reiterate: it is not my intent to intentionally omit any specific family members from inclusion. It is my desire that as presented, contemporary Kellys will have enough information to allow them to connect the dots, to establish their own paths of descent, and more importantly to re-connect with the family at-large. Let's say for example, a specific Kelly or his/her sub-clan is not presented, but a known relative is presented. Knowing his/her relationship to that relative allows that individual to extrapolate his/her own path of descent.

The birth years and ages presented herein, taken from Darlington Census as well as U.S. Federal Census reports, should not be expected to be 100 per cent precise, but generally appear to be accurate within (+/-) three years. If a month /day/ year/ is given, then it is a well-documented date and should be considered correct.

Family lore declares that Dublin Kelly married Nancy Robinson and that they represent the elder couple of this wing of Kellys. The 1870 U.S. Federal Census lists the household of Dublin Kelly and Nancy Robinson Kelly as shown below. Please note that the names in parenthesis were added by the author to promote clarity. The years of birth were calculated from the ages given in the report:

i.	Dublin Kelly	b. 1842
ii.	Nancy Kelly	b. 1837
iii.	Caroline Kelly	b. 1857
iv.	Esaw (Esau) Kelly	b. 1865
v.	Juna (Jane) Kelly	b. 1867

vi. Florrace (Horace) Kelly   b. 1868
vii. Lewis Kelly   b. 1825

The 1880 Darlington County Census lists Dublin and Nancy as 50 and 40 years of age respectively. The listing of their household in 1880 is shown below:

i.   Dublin Kelly   b. 1830
ii.   Nancy Kelly   b. 1840
iii. Caroline Kelly   b. 1857
iv.   Esau Kelly   b. 1862
v.   Horace Kelly   b. 1864
vi.   Jane Kelly   b. 1867
vii. Issac Kelly   b. 1871
viii. George Paris Kelly   b. 1873
ix.   Frankie Kelly   b. 1874
x.   Elam Kelly   b. 1865
xi.   Elsie Kelly   b. 1863
xii. Binah Kelly   b. 1848

As you can see there are some striking differences in the two census reports. One very obvious difference, as reflected in the 1880 Census Report, is the fact that Dublin and Nancy had three additional children after 1870. The most glaring difference is the inconsistency in Dublin's date of birth. The 1870 report indicates he was born in 1842, while the 1880 report indicates his date of birth is 1830. This is a substantial difference that has serious implications in the interpretation of the reports.

In addition, a gentleman named Lewis Kelly is listed as a household member on the 1870 Census but not the 1880 version. Lewis' very significant presence on the 1870 version is discussed later along with a discussion of Dublin's date of birth. There is good agreement on the dates of birth of the children between the reports.

Binah Kelly is listed as a member of the Dublin Kelly household in the 1880 Report. This is significant because the 2003 Kelly Reunion Booklet lists Binah as an offspring of Nancy and Dublin. As a matter

171

of fact the present consensus among some Dublin Kelly descendants is that Binah was a daughter of Dublin and Nancy. However, if Binah's date of birth as listed in the 1880 Report is correct, it is not consistent with her being a daughter of Nancy, nor the mother of Dublin or Nancy. Let me explain the reasoning. First of all, Nancy (b. 1840) is too young to be the mother of Binah (b. 1848); and secondly Binah's Kelly surname rules out her being Nancy's mother or sibling. It seems much more probable that Binah is a sister of Dublin. This discovery alters the Kelly genealogy chart and places her in the same generation as Dublin in the evolvement of this family.

Binah Kelly wed John Rives (b. 1828). The names of the children of John Rives and Binah Kelly, sister of Dublin Kelly, are:

i.	Ellen Rives	b. 1863
ii.	Clara Rives	b. 1867
iii.	Soloman Rives	b. 1869
iv.	Joseph Rives	b. 1872
v.	John Rives Jr.	b. 1875
vi.	Martha Rives	b. 1875

Issac Kelly married Amelia Brockington (b. 1856). The names of the children of Amelia and Issac Kelly, son of Dublin and Nancy Kelly, are:

i.	Joe Kelly	b. 1882
ii.	Annanian Kelly	b. 1884
iii.	Warren Kelly	b. 1887

George Paris Kelly Sr. wed Eugenia Sams Russell (b. 1878) just before the turn of the century, in 1899. This union was blessed with nine offspring, starting with Dellie in 1901. The names of the children of Eugenia and George Paris Kelly Sr., son of Dublin and Nancy Kelly, are:

i.	Dellie Kelly	b. 8/5/1901
ii.	Eugenia Kelly	b. 3/12/1905

iii.	Annie Kelly	b.10/10/1908
iv.	Mary Kelly	b. 5/22/1909
v.	George P. Kelly Jr.	b. 2/15/1910
vi.	Caroline Kelly	d. 5/12/1991
vii.	Sallie Kelly	b. 1922
viii.	James W. Kelly	b. 12/13/1924
ix.	Samuel E. Kelly	b. 9/3/1912 or 1914
		d. 10/29/1996

Eugenia also had two boys from an earlier marriage, Clarence Russell (b. August 1897) and Henry Russell (b. 1898). Her daughters, Eugenia married Matthew Freeman, and Annie married E.C. Mack. Unfortunately young Sallie died as an infant in 1922.

My closest ties with this wing of the at-large Kelly family were with George P. Kelly Jr. (b. 1910), James W. Kelly (b. 1924) and Samuel E. Kelly, the father of Vivian Kelly Wilds. As a young man, each of these older gentlemen would always find time to talk to me, to encourage me, to find out what I was doing. They sincerely cared about the course of my life. I think it would be correct to describe them as very people/family oriented men, a trait that eventually contributed greatly to their success in their chosen fields of endeavor. George Jr. was an insurance agent with the famous North Carolina Mutual Insurance Company. He used his career as a platform to benefit the community by raising community awareness in terms of long-term estate planning as well as the utilization of insurance coverage to benefit heirs of ancestral souls and for the defrayal of future educational expenses for the youth. He and his wife, the former Harry Lee Sawyer, were not blessed with any offspring, but they exhibited great respect and love for young people, casting a valuable web as mentors and advisors.

James became a man of the cloth, a very influential Baptist minister. His life story is a very enthralling. Here is a gentleman who at nearly fifty years of age was still committed to attaining a college education while being a father and provider for his family. He is a decorated World War II and Korean War veteran, having been wounded in the Korean conflict. History will show that James, like his brother George Jr., made very significant contributions to this country in the armed services, George Jr. in the Navy and James in the Army, and once back in South Carolina aided in the development of the city of Darlington.

James's initial foray into the education arena was as a student at A&T University in North Carolina in the 1940s. This was interrupted by the extended military service to the country. After an honorable discharge, he transferred his college credits and attended Morris College in Sumter, South Carolina, on a part time basis, where he graduated magna cum laude with a bachelor's degree in english in 1973, and a bachelor of divinity degree in 1974.

He was called to the ministry in the 1960s and was the senior pastor at Friendship Baptist Church on Chestnut Street for twenty years. James is acknowledged as a devoted civic and community affairs activist, having also served as an educator for nineteen years, a School Board member for six years and a member of the very important Darlington Cemetery Board for many years. There is no doubt that James W. Kelly cast a huge footprint and positively impacted the lives of countless citizens in Darlington for decades.

James married Celia Bull (b. 11/15/1926). The names of the children of Celia and James W. Kelly, grandson of Dublin and Nancy Kelly, are:

    i.   Reginald J. Kelly   b. 12/2/1961
    ii. Mable Lynn Kelly   b. 6/9/1966

Samuel E. Kelly (b. 1912 or 1914) wed Vermella Kirvens (b. 1919). The products of the union of Vermella Kirvens and Samuel E. Kelly, grandson of Dublin and Nancy Kelly, are:

    i.   Elizabeth Kelly
    ii. Vivian Kelly   b. 4/30/1943
    iii. Margaret Kelly   b. 7/24/1944
    iv. Sarah Kelly
    v. Vermella Kelly
    vi. Samuel Kelly Jr.

This clan of the family resided on Old Society Hill Road in the Mont Clair section of Darlington County on the original George Paris Kelly Sr. homestead. As the head of this important family in Kelly family history, Samuel vigorously espoused and demonstrated the mantra that hard work should not be shunned, that it along with education represented a road map to success. He was a consummate entrepreneur. Some would coin him slightly eccentric; I prefer to say he believed in himself, that he could deliver on many fronts. He operated a gardening service, a cleaning service, was a farmer, barber and brick mason, a man of many diverse skills.

Before he established his own barber shop, he worked at the renowned W. Harrison Barber Shop adjacent to the old Greyhound Bus Station in Darlington. Samuel was the first man to cut my hair professionally and served as my barber for most of my pre-teen years. I looked forward to going to the barber shop on Saturdays, not only because it was the place to be, but because I trusted him immensely and as a young man enjoyed his conversations. We are all aware of the significant role the barber shop plays in the African-American community, and I learned a lot from him during my visits there.

Samuel was an excellent barber, and built a reputation and a strong following as a sideman in the entertaining, informative, circus atmosphere at W. Harrison's shop. Out of his many endeavors, this position afforded him the best platform to be a positive force in the lives of many young black men in Darlington as a mentor and intelligence force.

Samuel and Vermella provided their offspring with the tools to lead productive lives in America. Elizabeth, the first born, married Donald Henderson a mechanical designer with General Electric. Elizabeth had a productive career as a legal secretary for thirty years in Washington, DC where they resided. Donald is deceased and Elizabeth has residences in Washington and Darlington. The name of the child of Donald Henderson and Elizabeth Kelly, great-grand daughter of Dublin and Nancy Kelly, is:

    i.   Donald Henderson II

Donald II attended Morgan State University in Baltimore, Maryland and currently resides in the Washington, DC area. He has two children, Dasia Henderson and Donald Henderson III, great-great-great grandchildren of Dublin and Nancy Kelly. Donald II is currently married to Alessandra.

Sarah resides in Willingboro, NJ, while Margaret and Samuel Jr. live in Darlington.

Vivian, their second daughter, married Franklin Wilds, a Darlington native, in 1967 in Philadelphia, Pennsylvania. The names of the children of Franklin Wilds and Vivian Kelly, great-grand daughter of Dublin and Nancy Kelly, are:

    i.   Nicole Renee Wilds
    ii. Karen Wilds

Vivian is a classic prototype descendant of this wing of the Kelly family at-large. Educationally conscious, God fearing, community oriented, and a college administrator, she currently resides in Washington, DC with her entrepreneur/politician husband. She has served as President of the DC Democratic Woman's Club.

Unfortunately their daughter Karen died as a baby. Nicole, who represents the sixth generation of this wing of Kellys, currently resides in Washington, DC. She is a Temple University graduate and Director of the DC Public School Drug Initiative Policy Program.

Margaret Kelly married Gary G. Gregg. The children of Gary Gregg and Margaret Kelly, great-granddaughter of Dublin and Nancy Kelly, are:

    i.   Martrell Denise Kelly b. 5/16/1973
    ii. Gary G. Gregg Jr.   b. 5/21/1976

Vermella Kelly married Sidney Jerome Smalls Sr. The children of Sidney Smalls Sr. and Vermella Kelly, great-granddaughter of Dublin and Nancy Kelly, are:

    i.   Sidney J. Smalls Jr.   b. 11/10/1970
    ii. Edward C. Smalls   b. 8/11/1978
    iii. Vermella M. Smalls   b. 4/19/1981

Dellie Kelly, the oldest offspring of George Paris Kelly Sr. and Eugenia, married Columbus Jones Sr. The ten children of Columbus Jones Sr. and Dellie Kelly, granddaughter of Dublin and Nancy Kelly, are:

i.	Columbus Jones Jr.	b. 9/2/1919
ii.	James Kirmire Jones	b. 12/27/1922
iii.	Anceline Jones	b. 1/10/1924
iv.	Wilbur Jones	b. 2/11/1926
v.	Glendell Jones	
vi.	Annie Mae Jones	b. 7/71929
vii.	Majorie Jones	b. 3/18/1933
viii.	Wendell Jones	
ix.	William Jones	b. 10/10/1935
x.	Jerline Jones	b. 4/4/1938

Dellie, who went to the Golden Shore in 2001, spent the bulk of her life on the old Kelly homestead on Old Society Hill Road in Darlington. Her oldest son, Columbus Jr., sometimes called Redman because of his reddish complexion, spent most of his adult life in Philadelphia, Pennsylvania, and lived to the ripe old age of ninety four. He was married to Ophelia Bostic. Most of Dellie's other offspring also departed Darlington at an early age, relocating to New Jersey, Baltimore, Maryland, New York and Pennsylvania. Glendell married Joyce and they live in New Jersey. Wendell who was married to Ann lived in Baltimore before relocating to Darlington later in life, while Marjorie lived much of her life in Buffalo, New York before relocating to Florence, South Carolina. Anceline married Arthur Williamson and they lived in Newark, New Jersey before relocating to the old family homestead on Society Hill Road in the late 1970s. This remarkable, active, senior ancestor at age ninety participates in a massive amount of volunteer work at many venues in Darlington. Annie Mae still lives in Philadelphia. James K. is the only one that remained in Darlington for the duration. Somebody had to stay home and James accepted that responsibility. He had a home on South Main

Street and managed the noted Doctor Sparks Drug Store during its heyday.

Frankie Kelly, the youngest daughter of Dublin and Nancy Kelly, lived to be ninety-two years old. Frankie was married to Willie Bailey (b. 1874). It is interesting that this ancestral couple was born the same year and went to the Golden Shore the same year, in 1966. The names of their children are:

i.   Carrie Bailey
ii. Frances Bailey
iii. Lanie Bailey   b. 4/9/1900-d. 4/8/1984

Lanie Bailey married John Wesley McPhail (1/ 9/ 1896-12/21/1963). The names of the twelve children of John Wesley McPhail and Lanie Bailey, granddaughter of Dublin and Nancy Kelly, are:

i.   Catherine McPhail   (1922-2013)
ii.   Zerline McPhail   b. 1929
iii. Edith McPhail   (1927-2001)
iv.   Eula McPhail   b. 1933
v.   Mae McPhail   b. 1935
vi.   Jessie McPhail   (1940-2014)
vii. Vera McPhail   b. 1941
viii. Pressley McPhail   b. 12/24/1924-d. 4/8/1990
ix.   Roland McPhail   b. 7/15/1931-d. 12/21/1987
x.   Willie McPhail   b. 1936
xi.   Paul H. McPhail Sr. b. 1938
xii. Laura Lena   (1923-1925)

This patriotic and educationally conscious family of Kelly descendants resided in the small town of Badin, North Carolina where John Wesley was employed at Carolina Aluminum Company. Six of the children are still alive today. Pressley served in the Navy during WW II and Roland, who resided in Griffin, Georgia, served in the Army during the Korean conflict. Vera who currently lives in Philadelphia, Pennsylvania, attended Barber Scotia College in Concord, North Carolina, and Mae graduated from North Carolina Central University before relocating to Brooklyn, New York in 1957.

Jessie graduated from Livingston College in Salisbury, North Carolina and was an educator in St. Paul, North Carolina before moving to Fairbanks, Alaska. Jessie wed Booker T. McClain. The names of the children of Booker T. McClain and Jessie McPhail, great-granddaughter of Dublin and Nancy Kelly, are:

    i.   Sylvia D. McClain   b. 6/22/1965

   ii.   Russell McClain   b. 8/22/1970

It is simply amazing that Paul McPhail and I were enrolled at Morehouse College at the same time and did not realize that we were related. He was raised in North Carolina and I spent my early years in South Carolina. Simply put, we just did not know our heritage. We discovered that we were cousins while sitting adjacent to each other at a family reunion dinner over forty years later.

Paul married Johnnie Price. The names of the three children of Johnnie Price and Paul H. McPhail Sr., great-grandson of Dublin and Nancy Kelly, are:

    i.   Paula McPhail   b. 11/1962

   ii.   Ann Marie McPhail   b. 4/20/1969

  iii.   Paul H. McPhail Jr.   b. 7/5/1971

In many regards, Ann Marie McPhail is a Kelly treasure and an example of the immense talent that looms in the Kelly family. The Atlanta, Georgia native has rapidly established herself as a seasoned artist, a versatile lyric soprano, both nationally and internationally. She has sung with the Houston Ebony Opera, Capitol City Opera, San Francisco Opera, Paris Comique Opera and the Atlanta Opera to name a few. The Clark Atlanta University and Georgia State University graduate recently won the prestigious American Traditions Competition in Savannah, Georgia and was invited to perform with the Savannah Symphony. Ann has the distinction of having performed alongside legendary Jessye Norman with the Ebony Opera during their annual AIDS Benefit Gala and was a guest artist at the unveiling of the Martin Luther King Jr. Memorial at Constitution Hall in our nation's capital.

In closing this section on the Dublin Kelly/Nancy Robinson Kelly wing of Kellys, I think it is appropriate to note that the offspring of the union of George Paris Kelly, Sr. and Eugenia Sams Russell and many of their immediate descendants were a very distinctive group. A careful examination of their resumes reveals a very interesting longevity trait. Dellie lived to be one-hundred, Columbus Jr. ninety-four, the matriarch herself, Eugenia ninety-two, Frankie ninety-two, Annie ninety-one, Mary ninety-one, James W. and Anceline ninety and counting, while a few others lived well into their eighties including the patriarch George Paris Kelly himself.

Scientists know from the mapping of the human genome that there is a genetic component associated with the aging process. From a biological vantage point that makes this interesting family observation merit further consideration. This particular ancestral Kelly family, including their descendants, could be prime candidates for DNA analysis in search of the presence of a longevity gene, for example a variation of the FOXO3A gene. According to Willcox et al (2008) this gene has been shown to have a positive effect on aging and longevity.

Carolina Kelly (b. 1833) married Sarah Jackson who was born in 1832. According to family lore they represent the elder couple of the second primary wing of Kellys. In order to promote clarity, since there appears to be more than one Carolina in the family genealogy, Carolina will be listed as Carolina Kelly #2 in most cases in this treatise. As of this writing we do not have a lot of information related to this wing. Some of their genealogy, courtesy of the 2003 Kelly Reunion Booklet, is presented on the next few pages. It is known that over a span of twenty-six years they were blessed with eight children. They had two while in bondage and six more after freedom rang. The names of the children of Sarah Jackson and Carolina Kelly #2 are:

i.	Marie	b. 1853
ii.	Hannah	b. 1855
iii.	Margrett	b. 1867
iv.	Rebecca	b. 1867
v.	Ann	b. 1871
vi.	John	b. 1875
vii.	Jan	b. 1876
viii.	Boyd	b. 1879

The 1880 U.S. Census cites the family of Carolina and Sarah Kelly as residing in the Back Swamp, Darlington, South Carolina. The census, shown below, is consistent with the 2003 Kelly Reunion Booklet listing from above, except that by 1880 Marie Kelly had already vacated the family nest and begun a family of her own. In addition, Jan is listed as Jane in the 1880 census. The years of birth were calculated from the ages listed in the census.

	Age	Year of Birth
Carolina Kelly #2	47	1833
Sarah Kelly	48	1832
Rebecca Kelly	12	1868
Ann Kelly	7	1873
Hannah Kelly	8	1872
Margrett Kelly	6	1874
John Kelly	5	1875
Jane Kelly	4	1876
Boyd Kelly	3	1877

I find it very interesting that the first male in Carolina's family was given the name **John Kelly**, a name that recurs frequently in the annals of the three purported wings. It appears so abundantly that I almost need to number them John Kelly I, John Kelly II, etc. in order to avoid confusion among readers. Is there a significance to this phenomena? Stay tuned, this interesting revelation is briefly discussed later herein.

Margrett Kelly married Washington Samuel, a union that established a close bond between the Kellys and Samuels in Darlington. According to the 1930 U.S. Census, the family resided in the Leavenworth section of Darlington. Townsend Samuel, a son of this family, is missing from the census report. It lists the family of Washington Samuel and Margrett Kelly Samuel, daughter of Sarah Jackson and Carolina Kelly #2, as follows:

	Age	Year of Birth
Washington Samuel	68	1862
Margrett Samuel	55	1875
Boyd Samuel	21	1909
Frank Samuel	19	1911
Isiah Samuel	16	1914
Maggie Samuel	12	1918
Lottie Samuel	8	1922
Irene Samuel	5	1955

Frank Samuel married Viola James. The children of Viola James and Frank Samuel, grandson of Carolina Kelly #2 and Sarah Jackson Kelly, are:

i. Ann Laura Samuel (Lighty)
ii. Lilly Mae Samuel (Bynum)
iii. Rose Lee Samuel (Williams)
iv. Buster Samuel
v. Frank Samuel Jr.

Lilly Mae resides in Darlington and Rose Lee in Columbia, South Carolina. Ann Laura who resided in Chicago, Illinois, went to the Golden Shore in 2002. Her son Darrell Samuel is married to Kathy Samuel and they reside in Noblesville, Indiana.

Frank Jr., who currently lives in York, Pennsylvania, and I were classmates at Mayo High School where we graduated in 1955. Frank married his high school sweetheart, Estelle Nettles of Darlington. The children of Estelle Nettles and Frank Samuel Jr., great-grandson of Carolina Kelly #2 and Sarah Jackson Kelly are:

    i.   Sonja Samuel
   ii.   Vernita Samuel
  iii. Frank Samuel III

Sonja has a son named Brandon and Vernita has two daughters, Essence and Bridgett.

Irene Samuel married Fred Poole, a lay preacher in Darlington. The names of the children of Fred Poole and Irene Samuel, granddaughter of Carolina Kelly #2 and Sarah Jackson Kelly are:

    i.   W. Poole
   ii.   J.P. Poole
  iii. Buddy Poole
  iv. Daniel Poole

Marie Kelly (b. 1853) married Cato Brockington (1849-1933). The names of the children of Cato Brockington and Marie Kelly, daughter of Carolina Kelly #2 and Sarah Jackson, are:

    i.   Lois Brockington   b. 1873
   ii.   Marie A. Brockington   b. 1875
  iii. Armstrong Brockington b. 1874
  iv. Retchel Brockington   b. 1877
   v. Baltimore Brockington b. 1879

Marie Kelly is referred to in an Ancestor.com listing as Mary and in Roseville Plantation Clarke Family records as Massie. According to published literature Cato is credited with fathering fourteen children and was married twice. It is my belief that the five listed above are the only ones conceived with ancestor, Marie Kelly.

From an article written about Cato Brockington by Lillian Clarke James, of the Roseville Plantation Clarke family, I learned that Cato, the youngest of Abram and Harriett Brockington's four children was a survivor of the War Between the States, and a war hero of sorts. It is said that when Cato was a mere twelve years old, the plantation owner, Peter Samuel Bacot, in a demonstration of his support for the Confederacy, loaned him to Major William Cannon of Darlington to serve beside the Major in the War. His duty was to be a "body servant" and attend to the major's horses, but rest assured he performed many other tasks more closely related to the War. The duties of body servants varied greatly. Basically Cato was charged with keeping the Major's quarters clean, washing his clothes, cleaning his uniforms, running errands, grooming and feeding his horses and tending to his wounds. Occasionally when the situation arose, although he was still a slave, he was expected to fight in battles. Legend has it he was at the First Battle of Bull Run in Manassas, Virginia, on July 21, 1861.

According to family lore, Cato had two favorite stories about the War that he enjoyed relating. The first one dealt with the First Battle of Bull Run (First Manassas). To fully appreciate this story we need to briefly re-visit Civil War History 101. Thomas Jonathon "Stonewall" Jackson, educated at West Point, was a high profile Confederate General during the Civil War. In some quarters he is regarded as one of the most gifted tactical commanders in American history who rose to prominence and the rank of Major General. It is said that he excelled in the First Battle of Bull Run. The story goes that as the Confederate lines began to weaken and falter under heavy assault by Union forces, Jackson's troops provided crucial reinforcement on Henry House Hill. A version of the battle published in the *Charleston Mercury* newspaper on July 25, 1861, and in other papers in the South, stated that their bravery inspired Confederate Brig. Gen. Barnard Elliott Bee, Jr. of South Carolina to the extent that he shouted to his own brigade, "look, there is Jackson standing like a stone wall. Let us determine to die here, and we will conquer. Rally behind the Virginians." Cato loved to relate that during the barrage of gunfire he personally observed and clearly overheard General Bee make that historic statement, just moments before he was killed. Hence, he witnessed the historic coinage of the moniker "Stonewall Jackson." Cato was indeed there in the heat of this famous battle, on the front line, as a mere twelve year old.

The second story related to the diet of the Confederate soldiers. Of all the rations he consumed as a body servant it was the "mush" that he remembered and joked about the most among family and friends. He liked to talk about how the Confederate soldiers did not have as much variety in their rations as Union soldiers and as such subsisted largely on cornmeal "mush" during the war. This mush was simple to prepare as it consisted merely of a mixture of cornmeal, salt and bacon grease which was boiled in water until ready to eat. It could be consumed hot or cold depending on the situation.

When the war was over Cato returned to Roseville Plantation where his parents remained. During that time he was a lay preacher and had his own small church near the plantation grounds where he often spoke about his experiences during the war. He also worked as a house servant for Peter S. Bacot and Ada White Bacot, as well as the Clarke Family when they took over the plantation after the death of Peter S. Bacot. With the Clarkes he served as a yardman, fed the livestock, milked the cows, cut firewood and worked the vegetable garden and flower beds around the house. The Civil War veteran went to the Golden Shore in 1933.

It is curiously ironic that Cato Brockington has turned out to be the great grand-uncle of Vivian Guyton mentioned earlier in this thesis. If you recall, Ms. Guyton is the unexpected researcher who emerged from the depths of the haystack, and proceeded to motivate and nudge me in the right direction during the initial phase of this ambitious, spiritually driven project. Somehow I feel the connecting of Ms. Guyton and I was not just a haphazard event, for you see although she and I are not blood relatives, it has become clear that we are related by marriage. Some of our ancestors toiled at the same plantation, are entombed in the same slave boneyard, and their spirits reside with us on a daily basis.

Rebecca Kelly married Robert Robertson (born 1850). The names of the children of Robert Robertson and Rebecca Kelly, daughter of Carolina Kelly b#2 and Sarah Jackson, are:

i.   Jane Robertson   b. November 1, 1880
ii. Fannie Robertson   b. April 1881
iii. Addie Robertson   b. Dec 1, 1887
iv. Andrew Robertson   b. 1888
v.   Thomas Robertson   b. June 1892
vi. Pattie Robertson   b. February 1893
vii. Furman Robertson   b. May 1884
viii.Henry Robertson   b. May 1895

Hannah Kelly (b. 1855) married another John Brockington (born 1855). This is a very interesting union in the annals of Kelly family lore primarily because of the names of the principals. Roseville Plantation had its share of Hannahs and John Brockingtons. The names of the children of John Brockington and Hannah Kelly, daughter of Carolina Kelly #2 and Sarah Jackson, are:

i.   Sarah Brockington   b. 1870
ii. Spencer Brockington   b. 1873
iii. Millie Brockington   b. 1875
iv. George Brockington   b. 1877
v.   Tonia Brockington   b. 1879

According to family lore some of Carolina's offspring, around the turn of the century, had a presence in an area currently known as the Snow Hill Community in Florence County, South Carolina, and branched out from there. They were farmers.

Boyd Kelly (b. 1879), according to census reports, once resided in the Savannah Grove section of Florence County, also known as Effingham, South Carolina. It is said that he was an excellent farmer, owning approximately fifty acres, more or less, in Savannah Grove. Boyd Kelly married Ameta Poole (b. 1880). This union produced eight children. The names of the children of Ameta Poole and Boyd Kelly, son of Carolina Kelly #2 and Sarah Jackson, are:

i.	Mable Kelly	(1899-1986)
ii.	Johnnie Kelly	(1901-2001)
iii.	Chamberlain Kelly	(1903-1979)
iv.	Hattie Kelly	b. 1907
v.	Abraham Kelly	(1917-1948)
vi.	Timothy Kelly	b. 1918
vii.	Margrett Kelly	
viii.	Elvira Kelly	b. 1921

Chamberlain Kelly (1903-1979) married Annie Laup Warren (b. 1905) in 1926 in Philadelphia, Pennsylvania. They lived a large portion of their lives on 135th Street, near Adam Clayton Powell Boulevard in Harlem, New York. The children of Annie L. Warren and Chamberlain Kelly, grandson of Carolina Kelly #2 and Sarah Jackson, are:

i.	Elizabeth Kelly	b. February 9, 1931
ii.	Chamberlain Kelly Jr.	b. 1933
iii.	James Kelly	b. 1935

Margrett Kelly married Alex Wilds. The names of the eight children of Alex Wilds and Margrett Kelly, granddaughter of Carolina Kelly #2 and Sarah Jackson, are:

i.	Joseph Wilds	b. 1937
ii.	Johnny Wilds	b. 1942
iii.	Barbara Wilds	b. 1943
iv.	Mabel Wilds	b. 1945
v.	Eugene Wilds	b. 1945
vi.	Charlotte Wilds	b. 1948
vii.	Julia Wilds	b. 1950
viii.	Soloman Wilds	b. 1951

Abraham Kelly (1917-1948) married Lillian. The names of the children of Lillian and Abraham Kelly, grandson of Carolina Kelly #2 and Sarah Jackson, are:

    i.   Delores
   ii.   Abraham Jr.
  iii.   William

Barbara Wilds (b. 1943), daughter of Margrett Kelly and Alex Wilds, married a Daniels gentleman. Barbara currently resides in Far Rockaway, New York. The names of the children of Mr. Daniels and Barbara Wilds, great-granddaughter of Carolina Kelly #2 and Sarah Jackson, are:

    i.   Johnathan Daniels   b. May 5, 1958
   ii.   Sandra Daniels   b. August 11, 1962
  iii.   Helen Daniels   b. November 11, 1963
  iv.   Vernita Daniels   b. April 10, 1967
   v.   Charles Daniels   b. April 8, 1979

Elvira Kelly (b. 1921), daughter of Boyd and Ameta Kelly married Eugene Augustus Warren. The names of the children of Eugene Warren and Elvira Kelly, granddaughter of Carolina Kelly #2 and Sarah Jackson, are:

    i.   Eugene Warren (died during childbirth)
   ii.   Brenda Warren

Brenda Warren married Wilfred Herrington from Hartsville, South Carolina. The names of the children of Wilfred Herrington and Brenda Warren, great-granddaughter of Carolina Kelly #2 and Sarah Jackson, are:

    i.   Winfred Herrington Jr.   (b. 1978)
   ii.   Shayla Herrington   (b. 1980)

Winfred Herrington Jr. married Redia Baxter. As of 2011, Winfried Herrington Jr., the great-great-grandson of Carolina Kelly #2 and Sarah Jackson, and Redia Baxter have one child:

    i.   Myles Herrington

Myles is the great-great-great-grandson of Carolina and Sarah Kelly.

This wing of the Kelly family is also very education conscious. It began with Elvira who graduated from Benedict College in the 1940s and ultimately earned a master's degree from The University of South Carolina. Brenda followed her mother's lead and matriculated at Benedict College also, ultimately earning her master's degree from Webster University. To cite a few others from this wing who attained a higher education, Eugenia Wilds-Selder also attended Benedict; Barbara Wilds-Daniels received an undergraduate degree from a college in New York City, while Winfred Jr. and Shayla Herrington finished Winthrop University in Rock Hill, South Carolina. Winfred Jr.'s bride, Redia, also graduated from Winthrop.

Elvira Kelly had an illustrious career as an educator in Darlington, having spent over thirty years in the Darlington County School System. When she ambitiously relocated to Darlington in the 1940s to launch her career, she resided at the residence of her cousin, Evelyn Kelly Bolden Brown, of the John and Hannah wing of Kellys, for nearly a year until she secured her own permanent residence.

Johnathan Daniels, a son of Barbara Wilds, married Jeanette. The names of the children of Jeanette and Johnathan Daniels, great-great-grandson of Carolina Kelly #2 and Nancy Jackson, are:

    i.   Keisha Daniels
    ii. Christine Daniels
    iii. Vanessa Daniels
    iv. Sharmiell Daniels

I am a descendant of **John Kelly Sr.** and **Hannah Harrison Kelly**. According to family lore it is currently believed that they represent the eldest couple of the third primary Kelly wing and this treatise focuses primarily on a few aspects of their lives and the lives of some of their descendants.

As I assess the accuracy of Kelly family lore to date, it is simply astounding how many events and occurrences related to early Kelly ancestors have been documented by this research. New information has also been discovered and a wealth of information passed along over generations via the oral channel has been confirmed.

Over the last decade numerous findings have emerged that redefine Kelly family genealogy as we know it today. The evidence in two of the most astonishing revelations that relate to the early life of John Kelly Sr. is based primarily on a mixture of a few documented facts, family lore and circumstantial evidence at this point. These disclosures remain to be unequivocally corroborated and confirmed as more extensive research is conducted.

It has been passed down, via family lore, that John Kelly Sr.'s father was named Carolina Kelly. An old, slightly discolored, sheet of paper in Evelyn K.B. Brown's cedar chest contained that single astounding declaration. A long time ago she put that statement in ink. However without any birth certificate, plantation birth record, census report, or death certificate to refer to, it is difficult to make the assertion with the highest degree of certainty. Death certificates were non-existent in South Carolina before 1915 except in a few towns where these records started being kept around the turn of the century. Let us not speak at all about birth certificates for the enslaved. Because of such constraints, I felt that the more circumstantial evidence I could uncover, the stronger the support for this very significant assertion. First and foremost, I needed to demonstrate that a Carolina Kelly even actually existed in that locale during the time frame in question, and secondly, if I could place him at Roseville Plantation during this period it would provide at least circumstantial support for this assertion.

It is simply incredible that such evidence crystalized in my hands in two forms. Firstly, there are two Carolina names on the list of Negro slaves owned by Richard Brockinton, shown in Table 3. It is very possible that one of these two men named Carolina is actually the putative father of John Kelly Sr. The likelihood of this being true is very high, considering the remarkable accuracy to date of Kelly family lore.

Further support of Carolina's presence at Roseville is provided by an entry from the 1839 Mechanicsville Baptist Church minutes which contains a reference to the death of a male slave, named Carolina, from Roseville Plantation. The minutes referred to his death on October 19, 1839, and suggested his year of birth as 1770. This projected date of birth and actual year of death, both are skewed in the proper direction for pinpointing this Carolina as a candidate for John Kelly Sr.'s father.

Another important clue that must be entertained is the fact that John Kelly Sr. used the moniker or alias John Carolina on numerous occasions on certain important documents later in his life. A few examples are presented and discussed in detail later in this chapter and in succeeding chapters. It was very common during that era for the enslaved to utilize their father's first name as their surname at times or even permanently. This in and of itself could very well indicate that Carolina was John's father.

In summary, with family lore as the primary elucidator, we have a supporting cast of documents which provide circumstantial evidence in support of the premise that Carolina Kelly is the actual father of John Kelly Sr. Mechanicsville church records place a gentleman named Carolina at Roseville at the time of John's birth, a gentleman named Carolina is on the list of slaves formerly owned by Richard Brockinton and lastly there are numerous instances where John used the moniker Carolina as his surname during the course of his life.

This represents an important link that documents Kelly lineage back into the late 1700s, and can be utilized to delve deeper into Kelly family history. Further research, utilizing ancestor Carolina Kelly's name and tracing it through Kelly slave owner records will allow historians and researchers to trace Carolina's path to Roseville Plantation and also possibly identify his parents as well as his spouse. It may also shed more precise light on the above mentioned relationship between John, Dublin and the other Carolina, who is referred to earlier in the text as Carolina Kelly #2.

As you have discovered there are numerous very illuminating revelations or findings that emerged from this research effort.

Discovering the historic plantation sites of the earliest known Bacote and Kelly ancestors is a milestone that probably stands at the pinnacle. However from a genealogy perspective, based on the facts as well as the circumstantial evidence cited above, probably the most noteworthy finding is the discovery of the apparent existence of an earlier generation of Kelly lineage. The family early beginnings may now be documented into the 1770s. It places a **Carolina Kelly #1** at Roseville Plantation, as the putative elder patriarch of the John Kelly Sr. wing, of the Kelly family and quite possibly the entire three Kelly wings as currently noted. This is a surprising, educational and spiritual discovery which amends presently inked Kelly genealogy, as it takes us deeper into Kelly family history, one step closer to the historic Trans-Atlantic passage. It is a very significant piece of the puzzle. If you don't think it is significant and you are a Kelly descendant, just take the ride up the promenade to the old restored Roseville Plantation mansion. Park the car, get out and anticipate a greeting by Carolina.

The evolution of this Kelly wing, for the purpose of discussion in this treatise, continues with the birth of the courageous **John Kelly Sr. 1804-1884-1886),** in the Darlington District, at Roseville Plantation. As outlined earlier, historical documents show that Peter Samuel Bacot inherited Roseville Plantation from Richard Brockinton and Mary Brockinton subsequent to their deaths. The 1857 cited document, shown in Table 3, that lists the Negro slaves and chattels owned by Mary Brockinton prior to transfer of title of Roseville Plantation to Peter Samuel Bacot, shows John Kelly Sr., his wife Hannah Harrison, and four of their children, John Jr., Lydia, Sarah and Mary as being housed at Roseville. This very important document was obtained from the court papers of Richard Brockinton, courtesy of the Darlington County Historical Commission. It supports information regarding John Kelly Sr. from the Mechanicsville Baptist Church tax records.

As stated earlier, when I began to compile data for this treatise, the ongoing consensus among contemporary family members was that John Kelly Sr. and Hannah Harrison were the forebears of the John and Hannah wing of the at-large Kelly family. As discussed later, they were married in 1855 and are generally acknowledged as the elder couple in Kelly family current genealogy.

However, during the early stages of this research, I instinctively felt that fifty years of age was a little old for the first marriage of a virile male during that period in American history. John was born on April 10, 1804. Something just did not seem consistent. Young strong bucks were just not allowed to roam around that freely; there was work to be done. The times encouraged large enslaved families, more to man the fields and generate income for the plantation. This opened up the possibility that John's marriage to Hannah could have been his second or maybe third marriage.

As such, it was not surprising when recent information from Roseville Plantation records found in the Bacot Family Papers and graciously provided by historian Scott Wilds, revealed that the union of John Kelly Sr. and Hannah Harrison (b. December 26, 1836) was preceded by an earlier alliance of John Kelly Sr. and Nancy Brockington (b. November 17, 1806). Both marriages occurred at Roseville Plantation. Regardless of my insight, this was still a thunderous disclosure.

What are the implications of this astounding new discovery? First of all it is indeed a welcomed revelation that will present a challenge to contemporary historians, and descendants of John Kelly Sr. to develop and establish a definitive Kelly-Brockington genealogy of the magnitude presented in Figure 2, Figure 2A, and the "2003 Kelly Reunion Booklet."

Secondly, this intriguing discovery which amends Kelly family history, adds a new wrinkle to Kelly genealogy. It portends a closer relationship between some African-American Brockingtons and Kellys of Darlington County and indeed obviously throughout America than previously acknowledged. Some contemporary Brockingtons and Kellys may be more closely related than they ever imagined. I say that with all due respect to our instincts and complex inner feelings as individuals. Many times there are reasons for feelings of closeness that we don't comprehend that are beyond the scope of our imagination. As a teenager growing up in Darlington there was a Brockington family that I did not really know very well but bonded with as a youngster. This was the family of Randolph Brockington Junior. Brock and I were teammates on our high school football team for one year. We always worked well together and espoused a tremendous amount of mutual respect for each other over the years. Although he was a few years younger than I, fifty years later we still have that closeness. Could this closeness be due to the similarity of our DNA sequences, could it be we are cousins?

More amazingly, this disclosure could possibly double or triple the heretofore acknowledged size of the Kelly family attributed to legendary John Kelly Sr.

It is my pleasure to present the beginning of the lineage of John Kelly Sr. and Nancy Brockington for the first time in a family history format. This new family of what we might term "newly found" ancestors will serve as a starting point for amending the genealogy of the afore-mentioned John Kelly Sr. wing of this Kelly family. One's first impulse is to deem them a "lost" wing of ancestors. I use the term "newly found," because just as we are aware of John's family with Hannah Harrison, there is no reason not to believe that descendants of his first family currently located in South Carolina and indeed throughout America have knowledge of his alliance with Nancy Brockington. Hence, in the strictest sense they are not a lost wing, but a loss of awareness of the extent of the relationship between contemporary descendants of the two families has occurred. So I pose the rhetorical question. Are the two families connected or disconnected today?

From Roseville Plantation Records, the children of Nancy Brockington and John Kelly Sr., son of Carolina Kelly #1, are:

i.   Lewis Brockington   b. August 1, 1827
ii. Tom Brockington   b. about 1830
iii. Jonas Brockington   b. May 15, 1833
iv. Olivia Brockington   b. about 1835
v.   Willow Brockington   b. January 7, 1837
vi. John (N) Brockington b. January 9, 1838

Their first child Lewis was born in 1827. It was very exciting to discover that Nancy's name and the names of all the children also appear in Table 3, which lists many of the Negro slaves previously owned by Richard Brockinton and Mary H. Brockinton. This further supports their presence at Roseville Plantation. As you can see, all of the offspring are listed above with the Brockington surname in the

Roseville Plantation books. Some may ponder, why the Brockington surname for some of the earliest Kelly ancestors? They have a valid point. This finding supports the premise that there were two sets of books when it involved the enslaved, the plantation books and the "public" books. Common law during the bondage era was that newborn slaves took the status or surname of the mother. However you will find examples to the contrary in the literature and even in this thesis, especially near the end of the era. Generally in plantation records, children of slaves were considered as belonging to the mother and were referred to as such. For example in Roseville Plantation records a reference is made to John H, (John and Hannah's son), differentiating him from John N, (John and Nancy's son).

In this treatise, usage of the term "married" when citing couples of the bondage era is not meant to infer that they were legally married. Loosely translated it means they were a couple, but because of my ultimate respect for them I will generally use the term "married." Marriage between slaves was legally forbidden. None of the slave holding states or the U.S. Government recognized a marriage between slaves as being binding in a court of law.

However, it is well documented that marriages between our enslaved African ancestors were known to have occurred, albeit sometimes in secret ceremonies at the plantations. We must remember that these individuals were plucked from a highly ordered society, a society where the concept of marriage and family was taken very seriously. These Africans were smart and proud, and they were committed to not allowing their innate culture to be totally dismantled. It is very clear that in order to survive their defense had to be constructed to bend but not break. It appears that more often than not these marriages were "respected" by the owners. It is also true, in some alliances or relationships the parties involved would just "shack up" and that was it.

The identity of all the descendants of John Kelly Sr.'s initial family is crucial to Kelly family history and is a work in progress. What better place to start than with the first offspring of this ancestral family.

The 1870 U.S. Federal Census Report, presented earlier in this chapter (p.121), cites a gentleman named Lewis Kelly (b. 1825) as residing with the Dublin Kelly family. Who was this Lewis Kelly?

What was his relationship to the principals in that listing? It was very prevalent during that period in history, when families basically remained on the same farm or locale for generations, to find fathers/mothers/siblings of the head of the household listed in the same census file as the head of the household. We know that sons and daughters generally are there to support and house their parents if the need arises, just as siblings support their brothers and sisters. After all, that is really the essence of the Black family.

It is my belief that Lewis Kelly's appearance on the census report as a member of Dublin's household may be a clue that Lewis is the father of Dublin, now freed from bondage and residing as a free man with his son's family. The reasons for this genealogy altering assertion are discussed below.

In order to support this assertion there appears to be three primary issues that must be addressed. First, could Lewis Kelly and Lewis Brockington be the same individual? Second, the age difference between Dublin and Lewis is crucial. Finally and very difficult to resolve, is whether Lewis Kelly was simply a sibling of Dublin's, a sibling of Dublin's wife, some other relative of Dublin's, or as asserted, the actual father of Dublin? In the Preface, I mentioned that during the course of the reconstruction of this family history, situations would arise where I would be forced to make assumptions in order to advance an idea or interpret information gathered. This is another one of those situations.

Could Lewis Kelly actually be Lewis Brockington, the son of John Kelly Sr. and Nancy Brockington, whose year of birth was listed as 1827? In my opinion there are two facts that suggest that they are indeed the same individual. First of all there is the recording of almost identical birth years in two, separate, important, historical documents, [Roseville Plantation birth records [1827], and the United States Census Report [1825] referencing the two monikers, Lewis Brockington and Lewis Kelly, respectively. These dates are well within the acceptable degree of variance when referring to birth years from that era. Secondly, if you carefully review Table 3, which is essentially the list of the Negro slaves who were housed at Roseville Plantation during the ownership of Richard Brockington and Mary Hart Brockington, you will find only one gentleman with the name of Lewis. There were two Marys, three Johns, and two

Carolinas listed on this particular document but only one Lewis. In my opinion, the latter observation, is the more compelling, that they are the same person, for you see Roseville Plantation was essentially the world of these enslaved ancestors, their small world, all day long, all years long, until it all ended. Based on the information at my disposal, their interactions, marriages and liaisons were essentially intra-plantational. There is no evidence of inter-plantational activity involving the enslaved at Roseville.

I acknowledge the fact that the proposed father of Dublin Kelly, the son of John Kelly Sr. and Nancy Brockington, is listed in the plantation books and early birth records as Lewis Brockington. Nevertheless, it is not incomprehensible to assume that Lewis acknowledged the reality that his father was a Kelly, and ultimately utilized Kelly as his surname, although the plantation books sought to tag a Brockington label on him. As discussed at length in this thesis the enslaved had a variety of options available to them in regard to surnames, including the usage of their father's surname as their surname. It is very interesting, as outlined in detail later, that Lewis's father himself used three different surnames during his lifetime. The 1870 census taker listed Lewis as a Kelly, we must presume at Lewis's request.

It is impossible at this point without additional documentation to ascertain with greater than 50% probability which census report is correct regarding Dublin's year of birth. However as a historical researcher, I am obligated, without bias, to investigate both possibilities. If one assumes the 1880 Census is correct, this would imply only a three year difference in their ages, unquestionably ruling Lewis out as Dublin's father. Could they be brothers? We already know from Roseville Plantations records that Lewis Brockington did not have a brother named Dublin.

However, if the 1870 Census has presented the correct information, it allows me the latitude to advance this interesting assertion that could very well provide a missing piece to Kelly genealogy. The fifteen-seventeen year age difference between Dublin and Lewis is in the right range to make him eligible for fatherhood and strengthen the probability of him being Dublin's father.

The fact that he is listed as Lewis Kelly in the 1870 Census, for the sake of our discussion here, rules out the possibility of him being a relative of Dublin's wife, Nancy Robinson. Based on that fact and the above reasoning and speculations I feel I have a legitimate case to make the proposal which has very interesting genealogical implications.

This is a thesis on the construction/re-construction of Kelly family history and as such contains proven as well as speculation-based suppositions. That is the nature of the reconstruction of family history. Such speculation-based suppositions have immense value, as they can serve as starting points for ambitious researchers and academicians with greater manpower and other resources at their disposal to refute or prove conclusively. I acknowledge that these findings do not conclusively nail down a father-son link between Lewis and Dublin however I feel they are strong enough to support the hypothesis that Lewis is indeed Dublin's father. Although the evidence is not etched in stone it is my belief that Lewis Kelly (Lewis Brockington) is the father of esteemed ancestor Dublin Kelly.

This startling disclosure sheds valuable light on the heretofore, indefinite relationship between the Dublin Kelly wing and the John Kelly Sr. wing. Yes, the wings are relatives, but to what extent are they actually related? If Lewis Kelly is indeed the father of Dublin Kelly then Dublin by definition is the grandson of John Kelly Sr. and that explains the close relationship of the descendants of these two men for over a century and a half. This discovery alters current Kelly family genealogy, as now Dublin Kelly instead of being a cousin of John Kelly Sr. is really his grandson.

A truncated version of the genealogy of the first family of John Kelly Sr. is presented in Figure 2A. This flow chart includes Carolina Kelly #1 as the patriarch of the John Kelly wing. In addition, John's son, Lewis is listed as the father of Dublin Kelly.

This enormous finding brings clarity to the evolution of the broader Kelly family. It establishes that the Dublin Kelly wing indeed has a special distinction, a unique bond that has been continuously conveyed and now we know why. They are descendants of John Kelly Sr.'s first family, representing one path of evolution of this family. So the earlier posed question is answered. The Dublin Kelly wing represents an extended connection between John's two individual families.

This revelation makes one ponder whether a possible similar relationship or connection exists with the Carolina Kelly/Sarah Jackson Kelly wing also. As mentioned earlier no one knows what the precise relationship was between John Kelly Sr. and the younger Carolina #2. Could it be that he is also a descendant of John, named after John's father? The definitive proof may reside in the depth of the extensive Bacot Family Papers at the University of North Carolina, Chapel Hill.

This does not necessarily alter the existence of the three current wings of the Kelly family as they exist today. What it does clarify is the nature of the relationship between the afore-mentioned descendants of the Dublin Kelly/Nancy Robinson Kelly and the John Kelly Sr./ Hannah Harrison Kelly wing. The two wings are more closely related than heretofore believed. This is a very exciting, and significant finding which merits consideration, further research, and additional documentation.

It seems evident that John Kelly Sr. anticipated the importance of the maintenance of a relationship between the offspring of his alliances/marriages. The machinery was installed early and put into motion during that period when our enslaved ancestor was over-perplexed with the contradictions between life and death, between family unity and family survival, between faith and reality. Nevertheless, in spite of the constraints, John sought to achieve extended family unity. What makes this even more compelling is that over two centuries after the birth of this icon, his extended family has remained an intact unit, against all odds.

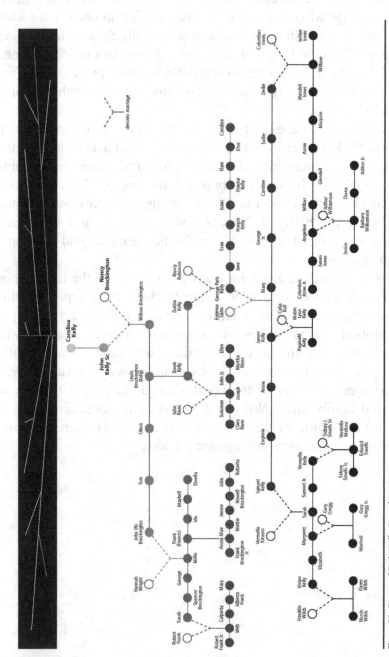

Figure 2A. Proposed Early Kelly Genealogy

Documentation of the offspring of John and Nancy's youngest child, John (N) Brockington and his descendants, has also been uncovered.

John (N) Brockington married Hannah Wright (b. about 1852). The 1880 U.S. Census lists this family as residing in the Back Swamp, Darlington, South Carolina. The children of Hannah Wright and John (N) Brockington, grandson of Carolina Kelly #1, are:

    i.   Sarah Brockington   b. about December 1869
    ii. Spencer Brockington b. about 1873
    iii. Millie Brockington   b. about 1875
    iv. George Brockington b. about 1877
    v.   Ida Brockington   b. about 1881
    vi. Maybell Brockington b. about 1888
    vii. Dinella Brockington b. September 1891
    viii.Francis Brockington b. May 1895

John (N) Brockington did not adopt the Kelly surname as I proposed earlier that his brother Lewis may have done, hence there is a wing of Brockingtons in Darlington, throughout South Carolina and indeed the country that from a patriarchal standpoint, as descendants of John (N), are a sub-clan of John Kelly Sr.'s family. In reality they are really Kellys. Some others are also presented below.

In addition, let us not forget the offspring of the females of that first family and the above cited female offspring of John (N) and Hannah. In reality these are Kelly females being represented with a Brockington surname. Their descendants also contribute to John Kelly Sr.'s lineage. I regret my inability to locate more information on these women at this time.

John (N) and Hannah's third daughter, Ida, aka Tonie, pronounced too-nie, went to the Golden Shore on December 12, 1918, at age thirty-seven, after an unsuccessful bout with pneumonia. Her Death Certificate cites her cause of death as "broncho-pneumonia from an attack of the influenza virus." Her parents are listed as John Brockington and Hannah Wright. It is believed she is buried in the "Colored Cemetery" in Darlington.

Ida was married to Doctor Wilds, son of Homer and Jane Wilds. To avoid any confusion I think it is important here to iterate that Doctor was married three times and Ida was his first bride. Ida is another thread that provides continuity to John Kelly Sr.'s legacy and it is interesting that she possessed the same unique nickname as her cousin Evelyn K. B. Brown, the iconic "Butterfly" featured later in this thesis.

As put forth in the Preface, family history can offer an explanation for an assortment of things. Since the recent re-discovery of the union of Ida Brockington and Doctor Wilds some interesting observations have emerged. It turns out that Doctor Wilds is the uncle of Janie Wilds, my family's adjacent neighbor in Darlington during my formative years. Our families developed a close relationship and were closely intertwined over the years. I had a special relationship with Janie's older sons, as we developed as athletes and students there on Chestnut Street. During this period mutual respect between the families soared to new heights. Leroy, Billy, Franklin, Peter and I developed strong bonds, and Franklin eventually married my cousin Vivian Kelly. Recent conversations with surviving Wilds family members reveal that we had no idea our families were previously linked. Does that past history explain the ease with which our families developed such closeness? Is it a quirk of fate that the families were again closely aligned? Maybe they were never disconnected. The old timers knew what was happening but somehow that information was just not adequately disseminated. Now the old timers are on the Golden Shore and we are at a loss to explain some family ties.

As outlined in the Preface, this highlights the importance of a rigorously outlined family history.

The 1900 U.S. Census lists John and Hannah's first daughter, Sarah Brockington, as married to Robert Frank (b. about 1864) and residing in the Palmetto section of Darlington, South Carolina. According to this report the names and years of birth of the children of Robert Frank and Sarah Brockington, the great-granddaughter of Carolina Kelly #1, are:

i.   John Frank   b. 1886
ii. Henry Frank   b. 1888
iii. Willie Frank   b. 1890

iv. Robert Frank Jr.   b. 1892
v. Marion Frank   b. 1894
vi. Calperta Frank   b. 1898
vii. Mary Frank   b. 1899
viii. Spencer   b. 1872

The report also cites a gentleman named Spencer, as residing with the family. Note the large difference in his birth year versus the other individuals listed. In this particular case, his year of birth does not support him as a candidate for the father of the head of the household or one of the children. It does agree considerably with the year of birth listed for Sarah's brother, Spencer, in the 1880 Census which leads me to conclude that Spencer Brockington probably resided with his sister's family in Palmetto during a period in his lifetime.

An interesting 1910 U.S. Federal Census Report also lists the household of Robert and Sarah Frank, great-granddaughter of Carolina Kelly #1, as residing in the Palmetto section of Darlington. The ages of the members of the family are cited and I have translated the ages to the year of birth for convenience in cross-checking the listings. Note that there is an addition to the family, a daughter named Alberta (b. 1900). In addition Sarah's mother, Hannah, is listed in the household of her son in-law and daughter. This is a similar situation to the earlier case involving Dublin Kelly and his putative father, Lewis, and adds credence to the conclusion drawn in that particular case. The Census Report is shown below:

Name	Age	Year of Birth
Robert Frank	50	1860
Sarah Frank	45	1865
Robert Frank Jr.	20	1890
Web Frank	16	1894
Calperta Frank	14	1896
Mary Frank	12	1898
Alberta Frank	10	1900
Hanna Brockington	70	1840

Robert Frank went to the Golden Shore on April 17, 1928 in Florence, South Carolina.

Web Frank, also known as Marion, went to the Golden Shore on August 11, 1936 in Florence, South Carolina. He was married to Hester Frank.

A South Carolina Death Certificate cites Sarah's other brother, George Brockington, as going to the Golden Shore on September 10, 1918, two months before his sister Ida. He also lived in the Palmetto section of Darlington. The certificate listed John and Hannah Brockington as his parents.

The 1940 U.S. Census shows Sarah's youngest brother, Francis (Frank) Brockington (b. 1892-1897), as married to Susan Brockington and residing in Georgetown, South Carolina. Francis was a World War I veteran. The names of the children of Susan and Francis Brockington, great-grandson of Carolina Kelly #1, are:

i. Frank Brockington Jr.   b. 1925

ii. Annie Mae Brockington   b. 1927

iii. Mattie Brockington   b. 1928

iv. Jennie L. Brockington   b. 1929

v. Howell Brockington   b. 1931

vi. John B. Brockington   b. 1933

vii. Roberta A. Brockington   b. 1936

The earlier generations of Franks and Brockingtons cited on the preceding two pages are examples of descendants of John Kelly Sr.'s first family who resided right in the back yard of where it all started, in Palmetto, Florence, and Georgetown, South Carolina. It is unfortunate that the at-large Kelly family as delineated in this treatise, the ones currently residing in Darlington, as well as those throughout America, is totally unaware of this group of relatives. The numbing reality is this is only the tip of the iceberg, undoubtedly there are numerous sub-sets of his descendants awaiting discovery. As far as I can ascertain no contemporary descendants of John Kelly Sr. and Hannah Harrison or Dublin Kelly and Nancy Robinson have any idea that John had an earlier family. It is a reality that needed to be uncovered before it became more deeply entrenched in the sands of time and totally escaped the history of this family. The genetic connection of the two families is real and will always exist. The challenge of contemporary generations is a greater recognition of this connection and the subsequent production of collaborations. It is very important that contemporary generations in these locales and elsewhere are identified and more factions reconnected.

Let's get back to the very fascinating life of John Kelly Sr. as he experienced a challenging transition from his heretofore unknown first family to a second well documented alliance. As mentioned earlier, the planter Richard Brockinton died in 1843 and his wife Mary Hart Brockinton ten years later in 1853. The enslaved first family of ancestor John Kelly Sr. was inventory and as such had cash values, represented as assets in their portfolio. Brockinton's estate inventory, dated October 16, 1843, as listed in the Darlington Inventory and Sale Book (1840-45) pp 243-247 cites them and their values in dollars as follows:

i.	carp John	600
ii.	Nancy	350
iii.	Lewis	375
iv.	Tom	250
v.	Jonas	250
vi.	L. John	175
vii.	Olivia	
viii.	Bellow	000 (Presumably Billow)

Mary H. Brockinton's estate inventory in 1853 lists John Kelly Sr.'s family and their values in dollars as follows:

i.	John, carpenter	950
ii.	Nancy	600
iii.	Lewis	950
iv.	Tom	950

v. Jonas	950
vi. L. John	850
vii. Billow	0

Note that John Kelly Sr. is listed as a carpenter in the estate inventory of Mary H. Brockington as well as her husband's ten years earlier. Also note the dramatic increase in the value of the other individuals. The value of L. John (little John) appreciated nearly five hundred per cent over the ten year span. That computes to a fifty per cent appreciation per year. According to Fogel and Engerman (1974) the dollar value of a male slave in the Old South in 1850 peaked at age 25 at approximately $800 and steadily declined as the person got older. At age 60 generally a male slave, dependent upon his state of health, was worth about $150.

It is interesting that John Kelly Sr. at nearly fifty years of age was still valued as highly as his "young buck" sons. This tells us something about the condition of this heralded ancestor, as he obviously was in great shape. To confirm that assertion he went on, as shown later, to beget another family, an even larger family, after the death of his first wife Nancy.

The period, 1853-1857, was a relatively pivotal period for Kelly ancestors at Roseville Plantation. The plantation was coming off one of its banner production harvests in years, but a lot of uncertainty was amiss due primarily to the pending execution of the will of Mary Hart Brockinton. Everyone at the plantation knew that change was going to occur; that some people would be relocated, to accommodate the heirs; that family structure as it existed was going to be disrupted or altered. To compound matters Nancy became gravely ill early in 1855. It is quite possible that the increased stress took its toll on this ancestral family and contributed to Nancy's early departure to the Golden Shore at age forty-nine in April, 1855. It is believed that this ancestral mother, possibly the elder matriarch of the broader Kelly family, is entombed in one of the unmarked grave sites in the Slave Cemetery at Roseville Plantation. I repeat, it is believed that the Eve, the ancestral mother of the Kelly family as we know it today, is entombed in the Slave Cemetery at Roseville Plantation.

When the will was finally executed in 1857, John Kelly Sr. was awarded to Peter S. Bacot, while his wife Nancy (deceased) and four of their children, Tom, Jonas, John and Billow, were awarded to Mary H. Brockington's niece, Mary Allston Jarrott, of Marion, South Carolina. After Mary Allston Jarrott's death these individuals were to be awarded to her heirs.

The execution of the will suggests that two of their six children (Lewis and Olivia) were no longer listed with the family, leaving one to assume that either they had their own families now, were sold, or had passed to the Golden Shore. As a matter of fact, evidence presented earlier in this chapter indeed suggests that Lewis fathered a son, Dublin Kelly, in 1842.

At this point the remainder of this ancestral family which had been together for over twenty-five years was subjected to one of the most horrendous, stressful scenarios attributed to the bondage era, where families were separated either by a sale of members to different individuals, or by execution of a will, which was the case here.

But that was not the end. It is very clear that even at that stage in Kelly history, faith and resiliency loomed large, that evidence of God's empathy was on display. In 1858, a very interesting equity court case was brought in Marion County, where the Jarrotts resided, to divide the slaves Mary Jarrott inherited from her "aunt," among her children. Kelly ancestors, Tom, Jonas, Billow, and John Brockington were among the enslaved named in the case. This was Marion Equity Bill #365, a long complicated document. The Commissioners in Equity ruled that the individuals should not be further divided because of the "interrelations" of some of the slaves owned by Jarrott, as well as the infancy of some of the Jarrott heirs. We must remember that this was just one year after the U.S. Supreme Court had rendered the inhumane Dred Scott Decision which decreed that our enslaved ancestors had no rights which any white man had to respect. It seems odd that the judicial courts, especially in South Carolina, were demonstrating compassion for these individuals and did not subject this ancestral family to additional separation. This included Tom, Jonas, Billow and John N who would have been about twenty years old at this time. This appears contradictory to much of the published culture of South Carolina and demonstrates the presence of the "Spirit" and some good, compassionate folk in that part of the Palmetto State at that time.

Since this was an equity case, it is noteworthy also that Billow was valued as a charge on the Jarrott estate, due to the fact that she was crippled and disabled.

As individuals each of us experience challenging life-altering moment(s) during our lifetime that crystallize our drive to operate at a higher level of action. First John's wife became critically ill; eventually passing on to the Golden Shore. A few years later his children were whisked away. John tackled the adversity the best way he knew how.

Like the mythical Phoenix rising from the flames, he emerged from the tragedy with renewed strength and empowerment. He was a survivor and while that fact in itself is simply remarkable, it is only a fragment of his story. What makes his story even more compelling is that in the midst of this very difficult ordeal he conquered his anger with faith, replaced his rage with determination and wiped out his despair with zeal. He believed the best was yet to come.

Following Nancy's death, a new Mary H. Brockinton's inventory, dated August 1856, in the Darlington Equity Bill 369, listed the individuals differently. John is listed in a family group that reflects a change in his status and family composition. Nancy went to the Golden Shore in April 1855 and it is revealing that her children Tom, Jonas, John, and Billow are listed separately. The entry of John Sr.'s second family in the 1856 Inventory is shown below with their dollar value:

i.	c. John	700
ii.	Leah	500
iii.	Hannah	850
iv.	John H	100

This document is very interesting, not only because it illuminates the beginnings of John's second family, but also because it underscores Peter S. Bacot's apparent respect for the institution of black marriage and family at least at his plantation. The fact that this plantation owner elected to list this group of individuals as a family suggests that he was an owner who acknowledged the institutions of marriage and family from a different perspective than the U.S. Government. The principals in this listing are, "c. John," or carpenter John, Hannah his second wife, Hannah's mother Leah and their first child John H. Again note that John H refers to Hannah's John to distinguish him from John N (Nancy's John), his older half-brother.

Although John Kelly Sr. was now over fifty years old the physical and mental status of this warrior was conspicuous. In the face of indescribable evil, disrespect for humanity and unimaginable pressure he held his head high and embarked with guile, vigor and splendor to build another family, an even larger version, as well respected, as talented, and resilient. John's journey continually serves to empower contemporary Kelly family members when faced with seemingly unfathomable situations.

I recall a passage from James Michener's #1 bestseller, The Source, where he talks about the great philosopher and theologian St. Augustine's declaration that the world is like an olive press. The premise is that man is constantly under pressure and the dregs of the action of the press contain the faint of heart while the pure oil represents the noble. He goes on to declare that pressure occurs throughout our existence through wars, siege, famine, and affairs of state. And might I add in John's case, bondage. There are those who grumble and complain of these pressures, eventually cowardly retreating to other less challenging states of mind. These individuals lack splendor. Then there is the individual who under the same pressure, does not complain but welcomes splendor. The friction of the pressure polishes him. It is the pressure that refines him and makes him noble. John's mentality as exhibited in many scenarios throughout this treatise compels me to place him in the latter category.

In 1855, **John's** second alliance to **Hannah Harrison** (b. December 26, 1836) was consummated. **Hannah** was the young daughter of Harry and Leah Harrison. While it may appear that John had an attraction for younger women, as his bride Hannah was at least thirty years his junior, remember that it was a common, accepted practice during that era for older men to marry much younger women. If we do the mathematics Hannah was nineteen years old when they wed, and John was fifty-one.

To the prolific union of Hannah Harrison and John Kelly Sr., sixteen children were born. The names of the children of Hannah Harrison and John Kelly Sr., son of Carolina Kelly #1, are:

i.   John Kelly Jr.
ii.   Lydia Kelly
iii. Harry Kelly
iv.   Serena Kelly
v.   Shadrack Kelly
vi.   Leahanna Kelly
vii. Mary Kelly
viii. Alfred Kelly
ix.   Caroline Kelly
x.   Georgianna Kelly
xi.   Esau Kelly
xii. Meshach Kelly
xiii. Peter Kelly
xiv. Abednego Kelly
xv.   Lucinda Kelly
xvi. Sarah Kelly

John Kelly Jr. was the oldest male offspring. Peter and Abednego died as babies. In the Kelly family tree version presented earlier in Figure 2, Esau is incorrectly listed as one of the quadruplets. In addition his year of birth and Alfred's is listed incorrectly as 1869.

An October 1, 1860 tax list included in the Peter Samuel Bacot Papers at the University of North Carolina, Chapel Hill, shows John (b. 1804), Hannah (b. 1836), John H (b. 1856), Alfred (b. 1858) and a Liddie (probably Lydia (b. 1859), as owned by Peter S. Bacot. According to historian Scott Wilds, Roseville Plantation records refer to John and Hannah's son as John H, with the (H) identifying him as Hannah's son.

As outlined earlier, the era of bondage was abolished in 1865 when Congress passed the Thirteenth Amendment to the U.S. Constitution by a vote of 119 to 56. At that point John Kelly Sr. and his family, as "free agents," settled on Old Georgetown Road, about five miles from Roseville Plantation, on what appears to have been original plantation land allocated to him. According to family lore and discussed in the "Elias Bacote" chapter, the Bacots were landowners who apparently allocated small parcels of land to their former slaves. The conditions of the allocations are unknown.

After gaining their freedom many freedmen and women encountered numerous financial and socialization obstacles in the free society. One of the crucial financial obstacles was the inability to handle and manage money, new territory for most of them since most had not been taught to read, write or count. However countless of them eventually acquired the necessary skills, allowing them to make giant strides. Apparently John belonged to the latter category.

After the Civil War ended, this historic Kelly family was unified in an attempt to weather the many socialization obstacles in their path. It is documented that John reconnected with his handicapped daughter from his first marriage, his child that had been so cruelly taken away in 1857. An August 17, 1866 Freedmen's Bureau Ration Book #3188, entry #244, lists Billow Brockington as follows: "Billoe Brockington, a freedwoman, 27 years old. Deformed and helpless. Has never worked a step, and cannot use her hands. Father's name John working with S.B. McBride who rents a plantation from Mr. Allston. Lives with her father on said place on Landers Lake 8 miles distant on Cashway Ferry Road. John has a wife and seven other children under 10 years old. Is recommended by S.B. McBride. Issued to Billow for ten days." This document and later census reports confirm that she resided with his second family during the rocky Reconstruction Era.

This finding addresses a seldom discussed issue in that it demonstrates that after the era of bondage was abolished, some families that had been separated as slaves found a way to reunite as freedmen/women. I am certain this was the exception and not the rule because in many cases the location of the sold individual was unknown to the grieving family. They could have been in another county, another state, another section of the country, who knows even another country. The prevailing perception of most Americans in regard to this separation of families via the sale of individual family members is that once the deal was consummated and the persons transported, there was no more getting together as family. That being said, it is very illuminating to discover that once a free man, John

Kelly Sr., probably with assistance from the Freedmen's Bureau, found a way to locate and reunite with his disabled daughter to insure that she would be properly cared for. By the grace of God, against all odds, they were once again together as father and daughter.

The Freedmen's Bureau document conclusively establishes that John Kelly Sr. worked at the Allston Plantation in 1866 initially after the War ended and that Billow received rations from the Freedmen Bureau for ten days. There are also other entries in the records of this branch of the bureau showing receipt of rations by her for ten day periods.

We read in American history books about the Freedmen's Bureau and the impact it had on American history in assisting the newly freed individuals in their transition. It is very enlightening indeed to have documented proof that Kelly ancestors cited in this thesis, like so many of their peers, were among those who benefited from the efforts of that benevolent organization. No longer will the Bureau represent a figment of our imagination, we have documentation that it assisted in the day to day survival of this Kelly family.

John Kelly Sr. was enslaved for over sixty years. I can easily visualize him on many occasions sitting on the floor, in the cramped confines of his one-room shanty, with twenty other occupants, dreaming of one day owning his own farm where he could utilize his expertise, and put into action his vast agricultural and carpenter skills in initiatives for his family's own personal gain. I sense very strongly that John was a "dreamer," a man with a plan, a prototype of the great achievers, against all odds, of his era.

Three years after slavery ended there were not many former slaves in a position in South Carolina to become land holders. In Darlington County you could count the number of black land owners on one hand. In 1868, after spending nearly his entire life as an enslaved individual, John was managing his own existence in an impressive manner. After handling his finances judiciously, he made his dream a reality with the purchase of 104 acres of prime real estate from E.J. Lide in Colfax Township. At this point, John Kelly Sr. officially counter-pinned his position as an "Iron Horse," a pioneering icon. This real estate was contiguous to what appears to have been his original post-slavery allocation there at Kelly Place, also later commonly referred to as "Mr. Jakes" or 557 Georgetown Road.

It is important that we emphasize that it was not a haphazard occurrence or quirk of fate that John emerged from bondage with the acquired occupation of carpenter. It addresses his character, his aptitude, his willingness and drive to capitalize on opportunities at his disposal. While enslaved he obviously was exposed to some occasions where he could learn the nuances of carpentry and wood work, and quite possibly he possessed some innate ability. Whatever the case, he had to be diligent and put in some hard work to develop skills which would establish his credibility as a true carpenter.

After the War there was great demand for his skillset throughout South Carolina as the State had to essentially be rebuilt. His trade fueled his financial capabilities and allowed him the insightful wherewithal to purchase land, the most prized commodity of that era.

See Figure 8. "Know all men by these present that Evan J. Lide of the County and State aforesaid for and in consideration of the sum of Two hundred and sixty five dollars to me in hand paid, have granted, bargained, sold and released and by these present, do grant, bargain, and release to John Brockinton, registered as John Carolina, all that parcel or tract of land known as the Red House Tract conveyed to me by A.H. Edwards Commissiones in Equity on the 12th day of December 1868. Bounded on the North by land of the estate of I. A. Fountain, East by Herring Creek, South by land formerly owned by William Fountain and West by the Public Road leading from Society Hill to Georgetown and containing one hundred and four acres..., etc.

Witness my hand and seal this ninth day of November one thousand eight hundred and seventy (1870). Signed E.J. Lide (LL)." That is an excerpt from the original deed of John Carolina legally finalizing the purchase of the 104 acres from E.J. Lide in 1870. John Carolina, aka, John Brockinton, was really John Kelly Sr.

Let us take a moment and look into some aspects of this historic purchase. This was an achievement that merits additional consideration on many fronts.

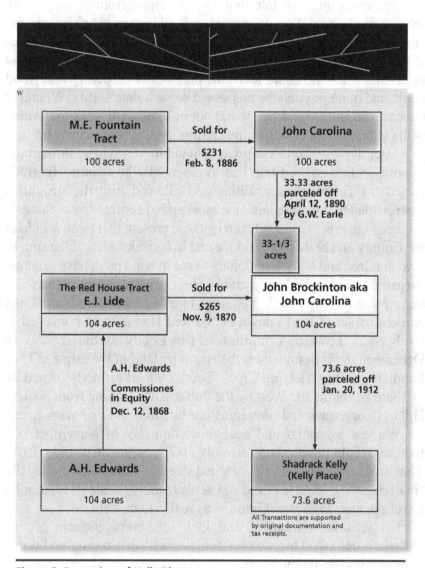

All Transactions are supported by original documentation and tax receipts.

Figure 8. Formation of Kelly Place

After the Civil War, white Southerners moved rapidly to minimize the freedom of liberated black Southerners. South Carolina began immediately to establish the Black Codes. These codes sought to limit the civil rights and civil liberty of John and his peers. One of the primary goals of the establishment was to keep them harnessed to the mule and tending the plantations. Among the numerous restrictions was the inability to practice any occupation, except farmer or servant under contract, without acquiring an annual license from a judge, and restriction from owning a firearm for their own personal protection.

However, on the other hand it is very interesting that some of the South Carolina Black Codes actually granted John and his peers a few more civil rights than they possessed during the bondage era. These codes declared that persons of color now had the right to acquire, own, and dispose of property; to make contracts, to enjoy the fruits of their labor and to receive protection under the law. In addition, for the first time the codes recognized the legality of black marriages as well as the legitimacy of the offspring.

We must also remember that this was at a time when Republicans, many of them African-American, had gained control of the South Carolina Legislature and were espousing more equitable treatment of all races and the encouragement of blacks to purchase land to farm. So the immediate climate was conducive for newly freedmen undertaking a successful foray into American society in South Carolina. In what appears to have been a short-termed inclusive culture, heralded ancestor John Kelly Sr. capitalized on the opportunity, amassed the capital and made his far-sighted move.

The phrase in the deed, "registered as John Carolina," was intended to clarify that the individual was using one name to record the deed to the property and another name when the property was later recorded. This purchase launched his career as an independent farmer and carpenter and initiated the evolution of Kelly Place. At that time the vast majority of farmers in South Carolina, black or white, were sharecroppers.

I believe the greatest challenge was not the politics, red tape or raising the capital for the venture, but the clearing of the forest and the tricky, swamp-like terrain leading to Herring Creek, for agricultural undertakings. This was no small task. The real estate came in the form of dense virgin forest containing trees of up to one-hundred to two-hundred years of age. Before any cotton, tobacco, corn, potato and melon crops could be planted these enormous specimens had to be removed, including the stumps, extensive root systems, ageless vines and undergrowth. This grueling project was very costly, time consuming and physically demanding and he had no free labor force to assist him. Needless to say, John's experience at Roseville Plantation paid dividends. He persevered and Kelly place became more than a dream, it became a reality.

The ownership of land in Darlington came with an array of perks. It is obvious that since farming was the number one vocation, the first requirement was acreage of fertile soil. However, it was about more than the physical presence of acreage. Ownership afforded the subtle edges of prestige, social status and credibility. If you owned land the doctor would make a house call; if you owned land the establishment viewed you through a different lens, you could get loans, you could vote with less confrontation, your actions in the community carried weight and set precedents. Even today there is still an aura associated with land ownership in the South and throughout America. John was forced to pay much more than the going rate to achieve this status as society still sought to limit black ownership. You could count the number of black land owners on one hand.

Hannah Harrison Kelly is also a legend in Kelly family lore. Figure 2 shows the birth years of most of her children except Mary and Sarah. The evidence is very clear from my research that she bore two children named Mary and Sarah. As stated earlier, their names appear on the list of slaves transferred to the ownership of Peter Samuel Bacot. This fact makes it a strong probability that they were born before John Jr. who was born on July 5, 1856. I was able to acquire less information on them than on any of John and Hannah's offspring. It is very interesting to note that Hannah gave birth for over two decades including two sets of multiple births. If we assume that Mary and Sarah were indeed older than John Jr., the data would suggest that she was a child bearing mother from the early 1850s to 1875, at which point she would have been a robust forty years old.

Information gathered from the Darlington County Historical Commission contained the following entry, which was recovered from the diary of a William Hutchinson, page 146, and it reads:

"John Carolina, a colored man, aged 67, and his wife aged 30, have been blessed with an addition to their family of four fine boys at one birth. Mother and children were doing well at last accounts, and were successfully attended by Dr. Horace Williamson. They live in Colfax Township. They were born June 2nd, 1869, in Darlington County."

The historic birth of the quadruplets was also reported in the June 16, 1869 edition of the Marion, South Carolina, *Star* newspaper, and quoted in the Darlington paper, *The Flag.*

The Darlington paper quoted the births, closing the item with a personal, local touch. It expressed excitement about the births and offers a subtle insight into the temperament of Darlington in 1869.

The clip reads as follows: "John Carolina, colored, aged 67, and his wife, aged 30, have been blessed with an addition to their family of four (4) fine boys at one birth. Mother and children were doing well at last accounts and were successfully attended by Dr. Horace Williamson. They live in Colfax Township, not far from the village, and we think there is no state of township that can beat that. This is certainly developing the country in the right way. Harrah for our side. We claim the championship. Let us have peace."

The names of the four fine boys cited above were **Peter, Meshach, Abednego and Shadrack.**

Please note that these births were attended by an established, white, doctor and not a black midwife, as that fact may have special significance. Blacks during that era generally used established midwives for such occasions. It may to a degree reflect John Carolina's bearing or respect in the community. You had to have some references, some status, or it had to be a special situation for a white doctor to travel to a remote black abode to render medical assistance during that stage of our history. Remember blacks were still not considered full human beings at that time. It is very obvious that this was a special obstetric event that merited special attention. The parties involved sought to insure, to the best of their ability, that no mishaps occurred during this complicated delivery. The lives of many African-American babies were lost during childbirth during that era, especially with the usage of midwives, as their technology was relatively archaic when compared to trained obstetricians. As evidenced by the 1870 Colfax Mortality Census, even though a doctor

217

was brought in for the delivery, two of the quadruplets only lived a short while. This particular census indicates that Peter died in July 1969, age one month and Abednego in September 1869, age four months.

Many contemporary Kellys who have knowledge of the birth of the quadruplets are unaware that these two essentially did not survive the birth process. The Colfax Mortality Census provided the proof for that important observation.

When these accounts were discovered there was immediate concern because it has been passed down via family lore that John Kelly Sr. is the father of the heralded quadruplets. The emergence of a man named John Carolina raised the author's antennas, as it suggested that maybe John and Hannah were no longer together in 1869, that there was a new man in Hannah's life.

Within about a month the 1870 Census of Colfax Township was uncovered. This report listed John Kelly Sr. as the head of that household. It became a challenge to generate an explanation for such wordage in the diary entry and newspaper articles. The question was who is this John Carolina? With your indulgence, I offer my view on the situation for your consideration.

The widespread usage of an alias during that era offers some insight and sheds some light on the situation. A common belief among many Americans is that the surname of a slave changed with a change in ownership. This was indeed a possibility, but not the rule. These individuals had a variety of options when it came to their adopted moniker. It is generally accepted that **John Kelly Sr.** actually did use the aliases John Brockinton, as well as John Carolina at times. Evidence presented herein clearly shows that **John** was at Roseville during a period when Richard Brockington was the plantation owner. It was not uncommon for slaves of that era to use their owner's last name as their sir name at times. To further complicate things, as stated earlier, **John's** father was named Carolina and at times he could have used his father's first name as his sir name, hence John Carolina, also a practice that other slaves, at Roseville Plantation and indeed throughout the South, were known to utilize. The usage of the owner's name, a father or grandfather's name as a surname was very common and acceptable during this period of American history.

It is very evident that John Kelly Sr. used multiple aliases during his lifetime. Numerous examples are presented during the course of the development of this treatise. One example already cited is the 1870 and 1880 Census of Colfax Township. In 1870, he used the name John Kelly Sr. while in 1880 he was listed as John Carolina. Another example is in the deed to his 1868 real estate purchase.

Page 386 of the 1870 Census of Colfax Township lists John Kelly Sr.'s family and their ages as follows:

i.	John Kelly	66
ii.	Hannah	34
iii.	John	14
iv.	Alfred	12
v.	Lydia	11
vi.	Caroline	9
vii.	Harry	9
viii.	Georgianna	7
ix.	Sarina	5
x.	Shadrack	1
xi.	Esau	3
xii.	Bella (Willow)	33
xiii.	Meshach	3

Two interesting aspects emerge from this census. First, Willow, now thirty-three years old, was still living with John's family. In addition, two of the quadruplets, as well as Mary and Sarah are not listed.

This census, which agrees with the ages presented in the Peter S. Bacot October 1, 1860 tax list, shows **John Kelly Sr.** and **Hannah Kelly,** to be sixty-six and thirty-four years old respectively in 1870. The census also lists both Harry and Caroline (née, 1861) and Esau and Meshach as twins. That was partially correct. In any case, it appears that Hannah was blessed with two sets of multiple births, a medical marvel. The reality is that Peter, Shadrach, Meshach and Abednego were born in 1869. The census report seemed to be at odds with reality, a communication problem which occurred frequently during that era of census taking, especially when the accurate accounting of black families was at stake.

The 1880 Census of Colfax Township, on page 11, contained the following listing:

i.	John Carolina	76
ii.	Hannah	44 wife
iii.	Georgeanna	17 dau
iv.	Serena	15 dau
v.	Evan (Esau)	13 son
vi.	Shadrack	11 son
vii.	Meshack	11 son
viii.	Leah	9 dau
ix.	Lucinda	5 dau

Some interesting observations emerge from this census report. The head of the household is listed as John Carolina, at the same age the head of this household in the 1870 census would have been in 1880. This supports the thesis that John Kelly Sr. and John Carolina were the same person. John's sons, John Jr. and Alfred, and daughter Caroline are no longer listed with the family. They appear to have moved on and established their own residences. Willow went to the Golden Shore between 1870 and 1880 and is also no longer listed. Two daughters, Leahanna and Lucinda were born after 1870. Meshack the other surviving quadruplet is listed as the same age of Shadrack confirming that the inaccurate citation in 1870 was a reporting error.

Earlier in this treatise we discussed the case of heralded ancestor, Matilda White, wife of Elias Bacote, who also matriculated for a period at Roseville Plantation when Peter Samuel Bacot, was at the helm. During that exercise we attempted to determine why her surname was White rather than Brockinton or Bacot.

Now a similar issue arises with John Kelly Sr., born at Roseville with a surname of Kelly. Why did John acknowledge the Kelly surname and not a Brockinton surname under these conditions? The simplest explanation is that at least his mother, and quite possibly also his father, Carolina, was sold to the plantation before his birth. They, as a couple, or Carolina alone arrived at Roseville with an established Kelly surname that the family elected to maintain for the rest of their lives. It is true that slaves, throughout the South, generally had that option. If this assumption is true then their names should appear on the early lists of slaves owned by Brockinton, possibly acquired from a Kelly family. This interpretation is plausible considering the fact that Darlington County history does show a Caucasian Kelly family firmly established in Darlington at that time. Carolina's name is on that cited list of slaves once owned by Brockington.

It is important to mention here that according to family lore, the two men listed on the preceding pages, **Dublin Kelly** and the other **Carolina Kelly, #2** (b. 1833), were housed at the same plantation as John during their years in bondage. The specific plantation was never iterated. As discussed earlier, it is probably more than a coincidence that there are two Carolina names shown in Table 3, the amended list of Negro slaves owned by the Richard Brockinton estate. In my opinion, these two men named Carolina represent **John Kelly Sr.'s** father and his putative cousin/grandson, adding more credence to the accuracy of Kelly family lore. Dublin is not on this list but his wife Nancy's name is present as well as Sarah's, the wife of Carolina #2.

John was born into bondage in contrast to being taken from the Mother Land. I cannot imagine living one's life in bondage, but in retrospect, if you had to be enslaved, it probably was less devastating to be born into it versus being stolen from Africa and forcefully relocated to America. I feel that one of the most dehumanizing aspects of that era on many Africans was the enforced separation from their family and their religion. Most religious individuals relied very heavily on their family and their God, then and even today.

It is simply amazing, when one considers the history of the core Bacote/Kelly family presented herein, that we have been able to demonstrate that paternal ancestors **John Kelly Sr.** and his future wives, **Nancy** and **Hannah**, as well as maternal ancestors, **Elias Bacote**, and his future wife **Matilda White**, all resided at Bacot plantations during their enslaved lives. Hannah's name, as well as the name of her parents, Harry and Leah is also included in the list of Negro slaves owned by Richard Brockinton. [See Table 3] Then as fate would have it, one of Elias's daughters would marry one of John's sons, a quarter of a century after slavery was abolished.

Darlington County history will reflect that post bondage Kelly and Bacote families, as well as their 20th and 21st century descendants, had and still share a sincere, deep rooted, respect and affection for each other. Their history is closely entwined via many parameters. Some still attend the same churches in Mechanicsville, churches like Providence and Pleasant Grove. This adoration was apparently unwaveringly established during the days of bondage.

To a certain degree, this addresses the nature, range and boundary of our forbearers' existence during the slavery and post-slavery periods in history. It is a point that is so often overlooked. Their world was very limited and although some slaves were allowed to leave the plantation and visit other plantations, their choices for selection of a relationship or spouse were limited to a very small area. In many cases, it was limited to the plantation where they lived. Forget about developing a friendship with a person from the other side of town, or even another town, or like today, another country. Roseville Plantation and the Cyrus Bacot Plantation was the restricted world of our Kelly and Bacote ancestors. Yet, even in such a restricted environment, love and evolution emerged victorious, Benjamin Bacot found Sara, Elias Bacote found Matilda White, John Kelly Sr. found Nancy Brockington and later Hannah Harrison, Carolina Kelly found Sarah, Jackson, Dublin Kelly found Nancy Robinson, Hannah Wright found John Brockington and a post-slavery generation later Minnie Bacote found Shadrack Kelly in the same vicinity.

John and Hannah are obviously two courageous individuals, who were born into bondage, survived the wrath of bondage, and raised a gutsy Kelly family whose descendants are still prospering today. I think it is important to acknowledge that they prepared the family for the future. To me, it is very clear that John and Hannah like many of their unheralded contemporaries recognized what was important for the survival of African-Americans. They possessed greater knowledge and skills than many would give them credit for. They were not "country bumpkins" or uninformed Negroes travelling along an unorganized path of doom and failure. Their models were consistent and fruitful.

One of the quadruplets born in 1869 would play a major role, as you will see later, in the development of Kelly Place. The oldest son, John Kelly Jr., was very instrumental in keeping the farm prospering during the early years. A portion of the lineage of this heralded ancestor is presented below and in Figure 12.

John Kelly Jr. (b. July 5, 1856) married **Susie Jackson** (b. July 1862), around 1877. Susie was the daughter of Jacob Jackson and Lina Moses. Some pundits say she is the "Aunt Sue Kelly," cook of David C. Milling [uncle of Dr. Chapman J. Milling] referenced in the historical tome *Darlingtoniana*, p. 154.

This ancestral couple built their home there at Kelly Place. The home was located near the present site of the Kelly graveyard on the wooded side of the lane leading to the graveyard. They had seven children who were born there. The names of the children of Susie Jackson and John Kelly Jr., grandson of Carolina Kelly #1 are:

i.	Frank Kelly	b. 9/1877
ii.	Julia Kelly	b. 7/1879
iii.	Jacob Kelly	b. 7/1884
iv.	James Kelly Sr.	b. 1891- d. 1971
v.	Dorsey Kelly	b. 9/1895
vi.	Kate or Rosa Kelly	b. 5/1893
vii.	Rena Kelly	

Frank Kelly (b. 9/1877), the oldest son of John Kelly Jr., married Rosa Fuller (b. 1878). The 1920 U.S. Federal Census lists them as residing in New Kirby, Dillon, South Carolina. This is the first known indication of an early Kelly ancestor relocating from the Back Swamp to nearby Dillon County. Family lore indicated that some family had moved to the other side of the Pee Dee River, but that belief although trusted, was undocumented. This documentation confirms that this Kelly family is entrenched in Dillon, South Carolina, and it started with Frank Kelly. It is incumbent upon the worldwide connected

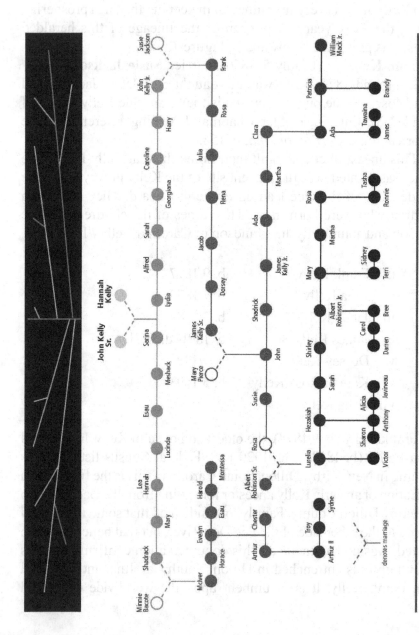

Figure 12. Kelly Genealogy: Lineage of Two Kelly Brothers

Kellys to re-connect with the Kelly descendants in places like Dillon, Palmetto, and Georgetown, South Carolina. Hopefully, this treatise as penned will serve as an impetus for such an endeavor and inspire a young Kelly descendant to undertake that ambitious task.

The 1920 Census listing of the family of Frank Kelly, great-grandson of Carolina Kelly #1, with their estimated birth years is shown below:

Name	Age	Estimated Year of Birth	Lifespan
Frank Kelley	42	1878	
Rosa Kelley	39	1881	
John Kelley	16	1904	(1904-1966)
Precilla Kelley	24	1896	(1896-1979)
James Kelley	12	1908	

John Kelley (b. 1904), son of Frank and Rosa Kelly, married Martha McGirt (10/6/1902-7/25/1995) from Marlboro County, South Carolina. The 1920 U.S. Federal Census lists him as age 16, married, and residing in the New Kirby section of Dillon, South Carolina. John, a farmer, had a variety of residences over the years, including New Kirby, Dillon, Key, Marlboro, South Carolina, and the Bethea and Latta sections of Dillon.

The 1940 U.S. Federal Census lists the ages and family of Martha Kelley and John Kelley (b. 1904), great-great grandson of Carolina Kelly #1 as follows:

		Age	Lifespan/EBY	Residence
i.	John Kelley	35	2/19/1904-12/6/1966	Dillon, SC
ii.	Martha Kelley	36	10/6/1902-7/25/1995	Dillon, SC
iii.	James T. Kelley	16	4/23/1923-5/22/1993	Phila, PA
iv.	Nellie Kelley	15	1925	
v.	Jesse K. Kelley	13	1927	
vi.	Rose Kelley	12	1928	
vii.	John J. Kelley	11	5/14/1930-5/27/199	Mount Joy, PA
viii.	Priscilla Kelley	9	6/30/1932-4/2/1969	Dillon, SC

ix. Frank Kelley   3   10/25/1936-11/16/2011 Dillon, SC
x. Jake Kelley   1   1940

The estimated birth year (EBY) was calculated from the ages cited in the census, while lifespan and place of residence were obtained on Ancestors.com.

Rose Kelly, also known as Rocetta Kelly, was married twice. Her first marriage was to Henry McKinnon, who died in 1971, and the second to John Henry Wiggins. The children of Henry McKinnon and Rocetta Kelly, great-great-great granddaughter of Carolina Kelly #1, are:

i.   Martha Mae McKinnon   b. 2/13/1946
ii. Mary Alice McKinnon   b. 2/6/1948
iii. Henry McKinnon Jr.   b. 2/21/1949
iv. Mollie McKinnon   b. 12/23/1953
v.   Henry James McKinnon   b. 10/20/1955
vi. Byron McKinnon   b. 3/7/1966

Henry McKinnon Jr. married Sandra. The names of the children of Sandra and Henry McKinnon Jr., great-great-great-great grandson of Carolina Kelly #1, are:

i. Christopher McKinnon   b. 4/26/1972
ii. Shanara L. McKinnon   b. 9/16/1975

Now let us go back across the Pee Dee River to the Riverdale Community, where James Kelly Sr. (b. 1891) married Mary Pierce (b. January 22, 1890), of the noted Ben and Susan Pierce family there on Old Georgetown Road. The ties between the Pierce family and the Kelly family are still very cohesive, over a century after this union was consummated. This legendary ancestral couple, who had eight children, is respectfully referred to in family circles as Big Mama and Big Papa. They lived their entire life on Old Georgetown Road in Riverdale. Mary went to the Golden Shore on August 26, 1961 and

James in January 1978. The names of the children of Big Mama and James Kelly Sr., great grandson of Carolina Kelly #1, are:

i.	Shedrick Shadrack Kelly	(10/3/1912- 3/4/1992)
ii.	James Kelly Jr.	(1915- 4/19/1977)
iii.	Rosa Kelly	b. 1/7/1920
iv.	Ada Kelly	b. 12/27/1922
v.	Clara Kelly	(2/29/1927-2013)
vi.	Susie Kelly	(7/15/1926-10/1/2003)
vii.	John Kelly Sr.	d. 12/22/1985
viii.	Martha Kelly	Died as a baby

Susie Kelly married Dence Daniels (1/19/1920-4/5/2003). Dence was also a Darlington native. They resided in Philadelphia, Pennsylvania. The names of the children of Dence Daniels and Susie Kelly, great-great granddaughter of Carolina Kelly #1, are:

i.	Hattie Carol Daniels	b. 12/25/1952
ii.	Evander Daniels Sr.	

Hattie Carol Daniels married Harry P. Richardson. The names of the children of Harry Richardson and Hattie Carol Daniels, great-great-great granddaughter of Carolina Kelly #1, are:

i.	Jasmine Daniels-Richardson	b. 12/28/1988
ii.	Jaret Daniels-Richardson	b. 12/28/1988
iii.	Tamara Daniels-Richardson	b. 2/4/1979

Jasmine attended Wilberforce University and is currently a hair stylist in the Philadelphia area.

Jaret, a 2012 Morehouse College graduate and an engineer in the construction industry married Yvonne Stewart in May 2013 in the City of Brotherly Love. They currently reside in Coatesville, Pennsylvania with their young daughter, Saania.

Tamara married Samuel McCullough. She is currently employed by the City of Philadelphia in business licensing and inspection. The names of the children of Samuel McCullough and Tamara Daniels-Richardson, great-great-great-great granddaughter of Carolina Kelly #1, are:

    i.   Samar McCullough
    ii. Samyra McCullough
    iii. Seth McCullough

Clara Kelly married William Mack (b. June 6, 1918). The names of the children of William Mack and Clara Kelly, great-great-granddaughter of Carolina Kelly #1, are:

    i.   Ada Mack   b. 1/22/1950
    ii. Patricia Mack   b. 1/22/1957
    iii. William Mack Jr.

Ada Mack, great-great-great-granddaughter of Carolina Kelly, married James L. Hamlin Sr. (b. June 4, 1939). The names of their children are:

    i.   James Hamlin Jr.   b. 11/11/1974
    ii. Tawaina Hamlin   b. 8/11/1978

Patricia Mack, great-great-great-granddaughter of Carolina Kelly #1, married James Gant (b. February 19, 1955). As shown in Figure 12 they have one daughter, Brandy R. Gant, who represents a seventh generation Kelly descendant.

To me it is very interesting how the same names were recycled within this Kelly family over generations. If you would allow me the latitude, I venture to speculate that this was due to the ultimate respect and camaraderie they possessed for each other, male and female. Sibling rivalries or second or third child syndromes were simply not in vogue. Survival was the order of the day. There was no time for any kind of complex psychological behavior or malarkey. You carried your weight, fought your own internal battles, and drank your moonshine or corn liquor, if that was your thing, but it was paramount that you earned the ultimate respect of the family.

Some of the sons of John Kelly Sr., including Meshack, Harry and Alfred, as discussed in more detail in the next chapter, departed Kelly Place to pursue their destiny away from Riverdale. It is unclear, years before the historic mass migration from the South by African-Americans, why they felt a need to depart the safety net of Riverdale. It is an unresolved issue often debated by contemporary Kelly descendants. Shadrack, John Jr. and Esau remained to ensure the success and long term survival of this revered residence which is still in the capable hands of a Kelly descendant today.

It has been difficult to obtain substantial information on John and Hannah's second son Alfred, born in 1858, and his descendants. The 1880 U.S. Federal Census does list him as residing in the Back Swamp, Darlington, South Carolina and married to Harriet Smith, born in 1860. Alfred was listed as twenty-two years old and Harriet as seventeen. His occupation was listed as a farmer. A Transfer of Title document, dated 1905, listed him as residing in Florence, South Carolina.

A Death Notice from the North Carolina State Board of Health, Bureau of Vital Statistics indicates that Harriet went to the Golden Shore on January 10, 1925 at the age of 65 in Wilmington, North Carolina. Alfred preceded Harriet in passing as her Death Notice indicated she was a widower.

Some of Susie and John Kelly Jr.'s offspring and descendants were successful farmers and sharecroppers at some of the large estate farms on Georgetown Road, on the other side of Louthers Lake, closer to the Florence County line. They were highly respected citizens of Riverdale for many decades.

John Kelly Sr., the great-grandfather of the author, went to the Golden Shore in 1886 and great-grandmother **Hannah** joined him on September 13, 1900, according to information found in the family bible.

As discussed in detail in the next chapter, after John Kelly Sr.'s death, Shadrack purchased the rights of three of his brothers to property which, according to court documents, was willed to them by their father. This property abutted John Kelly Sr.'s original post-bondage property. The strategic move kept this highly valued real estate in the portfolio of a Kelly and allowed Shadrack to eke out a more profitable existence. He eventually ended up owning a farm that encompassed seventy-three acres, more or less, there at Kelly Place.

Decades, even centuries from now when the question is posed, "what happened to that wing of the Kelly family of Riverdale/ Mechanicsville after the era of bondage"? History will reflect that the John and Hannah Kelly wing left Roseville Plantation "on a mission." They went to their post-bondage home at Kelly Place, commonly referred to among contemporary Kellys as "Mr. Jakes," and branched out from there to locations throughout America. For this clan, as free agents, it all started at Mr. Jakes. This accounts for the reverence given to Kelly Place in family lore, and why Kellys experience a special energy when they traverse the hallowed lane leading to the family graveyard, overlooking the valley and Herring Creek.

Earlier in this treatise we talked about the putative inheritance of family behavioral traits and patterns from ancestral generations. We talked about inherited behavioral characteristics of families, traits that remained intact through generations. We enumerated traits that Elias and Matilda Bacote appeared to have perpetuated. When we review a few aspects of John Kelly Sr.'s life, it is apparent that he was a calculating individual, a man who systematically, meticulously and legally juggled two aliases during his lifetime. In order to be successful at that, he had to maintain good records. It is very clear that this organizational trait and the careful maintenance of accurate records have persisted through generations.

John's son Shadrack recorded everything, including the planting location of specific crops on a yearly basis, dates of fertilization of crops, receipts from siblings and others for land rental, receipts from bank loans, deeds etc. Shadracks daughter Evelyn Kelly Brown was no different; she did not stray far from the tree. She owned a cedar chest that was crammed to the brim with all sorts of reminders of the past, even fifty year old bank records, outdated tax returns, telephone numbers from the 1940s and 1950s, and more importantly old historic documents of her grandfather's that were passed on to her for safe keeping.

The concept of inherited behavioral traits is very interesting. One day after I interviewed a senior Bacote family member, she looked at me with a quizzical stare and asked "are there differences between the Kelly family and us?" It was an issue I had not pondered, a difference between the two sides of my heritage, a good question. From my perch on both sides of the fence I have been afforded a comparative view of the nature of the two families and the nature of their existences. Although extremely close socially, and intellectually similar, they differ in many respects. At the risk of over generalization, I would like to cite areas where I feel there are differences.

The Kellys, with whom I have had much pleasure of association, when compared to the Bacotes, are much more captivating in a social setting. If you delete the exceptions, the Kellys overall are more outgoing, less reserved and appear to thrive in a social arena. They are also a very religious group of individuals. If you look at the numbers, a much higher percentage of them are pastors of churches, deacons, or church administrators, positions where you have to be spiritually committed.

It is generally accepted among behavioral scientists that successful, mentally healthy families have a ritualistic aspect to their agenda, traditions that serve to enhance their focus from a family standpoint.

Within that context, the afore-mentioned three Kelly wings still celebrate life as close cousins, a tradition established over two-hundred years ago during the era of bondage. The Kelly family, a comparatively large group, with its history of togetherness, places great importance on their biannual family reunions conducted presently at venues across the country. These well-attended gatherings where family members congregate, fraternize, and break bread together serve a very ritualistic purpose for contemporary members. They are a reminder of the past, and serve as a tool for transmitting family values, history and culture from ancestors to descendants. In addition they imply a future, and promote stability, togetherness and a continuity of sorts across generations. The highlights of the much anticipated gatherings are recognition of family members from each of the individual wings, celebration of recent family accomplishments, celebration of the ancestors, elders and youth, culminating on Sunday with the recognition of God.

These celebrations promote the continuity envisioned by legendary John Kelly Sr. in the 1800s and revisited in a very timely fashion in 1979 by a core of his descendants and extended family.

Over the last thirty years family reunions have been held in Atlanta and Columbus, Georgia, Bennettsville and Darlington, South Carolina, Indianapolis, Indiana, Detroit, Michigan, Hopewell, Virginia, King of Prussia and Philadelphia, Pennsylvania, Queens, New York, and Washington, D.C. These are all locations where at least one wing of this family is firmly established. The 2012 reunion was held in Columbus, Georgia and hosted by Patricia Gant and Reverend James Gant of the John Kelly Sr. wing. At these reunions, multiple representatives from each original wing are generally present.

When one examines the history of America and how African-American family continuity was so severely disrupted and disjointed during the era of bondage, it is simply amazing that this large family has maintained a measure of the concept of extended family. Initially, while enduring the wrath of slavery, on many plantations it was taboo to even contemplate the idea of extended family commitment. Today, as a result of Kelly culture, many extended cousins, four and five generations removed, know of one another and more importantly care about one another. Case in point, recently word was being disseminated among the family that Jessie Mae Kelly, a descendant of revered patriarch, Meshack Kelly, had gone to the Golden Shore. Jessie who was residing in Latta, South Carolina, is probably a 4th, 5th or 6th cousin to many contemporary Kellys, but they were genuinely affected by her fate. Although I did not know Jessie personally-had never laid eyes upon her-I went through a brief period of depression myself. That is the type of behavior which defines this family, a closeness that has been passed along almost like a genetic event for centuries.

Although the evolution of John Kelly's first family slipped through the cracks of contemporary family lore, at the next reunion in 2016 their story will be officially downloaded and re-inserted into the tradition.

The Bacotes rarely congregate in that manner as extended family. It appears to me that individual clans of the Bacotes do not reach out to other Bacote clans to the same degree as the Kellys. These observations lead me to believe that the Kelly family is more social, suggesting that this trait may be deeply entrenched in their behavioral mode and integrated into their DNA.

It is also very interesting when we examine behavioral patterns, that no post-bondage Kelly family members born around the turn of the century, or any members of the next generation of Kelly family members alive today, or their children speak of Roseville Plantation or, even more astoundingly, even know about the place and the role in played in the lives of our ancestors. Many of these family members spent major years on Old Georgetown Road, residing only a few miles from this place. It is well documented that ole man John Kelly's sons, Shadrack and John Kelly Jr., as well as many of John Jr.'s offspring, including James Kelly Sr. (see Figure 12) lived the majority of their lives on that scenic road. The reality is the legacy of Roseville Plantation was not verbally passed on by the emancipated John and Hannah Kelly or their prodigy. It is like the years spent there never existed, memories washed away from a corner of their brains, memories to be forgotten forever. They did not talk about it. It is very obvious that it was traumatic, that they were extremely humiliated and devastated. They made certain that the Roseville Plantation files in our brains were deleted due to lack of utilization or lack of traffic.

We often hear commentary about how cruel, inhumane, demeaning and demanding the life of an enslaved individual was. Experiences of that magnitude can be catastrophic and traumatic, the source of nightmares and sweaty dreams. Their experiences were psychologically similar to what Vietnam and Desert Storm veterans endured during the wars and to what Jews experienced during the Holocaust. How do we as human beings survive the after effects of such experiences without committing drastic actions? What human machinery allows succeeding generations to move on with a sense of dignity? One simple mechanism is to simply forget, it's the recollection that evokes the trauma.

I trust that the acknowledgement of Roseville Plantation in this treatise and the role I have indicated it played in the history of this family will not cause some entombed ancestral souls to "turn over in their graves."

It appears altogether fitting and proper that courageous John Kelly Sr., born a slave in 1803-1804, would have his name recycled and have a Kelly family member named in his honor three generations later. There is something to be said about the frequent recurrence of a name within a family genealogy. "What's in a name," you may ask?

In this context, it relates to something outstanding about the original individual. That person generally possesses some special talent or quality that ensuing generations revere, honor, respect and seek to reincarnate.

It was very surprising to discover that starting with John Kelly Sr. (b 1803-1804), even within the limited sampling of this treatise, there is a John Kelly in nearly each succeeding generation. It is ironic that John initiated the process himself, naming a son from both of his marriages after himself. His nephew, Frank Kelly, honored his oldest son with the name John. His great-grandson, **James Kelly Sr., and Mary Pierce Kelly** continued that tribute, naming one of their eight children **John Kelly, Sr.,** in honor of the legendary ancestor [See Figure 12]. The toughness, resiliency, Iron Horse traits and commitment to family of the former slave has truly captured the respect of ensuing generations of Kellys.

When the latter honoree was a young man, he left his job as a sharecropper to proudly serve in the United States Navy during World War II. "It was a duty he was very proud to have performed, protecting this great country," John would declare in later years. After the war he returned to Mechanicsville in 1946 and married the beautiful and charming Lizzie Daniels of Florence, South Carolina. It is not a coincident that they also named one of their sons John Kelly. For a while they resided with his parents, Big Moma and Big Papa, at their place on old Georgetown Road. Later they did a stint as sharecroppers at Celia W. Hymans place there on Old Georgetown Road. Life was good and they eventually moved to their own place on Indian Branch Road.

The children of the harmonious union of Lizzie and John Kelly Sr. #2, great-great-grandson of Carolina Kelly #1, are:

i.   Thomas K. Daniels
ii. Christopher Daniels
iii. Susie Kelly
iv. Lulu Mae Kelly
v.   John Kelly Jr.
vi. Elizabeth Kelly
vii. Alfred Kelly

As highly respected parents they placed great emphasis on religion and education in their lives and the lives of their children. The children attended school first in Darlington and later in Florence County. In 1961, after over a decade of farming the family happily moved "up town," to urban Darlington.

John went to the Golden Shore in 1985 after distinguishing himself as a youth leader at New Providence Baptist Church, Sunday School teacher, choir member and avid supporter of academic excellence. Because of his extraordinary commitment to the educational and spiritual development of youth in Darlington, the current, highly successful, John Kelly Memorial Scholarship Fund was established in his honor by Lizzie after his death. The fund has provided scholarships and financial assistance to deserving college students from the Darlington-Florence Pee Dee community for over 25 years.

Lizzie (b. 1919), the CEO of the Fund and one of the current matriarchs of the family is over ninety years of age now, and still resides at their home site in Darlington. She is very proud of the fact that having spent the bulk of her youth and life as a mother, housewife and homemaker, she had the tenacity to re-enroll in high school and ultimately attain her Mayo High School diploma in 1972 alongside her oldest offspring Alfred. That was a very special educational occasion for the family, and its ripple effects will be experienced for many generations. Lizzie has indicated it was one of the toughest and most rewarding tasks she ever undertook.

Alfred Kelly, the son of John Kelly Sr. #2 and Lizzie Daniels, married Sandra Mack from Lamar, South Carolina. Alfred, a distinguished builder in Darlington, is also an ordained minister. The names of the children of Sandra and Alfred Kelly, the great-great-great-grandson of Carolina Kelly #1, are:

    i.   Sherrie Mack
   ii.   Brandon Kelly

Elizabeth Kelly, the daughter of John Kelly Sr. #2 and Lizzie Daniels, married Jerome Parrott. The names of the children of Jerome and Elizabeth Kelly, the great-great-great-granddaughter of Carolina Kelly #1, are:

    i. i. Jerlonda Parrott
    ii. ii. Derrel Parrott

John Kelly Jr. #2, son of John Kelly Sr. #2 and Lizzie Daniels, married Sturvine. The names of the children of Sturvine and John Kelly Jr. #2, great-great-great grandson of Carolina Kelly #1, are:

    i. Evelyn Kelly
    ii. John Kelly, III

Evelyn and John III are great-great-great-great-grandchildren of Carolina Kelly. Evelyn married Cory Derry and they have two children. Evelyn is a medical technologist at McCloud Hospital in Florence, South Carolina. The names of the children of Cory Derry and Evelyn Kelly, the great-great-great-great-granddaughter of Carolina Kelly #1 are:

    i. Kaya Derry
    ii. Koven Derry

Kaya and Koven represent the eighth generation of Kelly lineage.

Lula Mae Kelly, daughter of John Kelly and Lizzie Daniels, married Johnny L. Jackson. Johnny went to the Golden Shore around 2006. The remainder of the family still resides in New Jersey. The names of the children of Johnny Jackson and Lula Mae Kelly, great-great-great-granddaughter of Carolina Kelly #1, are:

    i. Felicia A. Jackson
    ii. Johnny L. Jackson Jr.

Another of Carolina Kelly #1 descendants, a son of Big Moma and Big Papa, **James Kelly Jr.** (b. 1915), shown in Figure 12, wed Annie Alford (b. 1917). This important family in Kelly family lore also resided for many years on Old Georgetown Road, only a stone's throw from Roseville Plantation. James, aka Boisey, was an overseer at Fred Stems Place on Old Georgetown Road before relocating his family to Plant City, Florida, in 1960. He gained employment at Plant City Steel Company. Annie operated a very successful pre-school, child care nursery out of their home for many years, allowing numerous young mothers the opportunity to have a career.

The union of Annie and James Kelly Jr., great-great-grandson of Carolina Kelly #1, produced the following children:

i. Julia Kelly
ii. Annie Feen Kelly
iii. Sheryl R. Kelly
iv. Frank J. Kelly
v. Jackay L. Kelly

Julia and Frank's early education was in the Darlington School District while Annie, Sheryl and Jackay were educated in Florida. Sherel continued her education at Barbezon Fashion School and Annie is a graduate of the University of Florida. This was a very education conscious, Christian family, which demanded excellence from everyone. James went to the Golden Shore in 1977 and Annie in 1988.

The Kellys, as stated earlier, are a religious lot and this union produced two preachers. Julia is the wife of the late Rev. Artis Perkins who pastored Valley Grove Missionary Baptist Church in Miami, Florida for many years. Julia, very widely respected in Miami social and political circles, was a receptionist at American Dade Hospital Supply Company for a long time, before church duties took precedence. She currently resides in Miami.

Frank, a man of the cloth, now known professionally as Rev. Frank J. Kelly, lives in Sumter, South Carolina with his present wife Cynthia. He is a retired U.S. Air Force Major, and currently serves as a correctional officer for the State of South Carolina. Frank was initially married to Brenda who is deceased. The names of the children of Brenda and Frank J. Kelly, great-great-great-grandson of Carolina Kelly #1, are:

i. Frank J. Kelly II
ii. Shawn M. Kelly
iii. Michelle R. Kelly

Annie wed Richard Cox. The name of the child of Richard Cox and Annie Kelly, great-great-great granddaughter of Carolina Kelly #1 is:

    i.   Mercy Cox

Sherel Kelly wed Mark Gay and they reside in South Florida. The name of the child of Mark Gay and Sherel Kelly, great-great-great granddaughter of Carolina Kelly #1 is:

    i.   Tramel Gay

Another very important ancestor who merits attention in this treatise is Rosa Kelly whose position in the Kelly genealogy scheme is shown in Figure 12. Rosa spent a few of her early adult years in Baltimore, Maryland before relocating to Darlington. She married Albert Robinson Sr. and they spent many years as farmers at various locations on Old Georgetown Road before moving uptown. Rosa was a gentle, outgoing, compassionate woman who was known for her passion in lending a helping hand to the distressed during difficult times. Her many nieces, nephews and grandchildren flocked to her as they adored her and the ambiance she generated. A woman of immense faith she was a devout Christian and placed special emphasis on the family praying together. This remarkable ancestor was in the forefront of keeping the Kelly family organized and focused during the 1990s and early 2000s. She went to the Golden Shore on September 8, 2010.

The names of the children of Albert Robinson Sr. and Rosa Kelly, great-great-granddaughter of Carolina Kelly #1, are:

i.	Mary Robinson	b. 1/11/1942
ii.	Shirley Robinson	b. 8/17/1943
iii.	Albert Robinson Jr.	b. 6/5/1945
iv.	Martha Robinson	b. 7/1/1946
v.	Hezekiah Robinson	b. 8/17/1948
vi.	Sarah Robinson	b. 8/29/1951
vii.	Rosa Robinson	b. 12/5/1953
viii.	Lurelia Robinson	b. 5/30/1956

Mary Robinson, the oldest daughter of Rosa Kelly has the distinction of being one of the last Kelly family members to attend St. Paul School there in Riverdale when Mrs. Garner was the schoolmaster. She did a short stint there before transferring to New Providence School. Mary married James F. Gregg (b. December 10, 1937) in 1964 and they spent nearly two decades in Brooklyn, New York where she was employed with the New York City Transit Authority, before relocating to Darlington. The names of the children of James Gregg and Mary Robinson, great-great-great-granddaughter of Carolina Kelly #1, are:

    i. Sidney Gregg   b. 7/2/1969
   ii. Terra Gregg   b. 2/27/1972

Terra, great-great-great-great-granddaughter of Carolina Kelly #1, has a daughter Davondra Gregg, an 8th generation Kelly descendant.

Shirley Robinson, daughter of Rosa Kelly and Albert Robinson Sr., married Cleveland McLeod (b. April 29, 1948). The names of the children of Cleveland McCloud and Shirley Robinson, great-great-great-granddaughter of Carolina Kelly #1, are:

    i. Felicia Mcleod   b. 1/30/1971
   ii. Calvin Mcleod   b. 10/22/1972
  iii. Kimberly Mcleod   b. 7/28/1978

The offspring of most of the other children of Rosa Kelly and Albert Robinson Sr. are presented in Figure 12. Albert Robinson Jr., son of Rosa Kelly and Albert Robinson Sr. married Lela Lunn (b. October 26, 1945). The names of the children of Lela and Albert Robinson Jr., great-great-great-grandson of Carolina Kelly #1, are:

    i. Darren Robinson   b. 10/16/1965
   ii. Carol Robinson   b. 12/24/1967
  iii. Bree Robinson   b. 11/1/1984

Carol Robinson, great-great-great-great-granddaughter of Carolina Kelly #1, has a young daughter, Blair Robinson, who is an eighth generation Kelly descendant. Much of the future of this subset of Kellys rests squarely on Blair's shoulders, a truly charismatic young lady.

Shedrick Shadrack Kelly (10/3/1912-3/4/1992), a son of James Kelly Sr., married Ella Brown (9/16/1916-1/10/1988. The names of the children of Ella and Shedrick Shadrack Kelly, great-great-grandson of Carolina Kelly #1 are:

    i. Wilson Kelly Sr.   b. 8/2/1936
    ii. Rena Kelly   b. 9/27/1937
    iii. Shedrick Kelly Jr.   b. 3/1939

Rena Kelly (b. 9/27/1937) married Willie J. Martin Sr. and they resided in Darlington, South Carolina. The names of the children of Willie Martin Sr. and Rena Kelly, great-great-great-granddaughter of Carolina Kelly #1 are:

    i. Willie J. Martin Jr.   b. 8/16/1957
    ii. Vanessa R. Martin   b. 4/8/1959
    iii. Sandra J. F. Martin   b. 2/9/1963

Sandra J. F. Martin married Reginald Issac. The names of the children of Reginald Issac and Sandra J. F. Martin, great-great-great-great-granddaughter of Carolina Kelly #1 are:

    i. Paige A. Issac   b. 11/1/1995
    ii. Evan Issac
    iii. Tiffany Issac

Paige, Evan and Tiffany represent the 8th generation of Kellys starting with Carolina Kelly #1.

Wilson Kelly Sr. (b. 8/2/1936) married Blanche Brown. The children of Blanche and Wilson Kelly Sr., great-great-great-grandson of Carolina Kelly #1 are:

    i.   Wilson Kelly Jr.
   ii. Ronald Kelly

These two young Kelly men are great-great-great-great-grandsons of Carolina Kelly.

Throughout this treatise I have highlighted the activities primarily of the patriarchs of Kelly and Bacote families mostly because these men were more visible, from my perspective; nevertheless we know where the real power was held. Most of the male ancestors cited herein, held tough labor intensive positions on farms or in companies throughout this great nation. But in those Kelly ancestral families it was the mothers who provided the fiber that held them together and molded intensity, tenacity and dedication. Without sounding sexist, let me put it this way, "the men supplied the muscle and the women supplied the brawn."

The Kellys recognize and celebrate the very important achievements these women accomplished during the evolution of this family at-large. As a matter of fact in 2007 Rosa Kelly Robinson, Clara Kelly Mack and Lizzie Daniels Kelly were honored at a joyous family event for their outstanding contributions, not only to the family, but to the community as well. I know of no Kelly patriarch so fêted during his life.

CHAPTER FIVE

SHADRACK KELLY

The recently generated genealogy of Shadrack Kelly (née, 1869), his brother John Kelly Jr., the quadruplets, and their other brothers and sisters is presented in Figure 2 and Figure 12. These were very significant individuals in the genealogy of John and Hannah's wing of the original Colfax/Riverdale Kellys represented in this treatise. I regret that I don't have more information about them at this time. Most of them were the first post-bondage generation of this large family.

The looming query is how did they handle the adversity and responsibility of being a self-supported family? The social condition of post-bondage America engendered the concept of so-called inferior traits of African-American families. Western civilization sought, at all costs, to perpetuate as truth a notion that blacks represented sub-standard humanity. This climate of alienation was real and deeply affected the personality and consciousness of our early ancestors in both a positive and negative manner. First of all, it represented a challenge (early on) that had to be addressed and debunked at the individual level as a falsehood, if we were to survive as a family, as a people. That is why it is important today to elucidate and study how successful families and individuals maneuvered, counteracted and responded to that challenge. Shadrack and his siblings were in unchartered territory with the difficult mandate of not only traversing the extremely turbulent times but also preparing their offspring for a productive future of their own.

According to family lore, near the turn of the century, a few of the early Kelly ancestors departed Darlington County for greater employment opportunities in nearby Marlboro and Dillon Counties, and that lore has been substantiated. **Meshach**, one of the quadruplets mentioned copiously within this treatise, migrated to Marlboro

County, near the city of Bennettsville, to Brownsville, South Carolina where he met and married Nellie Jordan. The union of Nellie and Meshach Kelly, grandson of Carolina Kelly #1, was blessed with seven children:

i.	Wilbur Shadrick Kelly	(2/10/1910-6/28/1979)
ii.	Paul Kelly	b. 1919
iii.	Kenneth Kelly	
iv.	Rory Kelly	b. 1915
v.	Georgianna Kelly	
vi.	Nellie Mae Kelly	b. 1917
vii.	Louise Kelly	

The family listing above was retrieved from the "2003 Kelly Reunion Booklet" and the 1930 U.S. Federal Census Report.

Although Meshach and his family resided only thirty to forty miles away, the families of Shadrack and Meshach lost close physical but not spiritual contact with one another over the years. Visits were few and far between. We must remember that this was stagecoach and horse and buggy days, and traveling even forty miles in South Carolina during that period was a major ordeal for African-Americans. The trail from Riverdale to Brownsville was a potentially dangerous trek. The region was very remote; you could travel the entire route and not see anyone. God forbid you encountered some antagonistic stragglers, scalawags, carpetbaggers, or bounty hunters, and lest not forget the notorious night riders or klansmen. You might never be seen or heard from again. The culture of the old South was still very eminent. It was not safe on the road. In addition, there were no roadside inns, rest stops or safe havens were one could stop and generate new energy.

Meshach's oldest son, Wilbur Shadrick Kelly Sr. married Irene Pitillo. The union of Irene and Wilbur S. Kelly Sr., great-grandson of Carolina Kelly #1, produced twelve children:

i.   Wilbur S. Kelly Jr.   b. September 22, 1928

ii.   Freddie Lee Kelly

iii.   Charles Randolph Kelly

iv.   James Edward Kelly

v.   Jessie Lee Kelly   b. January 26, 1938

vi.   Jessie Mae Kelly   b. June 22, 1938

vii.   William S. Kelly   b. February 6, 1940

viii. Catherine Kelly   b. October 1, 1941

ix.   Paul Grover Kelly   b. May 22, 1943

x.   Jerry Kelly   b. January 28, 1948

xi.   Bessie Linda Kelly   b. October 30, 1950

xii.   Dorothy Kelly   b. July 22, 1951

According to family lore, Wilbur Shedrick Kelly Jr., also called Wilbur Shedrack, at the tender age of thirteen, obviously brimming with confidence and maturity left Brownsville to work as a water boy on the train in 1941, in his quest for personal fulfillment. It appears that this clan of Kellys, like other ancestral Kelly clans, sought to develop in the offspring a culture of independence, confidence, loyalty, and the drive to work hard to attain your goals. This courageous ancestor settled in Hopewell, Virginia, an industrial suburb of the tri-cities area of the Richmond-Petersburg region. He later found employment at the famous Hercules Chemical Company and worked there until he joined the United States Navy during World War II. Wilbur had an honorable career, having credibly served as a cook for the naval servicemen in Annapolis, Maryland, California and overseas.

After an honorable discharge from the Navy, the quiet easy-going gentleman, returned to Hopewell and his position at Hercules Chemical. He later married Mandie Easter (b. June 3, 1939).

The names of the children of Mandie Easter and Wilbur Shadrick Kelly Jr., great-great grandson of Carolina Kelly #1 are:

i.   Louise Kelly   b. August 3, 1957

ii.   Ada Kelly   b. June 12, 1960

iii.   Vanessa Kelly   b. October 20, 1958

iv. June Kelly   b. June 10, 1961
v.   John Kelly   b. December 18, 1963
vi. Monique Kelly   b. June 15, 1965
vii. Wilbur S. Kelly III

Wilbur retired from Hercules Chemical after over thirty years of service. He also worked in the construction business as a carpenter/ brick mason and assisted in the construction of numerous homes in the Hopewell, Virginia area. This very important ancestor went to the Golden Shore in August, 1979 but not before establishing himself as a force in Virginia. His confidence, boldness, courage and vision created another vital base from which the family could operate. Presently large contingents of Kellys, his descendants included, are flourishing in that region of Virginia. Wilbur was the initiator and catalyst in many regards, fulfilling a crucial role as the elder sibling of his clan.

Only two of Wilbur S. Kelly Sr. and Irene's offspring are alive today, Jessie Lee Kelly, great-great-granddaughter of Carolina Kelly, and the noted Reverend Bishop Jerry Kelly, great-great-grandson of Carolina Kelly #1. Bishop Kelly currently resides in Chester, Virginia.

Bishop Jerry Kelly married Brenda Herman (b. April 15, 1950). They have one son, Larelle Kelly (b. November 11, 1968).

It has become more and more apparent upon researching Kelly family history that the Kellys are very Christian orientated. Another notable example is Reverend Bishop Jerry Kelly, who has been consecrated and appointed Bishop of the Kingdom Dominion Fellowship of Churches and Network. He is also a Senior Pastor of Antioch Christian Center Church International in Virginia as well as a renowned motivational speaker, entrepreneur and author. Bishop Kelly also has a Ph.D. in Philosophy. He represents the new breed of Kelly descendants who have migrated from the cotton fields and tobacco plantations of America to the international stage.

Larelle Kelly followed in his distinguished father's footsteps, and is a noted pastor himself in Virginia. He is married to Jessica (b. August 30, 1969), who is also a minister. The names of the children of

Jessica and Larelle Kelly, the great-great-great-grandson of Carolina Kelly #1, are:

    i.   Jeree C. Kelly   b. 1/28/2000

    ii. Jocelyn C. Kelly   b. 8/11/2001

    iii. Brandon Kelly

Jeree, Brandon and Jocelyn represent the seventh generation of Kellys beginning with Carolina Kelly.

Jessie Lee Kelly, a daughter of Wilbur Shadrack Kelly Sr. and Irene, married Leroy Peterson. The names of the children of Leroy Peterson and Jessie Lee Kelly, great-great-granddaughter of Carolina Kelly #1, are:

    i.   Lee Roy Peterson   b. 5/15/1957

    ii. La'Ray Peterson   b. 7/17/1958

    iii. LaWana Rene Peterson b. 1/9/1961

LaWana Rene Peterson, great-great-great granddaughter of Carolina Kelly, has two sons, Jarrelle L. Peterson (b. November 28, 1982), and Ryan R. Peterson (b. March 28, 1992). These two young men represent the seventh generation of Kellys starting with Carolina Kelly #1.

La'Ray Peterson, great-great-great grandson of Carolina Kelly has two children, Kenya Peterson (b. March 29, 1978) and Valencia Peterson (b. January 20, 1989). They represent seventh generation Kellys.

Bessie Linda Kelly, daughter of Wilbur Shadrack Kelly Sr. married Rudolph Jones Sr. (b. June 18, 1948). The children of Rudolph and Bessie Linda Kelly, great- great-granddaughter of Carolina Kelly #1, are:

    i.   Rudolph Jones Jr.   b. 12/25/1967

    ii. Rodney Jones   b. 10/10/1969

    iii. Raqueal Jones   b. 2/25/1971

    iv. Rashelle Jones   b. 9/14/1972

Rudolph Jones Jr. married Verdell. The children of Verdell and Rudolph Jones Jr., great-great-great-grandson of Carolina Kelly #1, are:

i. Diamond Jackson
ii. Victoria Ford
iii. Shanine
iv. Renita Jones

Rashelle Jones married Marion Murrell. The names of the children of Marion and Rashelle Jones, great-great-great granddaughter of Carolina Kelly #1, are:

i. Ryan Jones   b. 5/3/1990
ii. Ryanna Murrell   b. 5/14/1991
iii. Mariah Murrell   b. 5/18/1995

Another of Meshach's sons, Kenneth Kelly, married Mandie. The names of the children of Mandie and Kenneth Kelly, great-grandson of Carolina Kelly #1, are:

i. Kathleen Kelly
ii. Georget Kelly
iii. Lee Kelly

Georgianna Kelly, daughter of Meshach Kelly, married a Davis gentleman. The names of the children of Mr. Davis and Georgianna Kelly, great-granddaughter of Carolina Kelly #1 are:

i. Marion
ii. Mildred
iii. William
iv. Herbet Kelly
v. Fred Kelly
vi. Agnes Kelly

Paul Kelly, son of Meshack Kelly, married Mary. The name of the child of Mary and Paul Kelly, great-grandson of Carolina Kelly #1, is Patricia Kelly. Patricia is thus the great-great-granddaughter of Carolina Kelly.

Nellie Mae Kelly, daughter of Meshach Kelly, married a McKinnon gentleman. The name of the child of Mr. McKinnon and Nellie Mae Kelly, great-granddaughter of Carolina Kelly #1, is David McKinnon. David is the great-great-grandson of Carolina Kelly.

Shadrach's sister, **Lydia**, shown in Figure 2, married Edward Ervin and they produced nine children. The names of the nine children of Edward Ervin and Lydia Kelly, granddaughter of Carolina Kelly #1, are:

i.	Willie Ervin	b. 1874
ii.	Marcus Ervin	b. 1878
iii.	Mareno Ervin	b. 1878
iv.	Baby girl	b. 1880
v.	James Ervin	b. May 1881
vi.	Mary Ervin	b. April 1889
vii.	Sarah Ervin	b. March 1891
viii.	Robert Ervin	b. March 1898
ix.	Baby boy	b. March 1900

Two of their babies died at birth.

Another sister, **Lucinda**, also shown in Figure 2, married Soloman Zimmerman in 1895. This union was blessed with five children. According to the 1900 United States Census, Lucinda was born in 1874 and Soloman in 1842. They lived in Mechanicsville and their daughter Lenora was born in 1897. The names of the children of Soloman Zimmerman (b. 1842) and Lucinda Kelly (b. 1874), granddaughter of Carolina Kelly #1, are:

i. Benjamin Zimmerman
ii. Bubba Zimmerman
iii. Ester Zimmerman
iv. Sadie Zimmerman
v. Lenora Zimmerman

Ester Zimmerman married William Sanders. The names of the children of William and Ester Zimmerman, great granddaughter of Carolina Kelly #1, are:

    i.   William Sanders Jr.
    ii. John Sanders
    iii. Hanna Sanders
    iv. Malloy L. Sanders

Another of Shadrack's brothers, **Esau Kelly**, also shown in Figure 2, married Amelia. They resided in Florence, South Carolina. Amelia was born in December 1866 and went to the Golden Shore unexpectedly at the tender age of thirty-five on February 15, 1901, in Florence.

Shadrack Kelly (son of John Kelly Sr.) and **Minnie Bacote** (daughter of Elias Bacote), the son and daughter of two of the "Iron Horses" were united in holy matrimony in Darlington County after the turn of the century, in 1903.

They established residence on the property where Shadrack lived as a child, at Kelly Place, now known as 557 Georgetown Road in the Riverdale/Mechanicsville section of Darlington, South Carolina. On a plot about fifty yards from the road, they constructed a modest but beautiful two bedroom home. The living room was reserved for special company and the master bedroom had a large fire place that endowed the room with a special serenity. The front porch extended across the entire front of the house which was erected on a foundation of twenty-four inch stone blocks. As of 2014 the old house is still standing, although unoccupied. Georgetown Road was previously known as Old Georgetown Highway or Road S-16-495. From Darlington one travels Route 34 East through Mechanicsville to Georgetown Road. Proceed south on Georgetown Road, about one mile to the old Kelly Place [Farm tract #3414] on the left.

The 1920 U.S. Federal Census lists the household of Shadrack Kelly as follows:

	Age	Estimated Birth Year
Shadrack Kelly	50	1870
Minnie Kelly	36	1884
Josephine Kelly	24	1896
Almeda Kelly	20	1900
Homer Kelly	18	1902
Evelyn Kelly	10	1910
Martel Kelly	7	1913
Harold Kelly	6	1914

The estimated birth year was calculated from the age cited in the Census. I acknowledge that most Census Reports are not 100 per cent precise, but this one is within an acceptable degree of variance of (+/-) two years. An earlier listing of the offspring of Minnie and Shadrack and a reference to Shadrack's two earlier marriages was presented under "The Bacote Side." They had two additional offspring, Esau and McIver, who died as infants. Martel refers to Montessa, and as outlined earlier Josephine, Almeda, and Homer (Horace) were offspring from Shadrack's previous marriages.

Their occupation was listed as farmers and they eked out a profitable existence at Kelly Place, which has a revered tradition in this family. The first reference to the area, that I observed, included it in a tract of one- hundred acres, more or less, as part of the estate of John M. Carolina [Figure 13]. A later deed lists Kelly Place as seventy three and six-tenths acres, surveyed March 30 and October 20, 1911, and deeded to Shadrack Kelly. Markers included an iron axle, iron stakes, specific pine and hickory trees and the noted Herring Creek which still flows along the eastern property line [Figure 14].

The fact that the old house is still standing, is a testament to the commitment of later Kelly/Bacote generations to the legacy of the family and its humble beginnings. Numerous homes from that era are no longer in existence, having been burned down, decayed to ashes, or bulldozed over. Residences that once gleefully bustled with

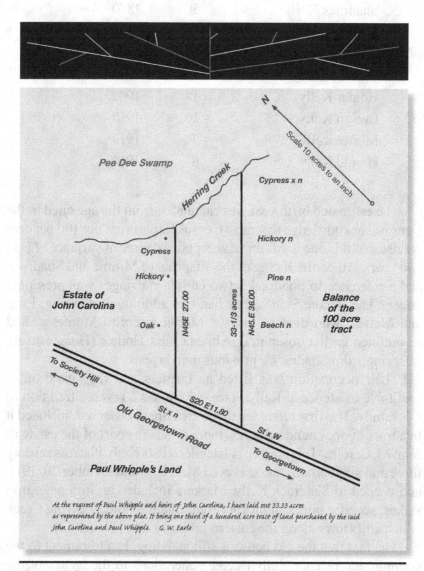

Pee Dee Swamp

Herring Creek

Scale 10 acres to an inch

N

Cypress x n

Hickory n

Pine n

Cypress

Hickory •

Estate of
John Carolina

N45E 27.00

33-1/3 acres

N45.E 36.00

Beech n

Balance
of the
100 acre
tract

Oak •

To Society Hill

St x n

S20 E11.80

Old Georgetown Road

St x W

To Georgetown

Paul Whipple's Land

*At the request of Paul Whipple and heirs of John Carolina, I have laid out 33.33 acres
as represented by the above plat. It being one third of a hundred acre tract of land purchased by the said
John Carolina and Paul Whipple. G. W. Earle*

Figure 13. South Carolina - Darlington County
Survey of land allocated by heirs of John Carolina

activity, with visitors for picnics, a fish fry, or other social gatherings are gone.

The family respects, honors and adores the old Kelly homestead. Evelyn K.B. Brown poured thousands of dollars and countless hours of diligence into the property over the last twenty-five years. She attempted to maintain its beauty, primarily out of respect for the past, and the courageous souls who made it a reality. However, despite her efforts, currently it is in disrepair. Plywood boards cover most of the window frames which are devoid of glass panes, and black insulation material protrudes in a few places, flapping in the wind, from gaps in the siding where boards are missing. Nature has essentially taken its toll on the house, as the weather and lack of proper maintenance in recent years has ravaged it badly. Sometimes the doors are seen ajar as intruders remove the locks to attain a night's sleep. Surprisingly, the interior and the tin roof are still very sound. Good neighbors, family members and forces at large maintain a watchful vigilance on 557 Georgetown Road, or it would just be overrun.

This vital landmark which once supported the life of a pioneering family in Riverdale is approaching extinction. An ambitious initiative has been undertaken seeking government support to place it on the National Register as a protected national treasure, a reminder of historic Riverdale. Georgetown Road, once the primary antebellum route connecting Charles Town, Society Hill and the Back Swamp region is wider now and beautifully paved as the area braces for a new era of construction, residency and re-vitalization.

I find the life of **Shadrack Kelly** to be, in many regards, even more intriguing and fascinating than that of Elias Bacote. Both of these real estate conscious men were very smart and cunning.

Their model was really very simple. Yet in many ways it was difficult to comprehend and implement. These two men said "let's go for it! Let's take some chances, some risk, and do what we have to do to be successful." They appear to have been no-nonsense types of men, who were probably a pain in the butt to some people, but I admire their aggressive approach.

Shadrack and Minnie lived on a tract, very rich in animal life. This property was bound on the south by land of Bessie Bacote Brockington and Handy Brockington, on the east by Herring Creek and on the west by Old Georgetown Road. It consisted of a significant portion of swampy woodland proceeding toward the Pee Dee River, with a huge drop-off between a portion of the farmable region and the swamp. A significant portion of the swampy region periodically floods from the overflow of the Pee Dee River and its tributary, Herring Creek. Sometimes the water can be up to 10 feet deep in that region (Figure 14), and according to legend, there were areas there that had quick-sand type properties, called bogs. Beware as you trod in this region.

The farmable region consisted of rich crumbly loam on clay subsoil, extremely fertile land from the bluffs all the way to Old Georgetown Road. Virgin stands of cypress, hardwood and rosemary pine covered the bottoms, while the bluffs contained the finest longleaf pines, hickory and white oak trees anywhere. Droves of large bucks, rabbits, wild hogs, raccoons and opossums roamed the valley while flocks of wild turkeys and ducks feasted among the great cypress trees in the marshy regions.

Herring Creek is a tributary of both Lourdes Lake and the Pee Dee River. When Shadrack was farming the property, each spring, around Easter, millions of silvery herring would migrate up the river on their "fatal honeymoon," and surge through the lake into Herring Creek. The narrow creek would literally be choked with so many fish, that they could be easily trapped, by wagon loads, in nets placed in the flowing water. For many decades the creek served as a source of herring for edible fish fare as well as fertilizer for farming.

A small active Kelly cemetery, which has about thirty-five to forty graves, that we are aware of, is located on the property. One of the best ways to learn about one's family history and the contributions of ancestors to American history is to visit cemeteries where they are entombed. **John Kelly Sr. and Hannah Kelly, Shadrack, Almeta, Montessa, Harold "Jake" Kelly, John Kelly Jr., and wife Susie Kelly, James Kelly Sr., and wife Mary Pierce Kelly, Esau Kelly, James Kelly Jr.,** his wife **Annie Kelly,** his son **Jackay Kelly,** and baby **McIver,** are a few of the Kellys known to be buried there. The remains of **Albert Robinson Sr., Rosa Kelly Robinson** and **Ronnie McLead Jr.** are also entombed there. Albert Robinson Sr. was the husband of the former Rosa Kelly. There are certainly many unknown grave sites there also.

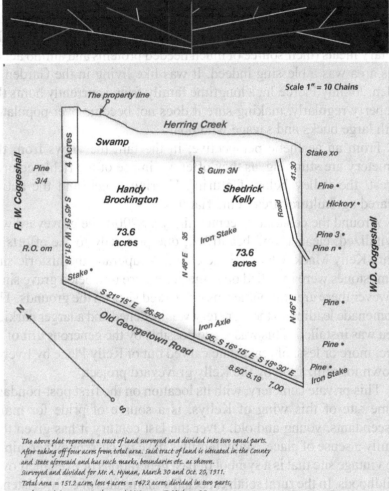

The property line

Scale 1″ = 10 Chains

Herring Creek

Swamp

4 Acres

Pine
3/4

R. W. Coggeshall

R.O. om

S 45° 51' W 31.18

Stake •

Handy
Brockington

73.6
acres

S. Gum 3N

S 21° 15' E 26.50

N 46° E 35

Iron Stake

Old Georgetown Road

Iron Axle

35, S 16° 15' E S 18° 30' E

8.50' 5.19 7.00

Shedrick
Kelly

73.6
acres

N 46° E

Road

41.30

Stake xo

Pine •

Hickory •

Pine 3 •

Pine n •

Pine •

Pine •

Pine •
Iron Stake

W.D. Coggeshall

N

The above plat represents a tract of land surveyed and divided into two equal parts.
After taking off four acres from total area. Said tract of land is situated in the County
and State aforesaid and has such marks, boundaries etc. as shown.
Surveyed and divided for Mr. A. Hyman, March 30 and Oct. 20, 1911.
Total Area = 151.2 acres, less 4 acres = 147.2 acres, divided in two parts,
each containing - seventy-three and 6/10 acres. T. Ettelson, C.E.

Figure 14. South Carolina - Darlington County
Survey of original Kelly Place

The old cemetery is regally perched atop a natural bluff which overlooks Herring Creek. When the creek overflows, water runs off into the valley forming what appears to be a natural seasonal pond that is interspersed with large billowing cypress trees. This generates a very fertile natural eco-system promoting the rapid growth of much needed young flora for the numerous fauna that inhabit the area. In the days of old, when the old timers hunted for much of the dietary meats (their source of much needed proteins and amino acids) this area was a blessing indeed. It was like living in the Garden of Eden. Johnny Pierce Jr., a longtime family friend currently hunts the property regularly, making sure it does not become over-populated with large bucks and savage wild boar.

From an aesthetic perspective, in the fall, the views from the cemetery are stunning, as they offer a glimpse of the richly colored forest, the valley below featuring Herring Creek and the active cleared agricultural area in the flat lands.

Around the celebrated, centennial year 2000, the graveyard was revitalized, cleaned and beautified, due primarily to the efforts of Clara Kelly Mack. Clara led the charge to upgrade the historic site. Tombstones were installed on some heretofore unlabeled grave sites; however there are still numerous unmarked sites on the grounds. The promenade leading to the cemetery was widened and a larger parking area was installed. This was made possible by the generous gift of an acre, more or less, of real estate carved out of Kelly Place by Evelyn Brown for utilization by the Kelly graveyard project.

This private cemetery, with its location on the first post-bondage home site of this wing of Kellys, is a source of pride for many descendants, young and old. Over the last century it has given this family a sense of place. Many families have no current ownership in the vintage site that is a symbol of past generations or even their own childhoods. In the rural south especially, many sites of early existence or occupation have been sold, engulfed by an expanding forest area, or dismantled by "progress" or industrialization, and as such have been reduced to figments of our imagination. All that is recognizable at many of these symbolic places now are distinguishable overgrown areas of old pine, hickory and chinaberry trees, where humble abodes once were so regally perched.

As such it is the desire of the contemporary Kelly family to properly manicure and maintain this historic, private, resting place for generations to come. If Kelly Place is ever sold to an outsider, the desire of the early ancestors was that a clause requesting the continued existence of the site with rights of continued access for the family guaranteed for the legal maximum of time, be penned into the legal document.

As outlined earlier, the marriage of **Shadrack and Minnie** produced five children. Unfortunately, only two of them survived long enough to become senior citizens. These two: **Evelyn Kelly Brown,** née May 13, 1909, and **Harold Jacob Kelly,** née July 19, 1913, were birthed in Mechanicsville with the assistance of midwives. They had fun childhoods frolicking in the swampy woodlands of Kelly Place, enjoying the cold water spring that was perched at the bottom of the deep ravine behind the Kelly graveyard, and developing knowledge of and a working relationship with the diverse spectrum of wild life with which they co-existed. Like many of their peers, they learned the inherent value of hard work and developed a strong work ethic at an early age. This asset would serve them well throughout their lives.

What was it like living in rural America for these ancestral farmers at this stage in the history of America? According to an article penned by Chapman J. Milling which appears in the book *Darlingtoniana*, blacks in Mechanicsville around the turn of the century were a happy people. According to Milling, "they spent a lot of time at church re-affirming their faith and their confidence in God."

Milling also stated that their needs were few and basic. "On their allotted tracts they raised much of their own food. Many had a cow or two, and all had a few chickens and a pen of hogs. The men hunted constantly and their tables were supplied with squirrel, raccoon, opossum, rabbit, venison, and a variety of fish. They cured most of their own bacon and raised a year's supply of rice on a small patch of land. They grew enough corn for the cattle and themselves. Behind every cabin was a small field of sugar cane from which delicious syrup was made in the fall."

"They had many festivities which occurred as regularly as the seasons. In midsummer when the crops were "laid by" there was much visiting and partying. Tobacco curing, which required sitting up at the barn for several nights, was the occasion for endless gossip and tall tales. There were fish fries, chicken bogs, and a lot of loving mixed with the rigorous work."

According to Milling, "cotton picking itself was the greatest game of all." This occurred from dawn to sunset and was a game of skill usually dominated by the females. A good cotton picker could turn in as much as three hundred pounds of seed cotton, while the average was about half that or one hundred fifty pounds. Some farmers would offer prizes or bonuses for the person who picked the most. However, the biggest prize was bragging rights which the serious pickers strove for.

I would like to take the opportunity to add some off-color, news tidbits I found in old *News and Press* newspaper editions from around the turn of the century, regarding blacks in Riverdale. Quoted directly from the newspaper as published, I thought they were rather comical, amusing and yet interesting, a sign of the times. They may sound like exaggerations or even fishy to some. I was not searching for material of this nature, but I have the knowledge, courage and inner strength to take the statements on their own merit. They may make you laugh, or make you cringe, but ultimately they offer a glimpse of the environment Kelly ancestors in Darlington County encountered on an ongoing basis.

1. "It seems as if the negroes are fully determined to make good crops too. We recently saw one pulling the plow and his wife plowing him."
2. "We understand that Mr. Evan Lide shot recently at a negro whom he caught stealing watermelons; so it seems there is somebody else besides our Wardsville friends who is going to have melons."
3. "There are more mean negroes down here than "Carter ever had oats," notwithstanding the fact that they have tri-weekly prayer meetings which last nearly all night."

4. "Boss Josey, colored, who operates T.S. Lucas farm near Mont Clare, did excellent work among the colored people of the Round
O section securing subscriptions of $1,200 for WW I Liberty Bonds."

5. "The colored people of this place have been greatly excited since the first convulsive shocks of the earthquake. They are sounding the gospel trumpet in every direction. They seem to blow long and loud, and spend the greater part of nearly every night, at their places of worship, and look so drowsy the next day that we think old Pluto would be entirely disgusted with their appearance."

6. "On Sunday, the 4th instant, while some colored boys were bathing in the Pee Dee River, near Cashua Ferry, one of the party, Lawrence Gregg, jumped from a springing board and struck his head and breast against a log or stump, killing him instantly."

7. "Some of the people of the neighborhood have not stopped grumbling about the No Fence Law yet. We were informed that there was a dispute between one of our colored men and a Republican a few days ago. The quarrel was put to an end by the Republican taking to the road. Thinking he was in a bad place he told his feet to carry him away and it is said they did as they were bid."

8. "Seeing accounts of the commencement exercises of so many schools reminds us of how badly we need a good Negro school in this part of the Township. We hope the people will consider what an important thing a school is, and that they build a good substantial school house and procure a competent teacher, so that the children will not grow up in ignorance."

One of the traditional highlights of the week was the trip to downtown Darlington on Saturday. Shadrack would oil the wagon wheels, prep the mules, gather his crew and take off on the wagon "to town." It would be an informal outing, and the attire was neat and casual. You wanted to look good because you never knew who you would run into. The farmers of Darlington County, including Riverdale would make the journey to pick up supplies, pay bills and enjoy themselves. This included shopping; tidying up their appearance with a haircut, and the females could get their hair done. The barber shops and hair salons were always packed on Saturdays. Other activities, in addition to people watching, included getting your shoes shined and catching up on the latest news. In later years, after the appearance of the movie theater they could take in a movie, which in most cases featured a western adventure depicting how the West was won and maintained.

Downtown Darlington fit the bill perfectly. The area was designed or constructed in the shape of a square, surrounding the court house, which contained a developing array of establishments until the area fully matured in the 1950s. In the beginning there was a general store, followed by clothing stores, grocery stores, barber shops, banks, drugstores, shoe stores, movie theaters, the county jail, tailor shops, ice cream parlors, as well as a few other establishments on the streets leading up to the square. The "Square" was a money making machine like the Strip in Las Vegas, and Saturday was payday. The entire area was constantly abuzz with activity as people stayed in "town" all day on Saturday cruising the Square afoot repeatedly until their feet wore out. It was a venture similar to visiting the mega suburban malls of today. It was an entertaining spectacle.

Saturdays and Sundays were basically leisure days, while the remainder of the week was devoted to rigorous farm work. Evelyn was not required to perform a lot of field work as a child, although as a teenager she picked her share of cotton at the farms on Georgetown Road. She was one of those fortunate southern girls who dragged a burlap sack during her teenage years, under the blazing South Carolina sun, picking cotton and harvesting pecans and walnuts. According to Evelyn, her primary tasks during her early years was tending to the chickens, turkeys and ducks, in addition to transporting water by buckets from the spring in the woods, to the house and to the thirsty workers in the fields. The water was primarily used for cooking, drinking, cleaning and bathing. This may seem very simple and forthright but it was a daunting task. It was about endurance and knowledge of the perils of the Back Swamp, as wildcats were indigenous to this region and snakes had a definite presence. The bucket of water was heavy and the goal was to minimize spillage. A direct route from the spring to the house consisted of a straight line from the spring, through the ravine, through the graveyard and the fields to the house, about one-hundred fifty yards in distance. However, if she elected to stay on the established path, the safest route to the spring, circling the graveyard and the deep ravine, it stretched to three-hundred to four- hundred yards. Sometimes she took the more perilous route, but more often than not she utilized the safer established path. This was a demanding and responsible duty which she enjoyed performing for the family.

This water carrier was also very proud of the fact that she could pick over two hundred pounds of cotton consistently on a daily basis, that she was not a one-day wonder. It was also important to her that the fowl grew fat and plump for consumption by the family. Later in her life, she talked about the fact that she believed her numerous responsibilities as a youngster contributed to the development of her commitment, character and desire to excel in whatever endeavor she undertook, that it had been a good learning tool.

The family regularly attended Pleasant Grove Baptist Church in Mechanicsville and the children attended grammar thru the sixth grade in Mechanicsville at St. Paul School, on Old Georgetown Road. Junius Bacote's wife, Josephine Bacote, as mentioned earlier, was a teacher at this revered school which served for many years as the only school for African-American children in that area of the county.

St. Paul School was a one-room, one door in, same door out, wooden structure. The boards that enclosed the structure always appeared unpainted. It was constructed because the good folk, white and black of Mechanicsville, around the turn of the century ascertained that the young black children in their community deserved an education; that the huge education discrepancy between the races needed to be eliminated. The community collaborated and worked to pool their individual resources, skills and time and the much needed school became a reality. It is said, the building which housed grades one through six was originally only open during the off-season months of December, January and February because the black youngsters were expected to work in the fields during the other months. Ms. Hattie Fields was one of the very early teachers before Ms. Josephine Bacote began her tenure.

The school had a large, wood-burning stove that was connected to a large pipe which extended to and through the ceiling, into the chimney. Male students would go into the surrounding forest and cut firewood to burn. It is said the building was usually very warm. This stove was situated near the front of the building, with the teacher's desk, which was situated on a raised platform, nearby. The front and side walls contained blackboards. Students were positioned in rows according to grade, with the first grade students closest to the teacher. There were usually about five students per grade in the early days. When one grade was reciting its lessons, the other grades would be kept quiet by performing non-oral tasks such as written arithmetic or grammar, writing the spelling assignment, or simply studying. In this manner each class performed its recitations during the day in an orderly fashion. It took planning to implement recitation periods for each grade as each class studied reading, writing, arithmetic, spelling, geography, history and english on a daily basis.

Kelly family members who attended there said it was an orderly, controlled environment, that it was a fun place which they joyfully walked to, with their book bags made out of old "overalls" material. That's denim, Folks. In later years, after it became clear what was happening to the children from an educational standpoint, the school year was changed to the normal nine month period. Most Kellys that spent their childhoods on Old Georgetown Road attended St. Paul School.

The project, along with other initiatives, was a huge success as the illiteracy rates of blacks in the area dropped from a high of ninety per cent in 1865 to around forty-five per cent in 1945. It marked the beginning of an ongoing struggle to combat the huge educational gap between blacks and whites in the county and serves as a testament to the resiliency of the citizens of Riverdale and the awesome power of interfaith and interracial communication and cooperation in communities across America.

Even though the schools were segregated, "separate but unequal" was the prevailing mantra. Race relations between whites and blacks while perhaps not idyllic, were more or less agreeable. In that small community there were quite a few interracial marriages, and each had large families, which is a real positive sign for that period in time. It has been written that in Mechanicsville during the Jim Crow era, blacks were treated like servants, but also as human beings possessing dignity and certain basic rights. The system was paternalistic, with both sides bearing responsibility for its success. Shadrack's daughter,

Evelyn, whose personality was shaped in that community, emerged as a non-prejudiced woman. Love and respect transcended color lines.

If one looks closely at the evolution of the Mechanicsville or Riverdale community with its higher than normal ratio of bi-racial alliances, it is clear that this was a special community. The camaraderie of the citizens was very unique, when compared to the remainder of Darlington County, and still is today. They know and respect each other, and support each other unconditionally.

Early in American history it is clear that blacks exhibited a significant presence at the predominately white Mechanicsville Baptist Church in Riverdale. According to church records, they were regular worshippers at the church during the bondage era when Roseville Plantation was a flourishing enterprise, and still are today. That in itself speaks volumes about the area. Transcripts of the old church's activities are richly endowed with information about individual slaves and later the black community. It seems extremely apparent that the religious climate of the area played a major role in shaping Riverdale and the Back Swamp and creating its unique culture and history.

After graduation from St. Paul School, **Evelyn and Harold** rode the family's horse and buggy seven to eight miles to Mayo High School in Darlington to begin the quest for their high school diplomas, an accomplishment both of their parents had the foresight to help them achieve.

Shadrack and **Minnie** embraced education as a vehicle to obtain liberty and self-fulfillment. They, like many other African-American families of their era, understood that their children's full potential would be realized through education, an opportunity that had so vehemently been denied our ancestors during bondage. They were adamant about their children gaining a full education and spared no expenses to that end. This is significant, because many youngsters from that area of Mechanicsville did not receive an adequate education simply because their family did not fully appreciate its long term importance, could not afford the expense of transportation to the school in town or needed the children at home to work on the farm. Shadrack and Minnie were indeed blessed to have the long term insight and resources to negate that obstacle. It should be noted that

Minnie, who possessed beautiful flowing penmanship, graduated from Mayo High School in 1900.

Shadracks daughter, Evelyn, often related how she and her brother Harold would board their horse and buggy carriage at 6 am for the bumpy trek to school. This was before the era of school buses for African-Americans. Many students had to walk several miles to get to school. In many regards, students riding a horse and buggy to high school in that era was like them driving a convertible BMW to school today. Maybe an old Corvette would be a better comparison because it has a rough ride also. On cold January and February days they would place hot cinders and coals from the fireplace into metal containers, and strategically place them near their feet for the chilly ride into town. Sometimes they packed lunches the night before, in anticipation of having a snack while on the road. Harold insisted on driving most of the time, especially when he wanted to impress the young ladies. I'm certain that trek was an extremely difficult ordeal, especially during the winter; they had to be determined, driven (no pun intended) and dedicated to reach their educational goals. We must remember here that they were not traveling on paved multi-lane highways. These were rut-laden, uneven, dirt roads, and there were no shock absorbers on the carriage. I can only imagine how thankful they were when the family relocated across the street from the high school in 1925. In my opinion, this was a tremendous accomplishment, an example of ultimate dedication to achieve against all odds. As Rosa Kelly Robinson so distinctly put it, "we just did what we had to do back then, there were no other alternatives in most cases."

It is stories like this that makes one fully respect the will to excel. It's all about "wanting it"; it's a mental thing. Can you even imagine riding in an open horse and buggy carriage for two hours in freezing weather to get to school? If you want it bad enough you will find a way. There are successful individuals out there every day, in all walks of life, finding a way. When I hear people, young and old, educated and uneducated, black and white saying "I can't do it, it's too difficult, it requires too much discipline and intensity, why should I put myself through that," I lament their unfortunate lack of fortitude, courage, wisdom and self-control.

Farming required a breadth of knowledge and depth of experience to create solutions for a myriad of problems. There was immense pressure to come away at the end of the year with a net profit. You had to find a way.

Shadrack struggled to protect himself against poor yields, droughts, hail storms, extreme temperatures, excess rainfall, insect infestations and other catastrophes. This was no joke, you had to be blessed, be determined, and be lucky as well as skilled.

Note that in 1909 Shadrack signed his name with an (x), while in 1913 he actually signed the lien as S. Kelly. Although he was an outstanding farmer, like many of his peers he had difficulty reading and writing. Armed with merely a 5th grade education, his accomplishments merit consideration and acknowledgement.

It is very interesting that Paul Whipple was the loan officer or facilitator at the Bank of Darlington when these loans were obtained.

Occasionally Shadrack and Minnie supplemented their income by selling timber from the forest portion of their property. One document dated September 1912, shows they entered into an agreement with D.T. McKeithan Lumber Company to sell their timber at the rate of $1 per thousand feet. In return they were to receive grade 3 flooring, sheathing and framing at a cost of $18 per thousand feet, to be delivered to Camp #1 on Cashua Ferry Road.

After Shadrack went to the Golden Shore and Minnie was at the helm of the farming operation, numerous tools became available for financial assistance to small farmers. The nature of the industry required huge outlays of cash in the spring of the planting season. To offset this obstacle, in 1934 Minnie obtained a Federal Crop Mortgage, shown in Figure 15, and in 1939 a Chattel Mortgage, which is presented in Figure 16.

FILE

Form 4-E—1934 BCL (Connecticut, Florida,
Maine, Massachusetts, Michigan, Pennsylvania, South Carolina, Vermont, West
Virginia)

45595

FARM CREDIT ADMINISTRATION
WASHINGTON OFFICE

FEDERAL CROP MORTGAGE

THIS INSTRUMENT GIVEN TO THE GOVERNOR OF THE FARM CREDIT ADMINISTRATION AS SECURITY
FOR AN EMERGENCY CROP LOAN MADE PURSUANT TO AN ACT OF CONGRESS
APPROVED FEBRUARY 23, 1934

THIS MORTGAGE, made this ____5th____ day of ____April____, 1934,
by ____Minnie Kelly____, a resident of ____Darlington____ County,
State of ____S. C.____, hereinafter called the mortgagor, witnesseth:

WHEREAS, the said mortgagor is indebted unto the Governor, Farm Credit Administration, Washington,
D.C., hereinafter called the mortgagee, in the sum of ____Sixty and no/100____ dollars
($ __60.00__), payable on or before October 31, 1934, at Washington, D.C., as is evidenced by a promissory
note of even date herewith, bearing interest at the rate of five and one half per centum (5½%) per annum until
paid.

Now, THEREFORE, In consideration of the premises and of the sum of one dollar ($1), receipt of which is
hereby acknowledged, the said mortgagor does hereby bargain, sell, convey, confirm, and mortgage unto the
said mortgagee or assigns the following-described property, to wit: ~~All crops planted or grown~~
____All crops growing or to be planted or grown____
or harvested during the year 1934, upon that certain piece or parcel of land in the county of ____Darlington____,
State of ____S. C.____ described as follows: consists of 30½ acres; bound
north and east by lands of A. C. Coggeshall; south by lands of Boyd Bacot
and Junius Bacot; west by lands of Ben Williamson.
together with any and all crops growing or to be planted or grown or harvested elsewhere in the above-
mentioned county and State during the year 1934 by the mortgagor, his agent, or agents.

To HAVE AND TO HOLD the property hereby mortgaged to the proper use and benefit of the said mortgagee,
successors, or assigns, forever.

PROVIDED, That if the mortgagor shall pay the said promissory note with interest, as aforesaid on or before
maturity, this mortgage shall be void; otherwise to remain in full force and virtue in law.

AND PROVIDED FURTHER, That the said mortgagor is to retain possession of the property herein
mortgaged until default be made in the payment of said note and interest on the condition that he shall take
care of the property herein mortgaged in a husbandlike manner.

If the mortgagor shall fail to make payment as in said promissory note provided, or shall break any of
the terms and conditions of this mortgage, or shall make any attempt to dispose of or to remove or permit
the removal of said property from the aforesaid county, the mortgagee or his agents may enter upon the premises where the property may be, take possession of, and/or sell said property, or so much thereof as may be
necessary, at private sale with or without notice, if permitted by law, or at public auction for cash, to satisfy
said debt and interest, and all expenses that may become necessary in the keeping, care, harvesting, and sale
of said property, after giving notice, as may be required by law, of the time and place of sale, and shall apply
the proceeds of such sale to the discharge of said debt, interest, and expenses, and shall pay any surplus to the
mortgagor or his assigns.

IN WITNESS WHEREOF the said mortgagor has hereunto set his hand and seal on the day and year first
above written.

WITNESSES:

Mildred Sauls

Ruth Jarrett

Minnie Kelly [SEAL]

STATE OF ____South Carolina____
COUNTY OF ____Darlington____

Be it remembered that on this ____5th____ day of ____April____ in the year
nineteen hundred and thirty-four, before me, the subscriber, a notary public in and for the said county and
State, appeared ____Minnie Kelly____ known to me to be the identical
person who is described in and who executed the within instrument, and acknowledged that he signed, sealed,
and delivered the same as his free and voluntary act and deed, for the uses and purposes therein mentioned,
without fear or compulsion of any person.

IN WITNESS WHEREOF, I have hereunto set my hand and seal this ____5th____

day of ____April____, 1934.

J. Carl Wright Notary Public.

My commission expires at the pleasure of the Governor.

This instrument to be of record in ____Darlington____ County.

Figure 15a. Front - Federal Crop Mortgage - 1934

AFFIDAVIT OF SUBSCRIBING WITNESS
(SOUTH CAROLINA ONLY)

STATE OF South Carolina
COUNTY OF Darlington } ss:

Personally appeared before me ___Mildred Taub___, and made oath that he saw ___Minnie Kelly___ sign, seal, and deliver the within conveyance for the uses and purposes therein mentioned, and that he with ___Ruth LaMotte___ in the presence of each other, witnessed the due execution thereof.

Sworn to before me the ___5th___ day of ___April___, A.D. 1934.

_____
Notary Public.

My commission expires ___at the pleasure of the Governor___

(TO BE USED IN VERMONT ONLY)
AFFIDAVIT OF MORTGAGEE

STATE OF _____
COUNTY OF _____ } ss:

The undersigned makes solemn oath and says: That he is the agent of the mortgagee named in the foregoing mortgage, that the said mortgagee has a valid claim against the within-named mortgagor in the amount of _____ dollars ($_____), representing the loan secured thereby; that the said claim is just and unpaid; and that the foregoing mortgage is given to secure the same without any design to hinder, delay, or defraud creditors.

_____
Agent for the Governor, Farm Credit Administration.

Subscribed and sworn to before me this the _____ day of _____, 1934.

_____
Notary Public.

My commission expires _____

(TO BE USED IN MICHIGAN AND VERMONT ONLY)
AFFIDAVIT OF MORTGAGOR

STATE OF _____
COUNTY OF _____ } ss:

The undersigned makes solemn oath and says: That he is the mortgagor named in the foregoing mortgage; that the said mortgage has an actual and adequate claim against him in the amount of _____ dollars ($_____); that the said claim is just and unpaid; and that the foregoing mortgage is given to secure the same without any design to hinder, delay, or defraud creditors.

_____
Mortgagor.

Subscribed and sworn to before me this _____ day of _____, 1934.

_____
Notary Public.

My commission expires _____

In consideration of a loan to be made by the Governor, Farm Credit Administration, Washington, D.C. (hereinafter called Governor), the undersigned (whether one or more hereinafter called undersigned) does hereby waive and relinquish to the Governor all or any rights, liens, claims, shares, titles, or interests which the undersigned now has or may hereafter have under whatever claim of right, in or to the crops described in the foregoing mortgage, or the proceeds from the sale thereof, to the extent of the claim thereto of the Governor, and does hereby covenant and agree that the enforcement of the undersigned's said rights, liens, claims, shares, or interest in the said crops shall be deferred until said claim(s) of the Governor is (are) fully paid, satisfied, and discharged. And for the consideration aforesaid, the undersigned does further covenant and agree: (1) That the undersigned has not nor will the undersigned transfer, pledge, hypothecate, sell, or assign any rent note, mortgage note, agreement, lien, sales contract, mortgage, pledge, bill of sale, judgment, or other lien or claim held by him against the said crops without first obtaining the written consent of the Governor, or his authorized representative, until the aforesaid mortgage upon the crops is fully satisfied; (2) That in the event advances are made to comply with the requirements of the Governor for the purpose of harvesting and marketing the said crops, it is agreed that the money so advanced may be repaid from the proceeds derived from the sale thereof prior to the satisfaction of any lien, claim, or interest of the undersigned. And for the consideration aforesaid and in conformity with the provisions of the Act of Congress approved February 23, 1934, impressing with a trust the funds loaned pursuant to the said act for the purposes specified therein, the undersigned agrees not to accept any of the proceeds of the above-mentioned loan to the said mortgagor, except such as may be paid to reimbursement for any advances of money or credit for farm supplies furnished directly to the said mortgagor.

AND PROVIDED FURTHER, That the said mortgagor may retain possession of said crops and chattels until default be made in the payment of said note or in the performance of any of the conditions hereof. But if the same is not paid when due, or if before said note is due the mortgagor shall attempt to make way with or remove said crops and chattels, or any part thereof, from the place where they now are, or shall neglect to take good care of the same and maintain them in as good condition as they now are; or in event the mortgagor shall breach any of the terms or conditions of this mortgage, then and in such event the mortgagee or __its__ agents shall have the right without suit or process to take possession of said crops and chattels, wherever they may be found, and may sell the same or so much as may be necessary at public auction for cash, after giving notice by advertisement __10__ days, and shall apply the proceeds of such sale to the discharge of such debt, interest and expenses, and the attorney's fees incurred by said mortgagee in the collection of the debt secured by this mortgage, the attorney's fees to be not less than __10__ per cent of the whole amount due; and shall pay any surplus to the mortgagor or __its__ assigns.

IN WITNESS WHEREOF, __I__ the said mortgagor, hereunto set __my__ hand and seal this the __10th__ day of __February__ A. D. 193 9.

SIGNED, SEALED AND DELIVERED
IN THE PRESENCE OF

Emma C. Woodruff
L. E. Abbott

Minnie Kelly (L. S.)
_____ (L. S.)
_____ (L. S.)

The State of South Carolina
COUNTY OF Darlington

PERSONALLY appeared before me __Emma C. Woodruff__, who, being duly sworn, made oath that he saw the within-named __Minnie Kelly__ sign, seal, and deliver the within chattel mortgage as __her__ act and deed, and that __she__ with __L. E. Abbott__ witnessed the execution thereof.

SWORN TO before me this __10th__ day of __February__ 19 39.

Notary Public for S. C.

Emma C. Woodruff

The State of South Carolina
COUNTY OF Darlington

Minnie Kelley

TO

Citizens Bank of Darlington,
Darlington, S. C.

NOTE and CHATTEL MORTGAGE
(NOTE ATTACHED)

Recorded this __10__ day

of __Feb__, 193 __9__.

in Book __527__, Page __67__

R. M. C.

OCT 14 1939

Citizens Bank of Darlington,
By_____ Cashier.

Mortgage of Crop and Personal Property—News and Press, Darlington, S. C.

$_____   _____, S. C., _____, 193____

FOR VALUE RECEIVED,   promise to pay to the order of _____

_____ DOLLARS,

($_____), in the following manner, to-wit: _____, 193___;

_____, 193___;

with _____ per cent interest after maturity. Failure to pay any installment when due shall render the whole

amount due, at the option of the mortgagee. In case of default _____ agree

to pay all expenses and attorney's fees incurred in the collection thereof, the attorney's fees to be not less than _____
per cent of the amount due thereon at the time of payment thereof.

Witnesses:

___

The State of South Carolina

COUNTY OF Darlington

WHEREAS, I am _____ indebted to Citizens Bank of Darlington

in the sum of - - - -Two Hundred and no/100- - - - - - DOLLARS,

($ 200.00), and have given _____ my _____ promissory note therefor, of even date with these Presents

and hereto annexed, payable as follows, to-wit: October 1 _____, 193 9;

_____, 193____;

Citizens Bank of Darlington, 193____;
Darlington, S. C.

NOW, in order to secure the payment of the said note and all other indebtedness now due or hereafter to be
contracted by the mortgagor with the mortgagee; and on consideration of the sum of FIVE DOLLARS ($5.00) to
me in hand paid, I do hereby bargain and sell unto the said Citizens Bank of
Darlington its heirs, successors and assigns, the following crops, goods, chattels and personal property, same being the property of the mortgagor and in his possession, being free from any encumbrance:

5 acres of tobacco,   10 acres of cotton,   8 acres of corn,
6 acres of oats,

1 black mare mule, named Mary, 12 years old, weight 1000 lbs.

1 disc harrow, 1 rake

Sundry Farm Implements

The crops above mentioned being planted or to be planted during the year 193 9 on the following described lands:
27 acre tract of land in my name on Mechanicsville Road
5 miles from Darlington

And I hereby contract and agree to cultivate and harvest said crops with ordinary care and diligence, and in the
event of _____ my _____ failure so to do, then the said mortgagee, or _____ its _____ agents, is hereby authorized and
empowered to enter in and upon said lands and cultivate and harvest said crop or crops whenever is its judgment
its interest renders it necessary so to do, in which event any expense to which it is put for such cultivating
or harvesting of said crop shall be charged to _____ my account _____, and shall stand secured by this
mortgage. And in the event of failure to plant, cultivate, and harvest said crops as aforesaid, such default and
failure on the part of the mortgagor shall, at the option of the mortgagee, render the whole amount of said indebtedness immediately due and payable.

TO HAVE AND TO HOLD, all and singular, the said crops, goods and chattels to the said Citizens Bank
of Darlington, its heirs, successors and assigns forever, the legal title to such crop or crops to
vest in the mortgagee immediately upon the same coming into esse.

In case of serious injury to said property or any part thereof, or the loss of any part thereof by death or otherwise, I agree to report the same immediately to the said mortgagee, and in case of _____ my _____
failure so to do, then and in that event the said mortgagee shall have the right at _____ its _____ option to treat the
entire mortgage debt as due and payable at once and take into its possession the property hereby mortgaged
and sell and dispose of the same as hereinafter provided.

PROVIDED, NEVERTHELESS, That if the said mortgagor shall pay to the mortgagee the sum or sums
hereinabove mentioned when due, then this mortgage is to be void; otherwise to remain in full force and effect.

Figure 16b. Back of Note and Chattel Mortgage

Each year they had to place their land or crops as collateral, if they did not garner enough profit from the previous year, to purchase seedlings, fertilizers etc. for the current year. Examples of this are shown in Figure 18 and Figure 19 where Shadrack obtained loans in 1909 and 1913 to purchase tons of fertilizer.

Nevertheless, for these ancestors land ownership was a valuable asset. It was like a blue chip stock. It appears the key was to optimize its utilization and use it as a springboard to diversify into other ventures like entrepreneurship, retail, production, real estate, the service industry, to get an education, etc. This was a slow process, a process that severely tested the will of all involved. Farming was a difficult venture, but when you sit back and analyze things, no vocation is a piece of cake, or a stroll in the park. Every vocation has its own set of pros, cons, rough testing times and pitfalls. Look at medical doctors for example. One would speculate that they have an easy life. However, when you look at it more closely, many doctors are almost always on call and doctors have one of the highest rates of suicide of any profession. Professional athlete's careers last only a few years, on average. Attorneys have a reputation of not being trustworthy. Corporate executives deplore the vicious culture of the workplace. Policemen and soldiers put their lives on the line every day. Look at the millions of unemployed Americans out there today, many on welfare. No one has an easy row to hoe. Our ancestors had to overcome their unique obstacles as every other generation does.

Regardless to how you describe their plight, one thing however is certain, farming was extremely physical and mentally draining. If one investigates the lives of the offspring of the early 20th century generation, the **Boyd Bacote** and **Shadrack Kelly** generation, of Bacote and Kelly farmers, it is very interesting that most of them did not elect to follow in their parent's footsteps. As a matter of fact, most of them got the hell out of "Dodge" as rapidly as possible, migrating to North Carolina, New York, New Jersey, Maryland, Detroit, Ohio, Connecticut, Pennsylvania, Washington, D.C., the Army, Air Force, Navy, even to nearby more industrialized Florence, South Carolina.

Shadrack and his post-reconstruction era peers, struggled through the period where their individual rights were scaled back and the institutions of Jim Crow had separated the races into separate and unequal worlds. They were older now, less vigorous and idealistic.

They witnessed the failure of the governmental machinery in place in the South to protect and enforce their rights as newly freed individuals or children thereof, and were resigned to stick it out, fight for their rights and implement change.

Shadrack's children, Evelyn, Harold, Horace and Josephine, participated in the Mass Migration. Recent interviews of some members of that generation who migrated revealed another interesting consideration. Disgraceful violence, lynching, night-riders and other forms of savage terror tactics carried out by the Ku Klux Klan, and other Jim Crow advocates, which often went unchallenged, were also primary factors that served to hasten their departure from South Carolina. It wasn't just the back-crunching nature of the farm work.

This was a difficult time for many of these intelligent, motivated ancestors. Their safety, educational and employment opportunities were questionable as they thirst for personal fulfillment and a better life. They, unbeknownst at that time, were at a crossroad in the evolution of this family, as they consciously reconciled themselves to making the decision to participate in the much publicized, risky Mass Migration to the North.

The massive exodus of Theodore, Cleo, Roy, Chaney, Boyd Jr., Rosalee, Mary Ida, Robert, Willie, Mae Ruth, et al (Bacotes), Harold, Evelyn, Clara, Suzie, Rosa, et al (Kellys) generation provides proof that this generation of these proud families did not resign quietly to the social, economic and political order of South Carolina. They did not believe in nor accept the approach to life the South had adopted, and departed Darlington County in great haste, at about a ninety-five per cent clip. They left, graciously bestowed with blessings from the family.

Some family members of that generation remained in South Carolina, in many cases because they felt a responsibility to the older family members. Bacotes like Colon, Buddy, Waddell, Norris, Handy, Sammie and others, as well as Kellys like James Kelly Jr. Ada, Shedrick, John, et al essentially stayed put. They felt an overwhelming commitment to the family and it's tradition as farmers. They remained to protect the legacies of Elias Bacote, John Kelly Sr. and John Kelly Jr.

Some historians will undoubtedly question the decision of some of that early 1900s generation to jump ship and migrate north and west. There will always remain some lingering queries from the brave family members who stayed put and endured the rampart injustice and indignity cast their way, as they "guarded the fort." Although I did not take part in that difficult decision making process, I really feel both factions followed their instincts. Some felt the urge to pursue other avenues of existence away from the soil. Some felt the wrath of the oppression and simply desired more progressive options. Others felt more secure and comfortable in the environment that they knew, they knew what to expect in South Carolina and did not desire to deal with all the unknowns that the industrial north and new frontier west offered. Some left and shortly thereafter returned to their roots in Darlington for a variety of reasons including family crisis, dissatisfaction, fiscal and health reasons, to name a few. The bottom line really is; it was a challenge for these ancestors to eke out a profitable existence anywhere in America at that point in American history. No matter where they decided to set up shop there were problems to be solved and obstacles to overcome.

Now, in hindsight, there was no right or wrong here; there were no winners, no losers. These people did what they felt the prevailing conditions compelled and mandated. They charted courses which they felt offered the best opportunity to improve the quality of life for their family.

However, out of this there is one certainty that emerges. The socio-economic and race related changes that occurred in South Carolina over the last seventy-five years were gained primarily because of the brave, tireless efforts of the many unsung heroes, black and white, who remained and worked exhaustively to foster and promote progress in the areas of commerce, justice and equality. Those of us that migrated cannot ever claim any responsibility for those accomplishments.

Farming during Shadrack's era was very labor intensive. From a financial point of view the profit margin was marginal, and black farmers suffered from the same economic issues that have historically endangered most small farmers throughout the history of America. The key was to minimize labor costs and enhance productivity. Historically our ancestors implemented this by having large families, and secondly; by working long, hard hours. For example Buddy and Marie Bacote had fifteen children, John and Hannah Kelly had 14, Elias and Matilda Bacote 10, Benny and Nannie Bacote had 8, Rosa Kelly Robinson and Albert Robinson 8, and Lydia and Edward Erwin had 9, to cite a few. Unfortunately Shadrack and Minnie were not blessed with their in-house labor force.

It is important for us to understand and fully comprehend that Shadrack Kelly and other ancestors cited above, stood tall to withstand and overcome the challenges of their generation and I strongly feel that the farming experience molded the family into a stronger group, a family more focused and determined to discover another route or vehicle to success, self-realization and fulfillment. It is similar to being terminated or unemployed in the present-day market place, and forced into entrepreneurial endeavors, where one creates a niche for himself or herself. The family did not collapse, rather it evolved. It proved that this family possesses what it takes to succeed; the most important requirements consisting of a real commitment, the willingness to work hard, the ability to adapt, and the will to persevere against all odds.

CHAPTER SIX

SHADRACK KELLY/JOHN CAROLINA

Let us take a more in depth look at the origin and history of Kelly Place, located in the historic Mechanicsville section of Darlington County, in Darlington, South Carolina. Then we can fully appreciate how the Kellys arrived at their present status. This section of Darlington County, as mentioned earlier, was once known as Riverdale, South Carolina, due to its close proximity to the Pee Dee River. Kelly Place has consisted of about twenty acres, to over two-hundred acres, to one hundred thirty three acres, to seventy-six acres, depending on the year surveyed. On the north bounded by land of Celia W. Hyman, east by Herring Creek (Pee Dee River Swamp), south by land of W.D. Coggeshall, or formerly Paul Whipple, west by Old Georgetown Road, surveyed by T.E. Wilson on March 30, 1911, same being ½ of track of land conveyed to Celia W. Hyman and **Shadrack Kelly** by T.H. Spain, master by deed bearing date 29 December 1911.

Evelyn K. Brown amassed a large collection of original documents, deeds, tax records and receipts that have allowed me to gain some insight into the history of how Kelly Place arrived at its present status. Numerous documents and tax records refer to a gentleman that we know by now as John Kelly Sr., also called John Brockinton, and represented as John Carolina.

In order to fully appreciate the historical evolution of Kelly Place [shown graphically in Figure 8] we need to closely examine some of these old documents. Tax receipts show the value of the tract over time.

- An 1874 tax receipt reveals that John Carolina paid $8.10 taxes on one hundred acres, containing four buildings, of said estate, valued at $440, to Ple Fludd Robertson, Darlington County treasurer.

- An 1884 tax bill listed John Carolina property as one hundred acres, four buildings, valued at $655. Taxes were $6.55.
- A tax bill, dated 1886, lists the John Carolina property as one hundred acres, four buildings, valued at $575. Taxes paid were $5.90.

1886 was a busy year in the evolution of Kelly Place. On February 8, 1886, M.E. Fountain of Darlington County, sold John Carolina one hundred acres, more or less, for $231. The land was bordered as follows to wit: north by the lands of John Carolina, east by Herring Creek, south by lands of Paul Whipple and west by Old Georgetown Public Road. See Figure 8. This tract was adjacent to the 104 acre tract already in his possession.

On the 15th day of June, in the year of our Lord, 1886, the last will and testament of John Carolina, late of said Darlington County, in this State of South Carolina, deceased, was proved, approved, and allowed of by Elihu C. Baken, Judge of Probate.

The will, registered as John Carolina, Darlington Will Book 12, pp.157-159, made in 1884, names wife Hannah Harrison and children John J. Kelley, Alfred Kelley, Lydia Kelley, Harry Kelley, Leah Kelley, Lucinda and Horace Kelley as heirs. No mention is made of teenagers Esau, Meshach and Shadrack, who at this stage were being schooled in the details and rigors of a mid-size farming operation in the Back Swamp. One sentence reads, "Daughter Georgianna Kelley has already received her portion." It references land he purchased in 1870 from Evan J. Lide but obviously does not mention the February 1886 purchase.

Genealogical extracts from the *Darlington News* [1885-1889 editions] extracted by Robert M. DeFee indicate that probate of John Carolina's estate occurred July 8, 1886 and was handled by Dargan and Dargan attorneys of Darlington.

A Creditors Notice extracted from that newspaper by Mr. DeFee reads as follows: "All persons having claims against the estate of John Carolina, late of Darlington County, deceased, will present them to Dargan & Dargan, attorneys, properly proven, and all persons to said estate indebted will make payment forthwith to the same parties, for John J. Carolina." It was dated July 7, 1886.

John Carolina went to the Golden Shore sometime between February and July in 1886.

Of the many tax receipts in Evelyn Brown's possession it is not until 1886 that the name John Kelly Sr., appears on one.

- A tax bill, dated 1886, shows that **John Kelly Sr.** paid $1.61 in taxes. No amount of land or value of land was given.

Obviously it was for less than the one-hundred acres cited above for John Carolina.

It is simply amazing, almost surreal, that two receipts for tax payments for the 1886 tax year, for John Kelly Sr.'s land holdings, were in Evelyn Brown's cache of documents. It is almost as if they were planted in this vast haystack, to be eventually discovered, to provide a vital clue to the puzzle. It is very apparent now that John Kelly Sr., the iconic Kelly ancestor, paid taxes on one tract as John Kelly Sr., and on another much larger tract using the alias John Carolina.

- A tax bill, dated 1889, lists the estate of John Carolina as two hundred acres (which included presumably the aforementioned one hundred acre and four buildings purchase from M.E. Fountain in 1886, as well as the 104 acre purchase of 1868), valued at $745. Taxes were $8.38.
- A tax bill, dated 1897, lists the estate of John Carolina as 133 acres and four buildings, valued at $835. Taxes were $9.60. Recognizing the fact that we don't have a complete record of transactions and taxes, the implication here is that between 1889 and 1897, the John Carolina estate disposed of sixty-seven acres and one building.
- A tax bill, dated 1899, lists the estate of John Carolina as 133 acres and three buildings, valued at $865.

It appears evident that John Kelly Sr. used the alias John Carolina, as a convenient legal, tax, and accounting tool, when dealing with certain of his real estate holdings. For business reasons, he and his family were careful not to comingle his small, post-bondage tract with his larger individual purchases of real estate. It is analogous to having two corporations or companies operating under one umbrella, with two different people listed as President or CEO, but actually controlled by one person. It is a legal tool employed by many entrepreneurial Americans even today, to navigate the financial environment. I think it is very interesting to note here that his will, a very important legal document, does not refer to him as "formerly known as John Brockinton," it cites him as John Carolina. It seems to be very clear as to what transpired here. John Kelly Sr. functioned via the utilization of three different last names, or one name and two aliases.

It is also very informative that in three separate legal documents involving **Alfred, Harry**, and **Meshack**, (brothers of **Shadrack**) John Carolina is listed as their father's name, not John Brockinton, not **John Kelly Sr.** Yes, you read correctly, under oath they legally recorded John Carolina as their father's name.

In Chapter Four, "The Kelly Side," evidence was presented that Meshack and Shadrack were from a set of quadruplets. The births were chronicled in the local newspaper, where the father was listed as John Carolina, "a colored man." In a family tree constructed by Kelly family members in 2003, and supported by 1870 U.S. Census data, **John Kelly Sr.** is listed as their father. There would appear to be a contradiction here if we fail to invoke the widespread usage of aliases during bondage and the Reconstruction Era by John Kelly Sr. and many of his peers.

Let's move away from John Carolina and the issue of aliases for a moment and continue with his son, Shadrack's, monumental and inspiring role in the development of Kelly Place during this time frame, as we unfold this interesting story.

Shadrack, the baby boy, demonstrated the capability and aptitude at a young age for managing a profitable farm. After a few years of rigorous training and grooming, it appears that he inherited the position of "Director of Farming" at Kelly Place as he accepted the huge responsibility of being the man in charge after the death of his father.

- An 1898 tax bill shows **Shadrack Kelly** paid $1.17 in taxes. No land shown.
- An 1899 tax bill shows **Shadrack Kelly** paid $1.35 in taxes. No land shown.
- This amount of taxes suggests possession of about eighteen acres of land, by my rough calculations.

It appears that after 1899 **Shadrack** was farming a larger amount of acreage in and near Kelly Place than the eighteen acres, which he paid taxes on in 1899, based on the following receipts.

- A receipt written in 1900 shows he paid his brother **Esau Kelly** $6 for rental of his land.
- A receipt written in 1901 shows he paid **Esau Kelly** $7 for rental of land.
- A receipt written in 1903 shows he paid **Esau Kelly** $7 for rental of land.
- A receipt written in 1906 shows he paid Esau $7.50 for rental of land.
- A receipt written June 28, 1912 shows he paid **Luecinder Hodges,** formerly **Luecinder Richardson** (an heir of his sister Serena Richardson), $16.96 for rental of land.
- A receipt written on May 25, 1912 shows he also paid **Phyllis Richardson** (an heir of Serena Richardson) $16.94 for rental of land.

Other receipts show that he paid his mom, Hannah, his siblings, and his siblings' heirs, for the right to farm their inherited parcels of land. An Agricultural Lease and Lien agreement between Shadrack and Hannah, dated 1900, indicates that in the year Hannah also departed this earth, he paid her $33 to rent twenty-two acres of the John Carolina (John Kelly Sr.) estate lands. A receipt dated December 10, 1907, shows he paid his brother, **John Kelly Jr.'s**, wife Susie $7.80 for the right to farm John Kelly Jr.'s share of the estate.

Shadrack was an ambitious black farmer; he worked all the land he could garner. He paid anyone, who would lease their land for agricultural purposes, as he withstood the challenge of not being a share cropper. It was not merely by chance that he was a forerunner of the independent black farmer in Darlington County, a man of vast expertise with a dynamic, long term plan.

It appears that between 1865 and the turn of the century many former enslaved Africans and sons of enslaved Africans opted for the less aggressive share cropper route for their lives. I am certain it was a tough decision, trying to decide what you should do with your life at that crossroads in time. Many doors simply were not open to them, access to credit was very limited, access to education was limited, and entrepreneurial opportunities were even more limited. However, like today, you had to have a vision, a support system, motivation, inspiration, and courage. I am certain the land-rich plantation owners were saying "stay with me, let's work together, I'll look out for you and your family. Continue to work my land; I'll make sure you have a place to stay and food to eat. There is no way you can survive out there without my support and guidance."

If one wonders how Shadrack developed and maintained his drive for success despite the many obstacles that confronted him, I sense that he had a strong support system and a strong vision, an independent vision, of where he wanted to be and how to make it happen. In addition, his wife Minnie was a strong-willed woman with a proud heritage. We are all aware of the legacy of black women being the family backbone and being there for their men, quietly and not so quietly nudging. Minnie was no different. Shadrack undoubtedly was also inspired by the independence of Minnie's brothers as well as the illustrious legacy of the two "Iron Horses" who preceded him.

The reward for making tough decisions, for putting your guts on the line, for vigorously pursuing your ideas and dreams, in most cases is not immediate. Sometimes there are cases where instant gratification is attained, however most of the time the results are only seen by the eyes of the historian many years or generations later. Shadrack deserves kudos; no doubt he demonstrated that he possessed the discipline to create and develop initiatives that would have generational-reaching implications.

There is one question I have for the sociologists and behavioral experts who may peruse this discourse. Out of the same household and environment, what is it that evokes the generational appearance of the Shadracks, or the Johns, in families in general, and differentiates them from the hell-raisers, criminals, lazybones, non-achievers and complainers in a family? If indeed Shadrack had a vision, the question is why Shadrack? Is it simply a bell-shaped curve, numbers game phenomena, is it God at work, is it fate or destiny, what is it?

• A 1901 tax bill lists the estate of John Carolina as 133 acres and three buildings valued at $865. Taxes were $10.81.

In 1902, **Shadrack** embarked on a series of key acquisitions from his brothers, **Meshack, Harry and Alfred.** He struck the same deal with **Meshack and Harry. Meshack,** who resided in Marlboro County, South Carolina, and his brother Harry who lived in Arkansas, sold their rights to their share in the 137 acres of John Carolina's estate to **Shadrack** for $100 each.

An excerpt of the Deed, filed October 4, 1902, states that "the land bordered North by lands formerly of J.A. Fountain, now the lands of C.J. Milling, East by Herring Creek, South by lands of Captain Paul Whipple and West by the public road leading from Society Hill to Georgetown, and being the lands of which my father, the late John Carolina, formerly called John Brockinton, died, seized, and possessed and one hundred and four acres (104 acres) of which was conveyed to him by E.J. Lide as John Brockinton registered as John Carolina, by deed bearing date the 9th day of November 1870 and recorded in office of the clerk of the court for Darlington County; and thirty three and one third (33 1/3) acres of which was conveyed by M.E. Fountain to my said father as John Carolina by deed bearing date the 8th day of February, AD 1886 which was recorded in the office of the Clerk of the Court for Darlington County." Meshack's wife Nellie signed off on the deal also.

Harry's deed which had very similar wording was filed October 24, 1902, and signed by his wife Elizabeth Kelly. They resided in Toltec, Arkansas. Shadrack was moving fast like a man on a mission.

• A 1902 tax bill lists the estate of John Carolina as 133 acres, two buildings, valued at $860. Taxes were $10.75.
• The 1909 tax bill lists the estate of John Carolina as 133 acres, two buildings, valued at $880. Taxes were $10.84.

A Transfer of Title document filed on March 21, 1905 and recorded in Book 43, page 206, in Darlington County, Darlington, South Carolina, states that **Shadrack Kelly** paid his brother, **Alfred Kelly** of Florence, South Carolina, $125 for Alfred's share, probably about eighteen acres, of the above 133 acre, more or less, tract of land, in 1903. I estimate eighteen acres because tax records suggest that Shadrack paid taxes on about eighteen acres, his share in that same tract. Alfred's spouse, Harriet Kelly, signed off on the sale also.

An excerpt from a March 21, 1905 document of Shadrack Kelly, Riverdale, South Carolina reads: "Dear Sir, Enclosed please find deed of Alfred Kelly to Shadrack Kelly, duly recorded...etc." Signed by W.F. Dargan.

An excerpt of that deed reads:

"All my right, title, interest and estate of, in and to all that tract of land situate in the County of Darlington and State aforesaid, containing one hundred and thirty seven acres, more or less, and bounded as follows, to wit: North by lands formerly of J.A. Fountain, now lands of C.J. Milling; East by Herring Creek; South by lands of Captain Paul Whipple, and West by the public road leading from Society Hill to Georgetown, and being the lands of which my father, the late John Carolina, formerly called John Brockington, died seized and possessed, and one hundred and four acres of which were conveyed to him by E.J. Lide as John Brockington, registered as John Carolina, by deed bearing date the 9th day of November, 1870, and recorded in office of the Clerk of the Court for Darlington County in Book EE, at pages 426 and 427, and thirty three and one third acres of which were conveyed by M.E. Fountain to my said father as John Carolina by deed bearing date the 8th day of February, A.D. 1886 which was recorded in the office of the said Clerk in Book No.1, at page 286."

Evelyn Brown also had that deed in her cedar chest. The addition of this land probably raised **Shadracks** total acreage to the seventy-three and six-tenths acres mentioned earlier. The ambitious Shadrack was the consummate, astute businessman, constantly acquiring valued assets to increase his growing real estate portfolio and more importantly, his farmable acreage. Note that unless there was a tremendous increase in the value of land in Riverdale between

1886 and 1902-1903, he compensated more, much more, per acre to his brothers, than was paid when the one- hundred acre tract was purchased in 1886 by his father. [See Figure 8] The original purchase was for $2.31 per acre, and he paid his brothers, by my calculations, $5.51 and $6.95 per acre. One can assume that Shadrack realized that the investment would reap benefits down the road, and he did not want to take financial advantage of his siblings. This speaks to his character, as he was an honorable man.

What is noteworthy here is that **Shadrack Kelly**, very similar to **Elias Bacote,** possessed an intense desire to re-make himself and his surroundings through courage, hard work and imagination. Both men obviously believed that you didn't have to be what the past made you. You can change things. You didn't have to be trapped by a past of inter-generational slavery, sharecropping or present-day welfare dependence. Their achievements substantiate the fact that America is indeed a place where you can not only dream about impossible or improbable ventures, you can actually turn them into reality, no matter their difficulty, no matter how great the odds.

An agreement drawn in 1910 shows Shadrack obtained a loan of $119.60 from the Peoples Bank of Darlington, where he was obligated to place a lien on his crop as collateral, signed by Paul Whipple. Whipple also signed a beautiful document to denote payment received in full from Shadrack. It was attested by a gentleman named Chap Moses. The surname is uncertain.

In November 1911, Shadrack had his portion of Kelly Place surveyed by T.E. Wilson for $12.50, paid to A. Hyman Jr. This included the portions purchased from his brothers. He successfully farmed that fertile tract until 1925.

One of the most interesting and important deeds owned by **Shadrack** was one for seventy-three and six-tenths acres recorded January 20, 1912 in Darlington County, deeded from Celia W. Hyman.

An excerpt of the deed reads:
"WHEREAS, Celia W. Hyman and Shadrack Kelly, of the County and State

Aforesaid, own and hold as tenants in common the tracts of land situate in the county and State aforesaid containing One Hundred

283

and Thirty Seven Acres, more or less, conveyed to them as tenants in common and joint owners by T.H. Spain, master, by deed bearing date the twenty ninth day of December, A.D. 1911 and

WHEREAS, the said Celia W. Hyman and Shadrack Kelly have agreed upon a division of the said tracts of land, have caused the same to be surveyed by T.E. Wilson, Surveyor, and their respective shares and interests as agreed upon marked out and designated upon a plat of the same, and

WHEREAS, they have agreed that each shall make a deed to the other of the respective tracts belonging to each of the said parties,

NOW THEREFORE KNOW ALL MEN BY THESE PRESENTS THAT I, Celia W. Hyman, of the County and State aforesaid, for and in consideration of the premises and of the sum of Five Dollars to me in hand paid by Shadrack Kelly, of the County of Darlington and State aforesaid, have granted, bargained, sold and released, and by these presents do grant, bargain, sell and release unto the said Shadrack Kelly all that tract of land situate in the County and State aforesaid containing Seventy Three and Six Tenths (73 6/10) acres, more or less, and bounded as follows, to wit: North by the lands of Celia W. Hyman, East by the run of Herring Creek, South by the lands of W.D. Coggeshall, formerly of Paul Whipple, and West by the old Georgetown Public Road, the same being designated on the plat of the tract of land described in the premises hereof as surveyed by T.E. Wilson, Surveyor on March 30, and October 20, 1911... etc."

All the receipts or deeds from financial activities of Kelly Place are not available, but through all these wheeling and dealing transactions, **Shadrack** was finally deeded seventy-three and six-tenths acres (Kelly Place) of land, a portion of the tract originally deeded to his father. This century old historic deed is still in the capable hands of one of his descendants. However, it is even more astonishing and amazing that the family has in its possession tax receipts and documents that certify and support the movement of tracts of land through the hands of John Kelly Sr. and the John Carolina Estate, from 1868 through 1911. See Figure 8.

These are original tax receipts and documents containing original stamps and raised certification, which are approaching a century and a half in age. It demonstrates the attention to detail and the disciplined record keeping that was passed down by the former slave.

Considering the many documents relating to the life of John Kelly Sr. and the probate of his property, in the family's possession, it is reasonable to conclude that he generously provided for his offspring in his will or before his death. The fact that Georgianna is mentioned in his will [presented earlier] and evidence that another daughter, Serena, owned a small tract, which her brother Shadrack rented from her heirs, suggests that he also provided for his daughters in the process.

The will is also documentation that John, a family man of utmost integrity, bequeathed four of his sons, leaving each what appears to be an estimated, modest, eighteen acre parcel of land from his estate on Old Georgetown Road. There is no evidence of Esau's involvement in the probate process as it relates to John Carolina's estate. However it is inferred from land rental receipts, which demonstrate that Shadrack paid his brothers Esau and later John Kelly Jr.'s estate to farm their land, that he also owned small parcel of land after his father's passing to the Golden Shore. Obviously John Kelly Sr., aka John Carolina, had his children's welfare at heart, bequeathing each an expanse of the most valuable commodity of their era, some acreage.

However, the true test of Shadrack's character and determination was that it took over a decade before he was legally granted the official deed to his purchases by the courts. Almost twenty-five years after his father's death, Celia W. Hyman and **Shadrack** culminated the efforts to legally place him in control of a large portion of his father's original estate. It is very clear that legal documentation was of paramount importance to all the parties involved and understandably so. We have Shadrack on record for legally acquiring the rights to three shares of said estate from his siblings over the years, and inheriting his own share of about 18 acres.

This joint effort served to unify the transfers of rights to shares of the John Carolina Estate, to **Shadrack**, by officially carving out the tract of seventy-three and six-tenth acres at the site of what would be called Kelly Place. It is unclear at this time as to what happened to the other sixty acres, of his father estate. Whether it was sold or ever legally deeded by the courts is unknown at this time. However, based on what has been ascertained about Shadrack, if the accounting is correct, it is highly probable that it was sold by the other heirs of the John Carolina Estate. It is difficult to comprehend anyone unjustly yanking anything away from this "Iron Horse" without legal documentation.

Why did the paperwork denoting legal transfer take so long? How smart of **Shadrack** and the **John Carolina Estate** to realize that his ownership needed to be documented, because my gut feeling is he was being allowed to farm some of the land, that had not been surveyed and legally transferred to him. How stressful that must have been. For over ten years he was forced to have enormous faith in the legal system, and trust in his attorneys even though he knew the system was flawed. It is indeed very possible that if he had not possessed the courage, bulldog mentality, savvy and determination to legally culminate the deal, it would not have been closed appropriately and this Kelly family history would have a totally different spin.

This undoubtedly was one of Shadrack's greatest and most far reaching, rewarding achievements. He took on and fought the powerful southern court system, which continuously utilized its power base to perpetuate Jim Crow ideals. For over a decade he waged a battle with this goliath and ultimately succeeded, against all odds, where so many had failed.

It was very commonplace for blacks to lose property or land that was legally and rightfully theirs during that period of Jim Crow, racial injustice and the denial of due process. He had heard stories of and seen cases where property was blatantly snatched and was determined not to be another statistic, another casualty.

Sometimes his peers were clueless, or simply overpowered, out-maneuvered and rendered helpless by the lack of financial resources or business acumen to handle complex situations. There were instances when blacks just lost confidence in the legal system because history had shown that it was heavily biased against them, so much so that they would not even appear at hearings even when petitioned by the courts. In many cases it was simply distrust that an attorney would not represent them in their best interest or proceed strongly enough in their behalf. The situation was not much different from what newly freed slaves found themselves in in 1865, following their liberation. They knew deals were secretly being consummated behind closed doors by the establishment.

In short, this restructuring provided a broader platform from which this Kelly family would operate for decades and subsequent generations, and offers an explanation for why and how Shadrack became an independent black farmer while his siblings and their descendants in Mechanicsville opted for a different approach.

Although Shadrack followed in his father, John Kelly Sr.'s, footsteps as a farmer in Riverdale, the road to success was a very embattled one. When he embarked as an independent black farmer many of the barriers and obstacles that his father and other freedmen encountered during their post slavery existence were still in place with a few updated wrinkles added. That in itself makes his achievements that much more dramatic and amazing. Success is not always measured in dollars and cents but rather, in many cases, in terms of the extent of the battle waged and the difficulty of the hurdles encountered during the journey.

Around the turn of the century, with Jim Crowism running rampant, the establishment ramped up the effort to make it more difficult for black farmers in the South. Maneuvers to force them into foreclosure were increased via the denial of educational, agricultural and financial resources. It is said that on occasion county supervisors or lending officials would simply rip up applications right there in their presence of the applicant and make statements like, "it would be best for you Shadrack if you just sold your farm to us. We are not going to loan you any money this year."

But Shadrack had an "ace in the hole" in his friend and neighbor for many years, Paul Whipple. Whipple, a banker, was a very well respected white, large estate land owner in Riverdale. At one point in time his plantation abutted the old Kelly Place on the south. [See Figure 4] It is interesting how often his name has appeared on financial documents involving **Shadrack**, either as an attester or loaner. This suggests that he had a lot of respect for Shadrack. Two examples are shown in Figure 18 and Figure 19 where Shadrack applied for loans to purchase tons of fertilizer in the spring of 1909 and 1913.

Captain Paul Whipple, as he was affectionately referred to, was originally from New Boston, Massachusetts. He had served as a captain in the Union Army during the War Between the States and at one point commanded a company of all black Union Army men. Obviously this experience had a profound effect on him. Local lore has it that after the war he settled in Riverdale, on Old Georgetown

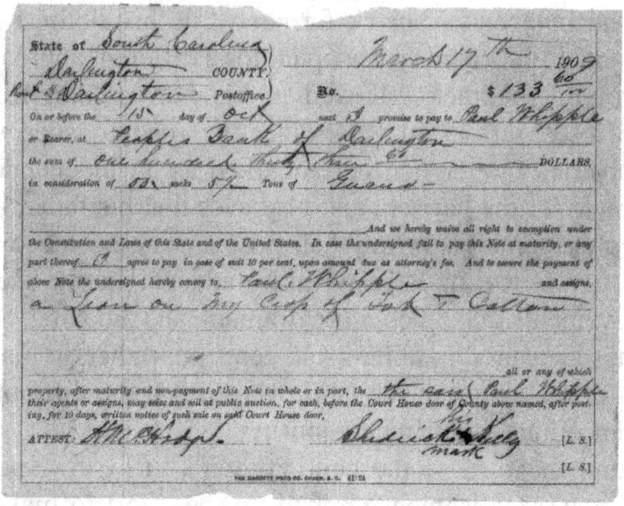

State of South Carolina
Darlington COUNTY
Rout 3 Darlington Postoffice

March 17th 1909
No. $133 60/100

On or before the 15 day of Oct next I promise to pay to Paul Whipple or Bearer, at Peoples Bank of Darlington the sum of One hundred thirty three 60 DOLLARS, in consideration of 52 sacks 5 1/2 Tons of Guano —

And we hereby waive all right to exemption under the Constitution and Laws of this State and of the United States. In case the undersigned fail to pay this Note at maturity, or any part thereof I agree to pay in case of suit 10 per cent, upon amount due as attorney's fee. And to secure the payment of above Note the undersigned hereby convey to Paul C. Whipple and assigns, a Lien on my crop of Tob & Cotton

all or any of which property, after maturity and non-payment of this Note in whole or in part, the the said Paul Whipple their agents or assigns, may seize and sell at public auction, for cash, before the Court House door of County above named, after posting, for 10 days, written notice of such sale on said Court House door,

ATTEST: A. W. McHodges — Shadrick his X mark Kelly [L. S.]

[L. S.]

THE DAGGETT PRTG CO. CHASN. S. C. 41124

FIGURE 18. SHADRACK KELLY 1909 APPLICATION FOR BANK LOAN

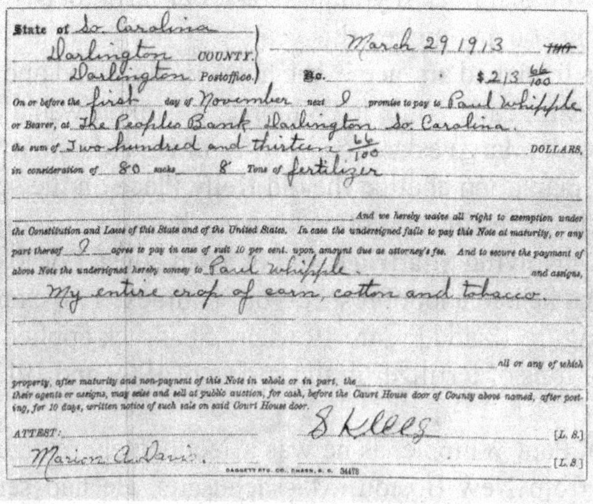

State of So. Carolina
Darlington COUNTY.
Darlington Postoffice.

March 29 1913 ~~191~~
No. $213 66/100

On or before the first day of November next I promise to pay to Paul Whipple or Bearer, at The Peoples Bank Darlington So. Carolina. the sum of Two hundred and thirteen 66/100 DOLLARS, in consideration of 80 sacks 8 Tons of fertilizer

And we hereby waive all right to exemption under the Constitution and Laws of this State and of the United States. In case the undersigned fails to pay this Note at maturity, or any part thereof I agree to pay in case of suit 10 per cent. upon amount due as attorney's fee. And to secure the payment of above Note the undersigned hereby convey to Paul Whipple. and assigns, My entire crop of corn, cotton and tobacco.

all or any of which property, after maturity and non-payment of this Note in whole or in part, the their agents or assigns, may seize and sell at public auction, for cash, before the Court House door of County above named, after posting, for 10 days, written notice of such sale on said Court House door.

ATTEST: — S Kelly [L. S.]

Marion A. Davis. [L. S.]

DAGGETT PTG. CO., CHASN., S. C. 34478

FIGURE 19. SHADRACK KELLY 1913 APPLICATION FOR BANK LOAN

Road, and during the course of his life made no effort to conceal a common law marriage to a black woman who bore him twelve children. It is said that he acknowledged all of them in his will, deeding each a "generous" tract of real estate. Like Paul Whipple there were other sensitive, non-prejudicial whites in that section of Darlington County also.

Among locals, it was said that Whipple had a fine plantation, kept good horses, and set a wonderful table. He died at his estate in Riverdale at the age of seventy seven in 1915, but not before assisting in establishing Shadrack as a force in the Riverdale community. Brights Disease was the cause of death.

Even though Shadrack lacked a formal education, he had a grasp of the law and knew how to conduct business in a legal manner. He kept all receipts, many that are currently in the family possession via Evelyn Brown. He even kept handwritten ones from his own brothers, and always utilized legal machinery to document the purchases of land from his brothers. In each transfer of rights to property, a deed was drawn and recorded by an attorney. It is said that Shadrack had a fighter's mentality and feared no human being. He was determined not to be bamboozled and outwitted by a system that was designed to allow such chicanery. His ancestors had toiled too diligently for over one-hundred years in the Back Swamp for him to acquiesce and throw in the towel so easily. An example of his mark (X) and signature are shown in Figures 18 and 19 respectively.

From a historical standpoint, there are some interesting aspects of Celia W. Hyman's involvement in the formation of Kelly Place. Mrs. Hyman was a prominent, well respected woman in Riverdale and indeed the entire Darlington community. Research reveals that she was born Celia Weinberg, lived from January 23, 1887-May 9, 1957, and wed Abram Hyman a prominent South Carolina businessman. During the early 1900s she owned a large amount of acreage adjacent to Kelly Place. Her name appears on some early Kelly family documents. I find it intriguing that she had to deed acreage to Shadrack to finalize the process of his attainment of title to his acquired real estate? It implies that one or both of John Kelly Sr.'s earlier one hundred acre plus purchases may not have been properly surveyed and/or recorded by the courts.

Conventional wisdom is that Shadrack was the ultimate perfectionist, a self-trained agronomist, even though he possessed less than a 5th grade education and signed his name with the mark (X) at times. He understood the importance of maximizing efforts to maximize yield. He learned in a short while the art and science of crop production, field rotations, and the importance of the efficient utilization of fertilizers. Figure 19 shows that in 1913 he purchased eight tons of fertilizer. That is 16,000 lbs of fertilizer. The soil required it and Shadrack complied.

The sandy soil of the region was his milieu and he did not allow anything to dilute or deplete the power of his soil. During the 1910s and 1920s this wise agronomist used crop rotations and cover crops to maintain the productivity of the soil, not only for him but also for future generations. Family lore has it that he walked the fields daily to stay ahead of disease and pest problems. There were no weeds in his fields to suck up energy, no suckers on his plants to divert energy from neighboring leafs, no insects on his plants to compromise their health, strength, and ultimate efficiency.

In a short while, Shadrack's virtuosity was recognized by other farmers in Darlington County; his skill was very highly admired. Old timers say that when the word got out that **Shadrack Kelly** was bringing a load of tobacco to the warehouse to sell, people would become curious, gather and tarry to catch a glimpse of his remarkable creations. They say he had a knack for growing those flowing, golden, long-stem leaves and his presentation had its own unique character. You farmers know what I am talking about. There is an art to the entire process, the art of knowing how long to color at ninety degrees and how long to dry those stems at 160-170 degrees. "Can I get an amen?" **Shadrack** comprehended the art and science of the entire process, he was like an artist, a virtuoso, they say. The bulk of his final product was tons of the finest grades of tobacco one could find anywhere, for the production of the finest cigarettes and cigars in America.

From a young age, he also possessed excellent motivational and organizational skills. Shadrack knew how to get the most productivity out of a work crew, and he had a knack for making a worker feel important, whether a family member or a day worker he had no difficulty getting help. From extended Kelly family members on

Old Georgetown Road to neighbors and associates, people enjoyed assisting him in the farm work: The word was he paid well. Some farmers would "work you to death" and then at the end of the day offer you less than the going rate. He relied heavily on day workers, we must remember the number of working hands in his own family were small. Minnie and Shadrack were very unlucky in their attempts to rear a workforce as two of their offspring succumbed to death as babies, another had infantile paralysis and died as a teenager, and their beloved daughter, Almeta, went to the Golden Shore at age twenty-three.

They had a lot of death to deal with as parents and it may have contributed to Minnie's development of dementia at such a relatively young age.

During a period in American history when most farmers worked until they actually went to the Golden Shore, **Shadrack**, born in June 1869, retired from farming in 1925 at the young age of fifty-six. After living his entire life in a rural Darlington County community one of his wildest dreams was to move "to town" one day. The move would have a dual effect. First, and probably most important to Shadrack and Minnie, it assured a quality education for their children, eliminating the demanding daily eight mile trek to Mayo High School. Secondly, they longed to experience the availability and conveniences of city living, not just on Saturdays but on a daily basis.

Minnie and Shadrack worked hard and invested wisely and in 1925 relocated from the rural Riverdale section to the more urban Darlington Township. It appears that they optimized the utilization of their assets well. Shadrack's past history demonstrated that he possessed an understanding of the immense value of land as a tool for financial security. He had invested heavily in real estate. At one point, he owned three intermediate size properties on South Main and Guess Streets, investments which he planned to utilize as sources of income during his retirement.

Another of his investments was the plat located at 501 Chestnut Street, Darlington, South Carolina, the family home site until 2009, when the property was sold. They commissioned the construction of a beautiful home there by Daniel Lumber Company for $1,368.70 in 1925.

It appears that African-Americans had a strong presence in the construction industry in Darlington at that time. For a builder they had their choice of four black general contractors, W.H. Abrams & Son, Willie Williams, Rufus Lomax and Leroy Stubbs. They selected the legendary Stubbs. Like the late Lawrence Reese, ancestor of Ruth Reese Fiuczynski and family, Mr. Stubbs played a major role in the construction industry in Darlington.

Their modest home consisted of six rooms with a screened in side porch, in addition to a front and rear porch that contained a conveniently located pump that pumped fresh, drinking quality, water from a well located below the house.

This may seem mundane to many today, but think about it. They no longer had to go away from the house to get water. The family had evolved from transporting water from a remote spring down in the woods, to having it at the house. It was like having running water in the home which I am certain was not yet available in their community at that point in history. The new home also did not have an indoor bath room and shower as we know them today. A large tin tub was their shower, so jump in, the water is nice and warm.

The two front rooms were trimmed in light oak, balanced in a side trim of mahogany wood. Family records show that Minnie Kelly paid cash for the new home, counted it out on the table. This accomplishment represented a new beginning for **Minnie and Shadrack,** a Bacote/Kelly family.

They made their calculated move just four years before the bottom fell out of the U.S. Stock Market, as the American economy collapsed with the onset of the Great Depression in 1929. Like millions of blacks in the South, they had endured the inhumanity of the propagation of Jim Crow laws and segregation with immense inner moral strength and a calm dignity. Against all odds, through determination and the will to succeed, to demand and attain justice through the legal system, they prevailed in attaining due process with regard to Shadrack's legal rights. How fortunate they were indeed, to be able to capitalize, to utilize their savings, as four years later their cash would probably have been devoured by the banking system. Many Americans lost their hard earned life savings during that period as banks folded and declared bankruptcy.

From the early beginnings Darlingtonians have always been an industrious breed and it was no different in the 1920s. The city possessed a thriving business economy that served Darlington and Florence Counties. For the sake of antiquity, some of the businesses that contributed to the bustling economy are shown below.

Name of Business	Specialty	Telephone or Location
Garrison Auto Company	Auto repairs and supplies	327
Smith Auto Paint Works	Auto painting	N. Main St
Albert Samuel, Tailor	Tailoring services	162
Fred Lucas	Electric service, and auto repairs	211 S. Main St
C. E. Gardner	Auditor, public accountant	471
Metropol & Holloday	Fruits and produce	S. Main St
W.H. Abrams & Son	Building and construction	
C. C. Stratton	Paint Contractor	242 Ave B
Liberty Theater	Movies	Public Sq
W.C. Edwards Ins. Agency	Insurance coverage	356
Hills Drug Store	Candies, soda fountains	44
Darlington Baking Co.	Bread, rolls, cakes, pies	
Daniel Lumber Co.	Building supplies	
Wilson & James	Hardware, supplies, stoves	
Darlington Drug Co.	Drugs	
Nicks Bus lines	Transportation	
Owen-Woodward Co.	Auto tires, gas and oil	96
Darlington Bonded Warehouse	Cotton storage	326

Willie Williams	Building contractor	468
Peoples Grocery Co.	Groceries, feed, hay	152 Pearl St.
Gardner-Green Co.	Fire Insurance	471
The News and Press	Newspaper, office supplies	67
W.D. Coggeshall Co.	Dry goods and notions	Public Square
Coggeshall Hardware Co.	Hardwares, farm supplies	
The Bank of Darlington	Banking	Public Square
Coca-Cola Bottling Co.	Coca-Cola in bottles	
C. R. Chestnut	"Colored Undertaking"	Grove St
Perpetual Bldg & Loan	Banking	
Earle B. Wilson	Auto tires, tops, and upholstering	Sycamore Street
Bonnoitts Haberdashery	Men's clothing	Public Square
Anderson's Meat Market	Fresh meats	Pearl Street
Darlington Furniture Co.	Furniture	384
Hartwell Black	Brick/cement work	332

Shadrack Kelly went to the Golden Shore in 1929 at age sixty, after four years of enjoying the many services the city offered as well as his new post-retirement home with "in-house water." He passed on a legacy and a rich tradition that is still intact today.

CHAPTER SEVEN

EVELYN KELLY BOLDEN BROWN

Up to this point we have revisited, albeit relatively superficially, the lives of three "Iron Horses" of this family history where we spanned the Era of Bondage, the Reconstruction and Jim Crow Eras. Now we shift the focus to a fourth important figure, **Evelyn Kelly Bolden Brown**, the daughter of Shadrack Kelly who was the son of an African-American slave. Her interesting life spanned nearly a century, beginning in the early 20th Century and extending into the Modern Civil Rights Movement and the early 21st Century.

Many contemporary Kelly and Bacote family members are unaware that Evelyn was lovingly referred to as "Toonie" by the old folk. As discussed under "The Kelly Side" her 1st cousin, Ida Brockington, a descendant of her grandfather's first marriage, also responded to that unique moniker. There is usually a special significance to a recurring nickname in a family and from a retrospective standpoint it would be great to know the implication of "Toonie" in Kelly family lore.

Initially I had mixed feelings about the effect a recapitulation of Evelyn's story would have on surviving family and the public at large. If I wanted to write about important female Kelly ancestors from her era I could have just as well addressed the lives of Rosa Kelly, Clara Kelly or Irene Pitillo Kelly to name a few. Each of these women are deceased and recorded very challenging and interesting existences also.

Shadrack's daughter was a woman, who at an early age endured the premature death and demise of quite a few of her young siblings; a woman who witnessed the disastrous effects of a Jim Crow society on the life of the black woman in South Carolina; who appreciated and understood the importance of education; who participated in the historic mass migration to the North; whose husband died unexpectedly at an early age; who endured the debilitating illness of one of her young sons; who was a single mom for a few years and found love again; who was an entrepreneur, educator and community activist; who was a Christian woman that truly cared about others. Many would say her life was anything but uneventful and unchallenging. To many she was an unheralded hero and an iconic family figure.

I questioned the inspirational merits of her story, as it seemed so personal and in many ways painful, and pondered why she took on everyone's problems and sincerely cared so deeply for all people. How could it be inspiring, considering all the tragedy and pain she encountered? Then it hit me, there are many individuals like Evelyn Kelly Bolden Brown in this country who can relate to her story, who have felt or currently feel similar pain, who have suffered disastrous life-altering losses who deserve to be aware that they can overcome and still lead productive lives. The lesson from her story is not rocket science. It is very simple: "identify a career choice that is proactive, positive and beneficial that you enjoy doing, something which also serves to benefit and service others and fully commit to it."

Every period in history is characterized by some form of unrest, conflict, injustice and institutionalism that impacts the lives of one group or another. As we evolve as a worldwide society, rebellions occur constantly and initiatives are put into place to correct the wrongs, to rescue the oppressed, to resurrect the communities and the minds of the countrymen, and to create a more perfect society. A primary example is what is occurring presently in the Middle East.

Evelyn lived during a tumultuous era, a period vastly different from that which her father and grandfather endured. Her journey occurred during an intriguing period in American history for all Americans, but especially for African-Americans. History shows that America evolved from the problematic *Plessy v. Ferguson* doctrine, to desegregation, to the battle for equal rights for all citizens. There was indeed conflict and unrest as America was busy at work making adjustments and changes to the prevailing culture, subtle and not so subtle changes that changed the course of history. The three-hundred year period where race was the overriding factor in determining one's career or life choices in the Western Hemisphere was essentially facing major confrontation. Racial lines, as they once existed, were poised to tumble with the onset of integration and interracial alliances.

In order to understand and have a fuller appreciation for the life of this ancestor, one needs to understand what was occurring socially and politically in this country. The 30s, 40s, 50s and 60s were clearly unique, pivotal periods in our history. Change was underway as numerous barriers were being dismantled.

In an attempt to comprehend the institutional patterns that Evelyn encountered and endured during her early, formative, and young adult years I turned to a 1965 publication by J. Milton Yingers, entitled *A Minority Group in American Society*. Yingers presents a short list of important judicial and Supreme Court decisions which harassed Jim Crow, narrowed the basis for segregation, and reduced the disenfranchisement of African-Americans.

As early as 1915, when Evelyn was a mere youngster, the Supreme Court declared that "grandfather clauses" patently designed to prevent Negroes from voting, were unconstitutional.

Yingers affirmed that "in 1917, laws that required housing segregation were prohibited and in 1948, the Court ruled that private restrictive covenants designed to preserve segregated areas could not be upheld in the courts." He goes on to suggest that "one of the major decisions of this era was handed down in 1944, when the 'white primary'- the basic device for the disfranchisement of Negroes- was forbidden by the Supreme Court. Beginning in 1938, and reaching a climax in 1954 with its decision outlawing segregation in all public education, the Court set into motion the process of school desegregation. *Plessy v. Ferguson* was finally dismantled by the government, as the fact was finally acknowledged that segregated facilities were inherently unequal."

Yingers also alluded to the fact that in "1946, segregation in interstate travel was banned: and in 1955 the court ruled against segregation in public recreational facilities. In 1963, the constitution was amended to forbid a poll tax as a voting requirement in Federal elections." For those who are unaware, the Civil Rights Bills of 1957, 1960 and 1964, dealt primarily with voting rights, public accommodations and economic opportunity. They were the first of that nature passed by Congress since 1875 when Evelyn's father was six years old.

This cadre of laws and rulings, including some not presented here, although not readily accepted, not conformed to by many Americans, or rigorously enforced by the government, empowered Evelyn and her peers and established the tone for critical diverse employment and economic opportunities unavailable to previous generations.

Upon **Shadrack's** death in 1929, his wife **Minnie** took control of the family and of course Kelly Place. **Josephine Graham,** his daughter by a previous marriage, was deeded her inheritance from that tract. Shadrack's cherished daughter Evelyn was now a vibrant twenty year old woman. Some interesting aspects of her early life on the farm in Mechanicsville, as well as early educational experiences were chronicled earlier in this thesis under the "The Kelly Side."

Education appears to have been an important priority of the matriarchal side of her family from the early beginnings. Although the first post-slavery generation of Bacote men did not finish high school, the Bacote women earned high school diplomas. Armed with a strong, family, education tradition and a cognizance of the critical role education would play in the new society, after graduation from Mayo High School in 1930, **Evelyn Roberta Kelly,** the daughter of the son of a slave, became the first member of the Bacote and Kelly families, that I am aware of, to attend college. She matriculated at The Colored Normal Industrial Agricultural and Community College in Orangeburg, South Carolina, which later became the noted South Carolina State College. It is worth noting that her presence at South Carolina State set a precedent, and represented the beginning of a pipeline of Bacote men and women at this revered South Carolina institution during the 30s and 40s. She was a role model for many of her younger cousins as well as unrelated contemporaries.

After completing the studies prescribed in the Two Year College Program, she received a degree in home economics in the spring of 1932. Evelyn then decided she needed to generate some income, so she taught at St. John School and Brockington School in Florence County, South Carolina during 1932 and 1933.

For Evelyn, as it was with many other members of the Bacote and Kelly families and indeed many Blacks from the rural postwar South, slightly disenchanted and disenfranchised, the lure of the North was irresistible. Here was an opportunity to begin a new life, with less oppression and freedom from the aches and uncertainties of an agrarian society. Armed with her degree in home economics, she departed Darlington to pursue employment and social possibilities in New York City. As the culture of the country would have it, she first found employment as a house keeper for a prominent white family. Although she possessed a college degree, that was the best offer she could attain at that time. Not to be outdone, after beating the pavement relentlessly for many months during her spare time, she was able to capitalize on skills acquired during her college days, finding gainful employment as a seamstress at one of the many sweatshops in Manhattan.

It was in Harlem, New York, where **Evelyn** met **Chesterfield Harcourt Bolden**, a raging Bajan from Barbados, British West Indies, who had arrived in New York City in the early 1930s. He had stowed away on a steamship in Bridgetown, Barbados. Legend goes that when the large liner entered Ellis Island he jumped ship and swam ashore, avoiding customs. He must have been a strong accomplished swimmer to pull that daring venture off, because the Hudson River is a murky treacherous body of water that reeks with strong undercurrents. The years of practice in the Caribbean Sea honed his skills and ultimately paid dividends.

Barbados is a relatively large, quaint coral-capped island of unique geological formation located outside the Antillean archipelago, in the Caribbean Sea, off the northern coast of South America. It is noted for its beautiful beaches, gently undulating landscape, sugar cane, and Mount Gay rum. It is a very serene, stately, 166 square mile island, currently consisting of about 270,000 beautiful people. Barbadians boast of having the highest education level (K-12) of all the Caribbean Islands and a ninety-five per cent literacy rate, a testament to the high priority placed on public education by the government as well as the populace at large. The people are very serious about education; it is a culture.

During the European slave trade era, Barbados served as a holding location for "rebellious, strong willed" captives from Africa. Bajan lore has it that if a strong-willed captive was "broken," he/she was then transported to the slave markets in America to be sold. If the captive's resolve was too great and he/she was deemed unbreakable then he/she remained in Barbados and worked the sugar cane industry. This led to the emergence and selection of an island of special people, strong-willed and proud. As you navigate through the neighborhoods, you cannot resist becoming impressed by the sense of strong community values.

Chesterfield located his aunt, Maude Sargent, who was living on Jefferson Street in Brooklyn, and she welcomed him with open arms. Maude and Chesterfield's mother were sisters. He was in America to fulfill his destiny, to find employment, to pursue his dreams and ultimately set the stage for a new generation of the Kelly/Bacote family.

He voluntarily left a promising future in Barbados, his belongings, his parents, **Ethelene Sargent Bolden and Melville Bolden,** his sisters **Ermine and Gwen,** a young baby **(Ometa Harding),** his first cousin and best friend **Richard Sealy,** first cousin **Carl Bolden,** his old car, and a host of memories. It was a huge step when he departed, not knowing whether he would ever return. During that period, international travel was very costly and time consuming. People did not travel back and forth to the West Indies as they do today. The entire family was saddened for decades as reflected in their letters and photographs. Undoubtedly he was their prince. They expected great things from him: an industrious, talented, young man.

There is no stronger example of their feelings for him than exemplified in a classic letter penned by his mother to him on June 15, 1943, just months before his unexpected journey to the Golden Shore. It speaks volumes about his family, Barbadian culture, who he was, how the community regarded him, and his stance on family. The entire touching communication is presented below in its original format.

He was the product of a family that over the years has distinguished itself politically in Barbados. His dad served as a fire chief. His first cousin Richard (Dick) Sealy, who I had the pleasure of meeting for the first time in 1982, was a local politician in Bridgetown, the capital of the country, during the 1950s. Another cousin, C. Lindsey Bolden, a noted attorney and statesman was a Member of Parliament and served as Speaker of the House of Assembly from 1984-1986. The Bolden family tree exhibited in Figure 17 shows that the family has expanded globally with family members currently residing in Long Island, New York, California, Canada, Georgia, Barbados and the Bahamas. Although not shown in this figure, Bolden family members are also firmly established in Trinidad and England.

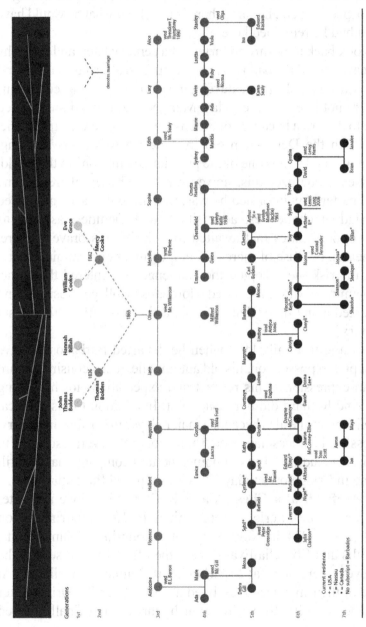

Figure 17. Lineage of Bolden Family in Barbados, America and Nassau

On numerous occasions Dick related that "Chesterfield was the smartest of them all," speaking of the youngsters in the family at that time, and there are some smart Boldens in Barbados. Continuing in that retrospective vein, he said "there is no telling what he would have achieved had he remained here."

We look back now, three quarters of a century later, and ask, why did he leave scenic Barbados? As beautiful and alluring as the island is, it was a relatively poor, developing country. Living conditions there were not like they are today. Many young Barbadians wanted to come to America because conditions at home were very traumatic. Even though the Depression era in America was overwhelming, America was and still is one of the premier destinations in the world. Chesterfield recognized this. However, I do not believe there was any way, no matter how informed he was, that he could have anticipated the myriad of challenges, adversity and difficulties, as well as the new opportunities that awaited him during his brave venture. Nevertheless, because of increased employment opportunities here, he took the risk; he accepted the challenge and entered the game. Dr. Benjamin E. Mays, the noted Morehouse College President and orator stated many times that "it is not a sin to fail, the ultimate sin is not to try."

According to family lore, when he departed Barbados he gave his most prized possession, his old automobile, to his cousin Richard Sealy, an expression of his respect and expectations for his young cousin. And Richard did not disappoint. In addition to his political accomplishments he also became a major player in Caribbean history, a successful businessman, and the owner of several successful enterprises including a funeral home and taxi company that are still operating in Bridgetown today. Dick was a proud Barbadian man.

Chesterfield, aka Chester, and Evelyn fell in love and after dating for a short period, were united in Holy matrimony on December 10, 1934 in New York City. Longtime Bajan friends, Philip Ellis and Cornelia Evans, were the official witnesses for the small joyous ceremony at the Manhattan Municipal Building. At the time of their marriage they lived at 1793 Riverside Drive. Later they resided on 110th Street in Spanish Harlem, and finally moved

4

a fellow from st James his *name*
~~marry~~ came to see *us* and tell *me*
he promise you he would
come ~~around~~ and look for us
that time you was in NY
and I answer that letter but
it came back you had
remove to South
now I must close whilot
myself your ~~If~~ Father
the children and all

enquring friends
send our best love
and respect for yourself
and family re~~maining~~
your loving ~~mother~~ ~~Ethelind Dottin~~

1

15th 6, 43

Barks Hall
Prince of Wales
St Michael

Dear Chester

This my letter comes hop-
ing to met yourself and family
well as it leaves all with me well
thank God I guess you must be
wandering if I had receive your
letter in time for the wedding
I recieve it quite safe also the
15 dollars and in good time
for the wedding Ernie been
to the wedding every body say how
nice she looked that she was
from Paris, Gwen made the
bride's dress every body gave
her credit Bury had a nice
wedding she send to remember

3

the children is getting on and what
they are doing I am always
talking about them, Ches you
know I love you and I pray
God one of these days he may let
us see each other face to face
before I die if it is his will
now let me thank you for
what you send and pray what
you give me the Lord may
not let you lack of it and
increase the remainder
what about those boy
friends of yours does
you see them Johns family
always asking one about
you, sometimes ago

2

to you, Mr and Mrs Gaskins
tell you they are still living
the same place and give you
they best regards. well boy we
are still fighting to live some
days bright some dull things
are still very high and dear I heard
Trinidad is in good swing with
work lots of barbadians going
down there I pray God that
work will open some where
that the poor people wouldn't
suffer Eric is one that gones
what about Evelyn tell her
I havent san her writing
hand for a long time so
write me and tell me how

to 145th Street and Seventh Avenue, (which is also known as Adam Clayton Powell Boulevard in Harlem) one building from the corner on 145th street. Many say it was exciting in Harlem at that time; the Harlem Renaissance was underway and many blacks in the Arts, from all around the country, found their way there. Notables like Paul Robeson, Romare Bearden, Jacob Lawrence, Countee Cullen, Nora Douglas Holt, Dizzy Gillespie, Zora Neale Hurston, James Baldwin, James Weldon Johnson, Aaron Douglas, James Van Der Zee, Paul Lawrence Dunbar, Billie Holiday, John Coltrane, Charlie Parker, W.E.B. DuBois, and Florence Mills, to name a few, contributed to Harlem's ambiance.

Evelyn said life was very engaging; both of them liked jazz and they frequented hot spots like Mintons on 118th Street, between St. Nicholas and Seventh Avenue, as well as the famed Smalls Paradise. **Chesterfield** found time to undertake a short lived, amateur pugilistic career. He fought in the New York City Golden Gloves Tourney at Madison Square Garden a couple of times. However, an unexpected, stunning KO drove him from the ring forever, never to return. That happens a lot, a young fighter gets knocked out and the overwhelming experience is too traumatic to recover from.

Even though they were young, and in a mecca like New York City they did not betray their Christian roots. They became members at Abyssinian Baptist Church, presently located in Harlem at 132 Odell Clark Place (also known as 138th Street) between Adam Clayton Powell Jr. and Malcolm X Boulevards. Abyssinian was founded in 1808 by a group of free African-American and Ethiopian merchant sailors and the first church was located in Lower Manhattan near the financial district on Worth Street.

Evelyn and Chester enjoyed a rewarding Christian experience at Abyssinian which was at the forefront of the black empowerment movement in New York City. Adam Clayton Powell, Sr. was the distinguished senior pastor at that time. Adam Clayton Powell Jr. the famed civil rights attorney and Supreme Court Justice also served in that capacity at Abyssinian for many years.

This illustrious church, with its rich history in the Civil Rights Movement is presently under the leadership of Reverend Dr. Calvin O. Butts III, a college president, community activist, Morehouse college graduate, and a member of Kappa Alpha Psi Fraternity, Inc.

Dr. Butt's outstanding leadership skills and message continues to make Abyssinian a favorite religious destination of contemporary Kelly and Bacote descendants in New York City.

Chester was employed as an elevator man/handyman. He gained employment the old fashioned way and defrayed their apartment rental expenses by serving as superintendent in the building where they originally resided on Riverside Drive. His duties entailed fueling the furnace when required, as well as performing electrical and plumbing repairs throughout the building. Some of his old, relic-like plumbing and electrical tools are still in the possession of his descendants today, as he was proud of his skills, and desired that they would eventually be passed on to his offspring.

Arthur, the first son of this unexpected, international union was born on July 21, 1938, at Columbia Presbyterian Hospital in Manhattan. I say unexpected because none of the conservative Darlingtonians expected Toonie to go to New York City and marry a West Indian man! The happy couple welcomed their handsome son with opened arms, showing him off proudly, on the weekends, to their relatives and friends throughout the city.

However, life in New York City proved too much for the man who was prince. Having grown up in the lush, pleasantly warm, environment of Barbados, BWI, on Prince of Wales Road, in the Parish of St Michael, in the Christ Church community, he struggled with the harsh winters there. This eventually led to difficult ear/nose/throat problems, which along with his mother-in-law **Minnie's** failing health, led to their decision to relocate to the weather friendly confines of Darlington, South Carolina in 1941. Their second son, Chester, was born there on August 23, 1941.

One of the more fulfilling and ironic aspects of their journey in New York City is that eighty years later, their only granddaughter and her husband not only reside on Adam Clayton Powell Boulevard, they are owners of a building on the noted Boulevard, only a few blocks away from Grandpa's original basement apartment. They, along with other Kelly descendants, represent a newly prepared breed of New Yorkers in Harlem, a breed that has migrated from the sugar cane and cotton plantations of the Western Hemisphere to the corporations and board rooms of America.

It is very clear that in everyone's life there is some adversity, some decisions and hurdles that we must meet head on in order to advance to the next level. We have seen numerous examples of this phenomenon already in this treatise. Evelyn's mother, Minnie, developed dementia, a form of adversity that many families have to cope with, and the Kellys and Bacotes in Darlington dealt with the illness and took care of Minnie.

With all due respect to Minnie, according to family lore, there were a couple of incidents relating to her dementia that, in retrospect, were comical then and still today evoke a laugh or two among contemporary family members. The first is "the eggs story."

Minnie's brother Benny and his wife Nanny wanted to send Minnie some fresh country eggs. Their neighbor on the Pocket Road had the eggs at his farm. They sent their son Sammy to get them, but the neighbor's dog attacked and maimed Sammy, scared the hell out of him. But Sammy, being the eventual dependable Kappa Alpha Psi man that he was, protected the eggs and escaped with the package intact. Now tattered clothes, broken skin and all, he went to deliver the eggs to Minnie. He related to her what had occurred, but she discounted it and berated him repeatedly about his appearance. She could not get past his uncustomary, disheveled appearance, and forbid him to enter the house, raised hell, took the eggs and told him to vamoose. Sammy laughed but was very disappointed; after all he had gone through to make the delivery.

It is a story related many times by Sammy when he referred to memories of his aunt. It was always funny because the family, which respected her immensely for her many contributions, knew at that stage her mind misfired sometimes and often found humor in her actions.

The second is "the street plow story." Originally Chestnut Street was a dirt street and the street plow would come by periodically to eliminate newly formed ruts. Her mind being what it was, she was extremely afraid of the plow. The plow was indeed hideous looking, appearing like a huge comic book space monster. She would be babysitting her grandchildren, Arthur, Chester, and their cousin

Gladys, and had made them terrified of the plow also. When the plow neared the home, for some strange reason, she would put them out. Directing them in her terrified state, to take refuge under the house until the plow disappeared. After the plow had vacated the area she would then let them back in. Of course by now they would be crying, angry and very confused by her behavior. Conventional humor among family was that maybe she thought the plow was going to level the house, so she was, in her confused state, protecting the children from danger by evicting them, while she "stayed with the ship."

Dementia or none she loved her grandchildren and the family found humor in the manner in which she handled the situation.

The stint in South Carolina was a very rocky one for Evelyn's family, and Chesterfield did not handle the adversity very well at all. He eventually became abusive to her. It appears that his failing health, traveling long distances throughout the dangerous South for employment as a carpenter, his jealousy trait, the new environment in South Carolina, with the natives' reputation for dealing adversely with outsiders who spoke with an accent, and having been reduced from a prince to a pawn; all took its toll on him. Barbadian men are extremely proud individuals, and he, an honorable man was no different. Nevertheless, he sacrificed his life for a new generation of Kelly-Bacote-Boldens and even though his sons never got the opportunity to get to fully know him, he garnered their respect and admiration. He was an extremely hard worker, who gave greater than one hundred per cent always, and was a no-nonsense type of individual who refused to accept any excuse for failure to achieve one's goal.

Chesterfield went to the Golden Shore two years later in 1943 at the tender age of thirty-nine. Somehow it seems unfair that this courageous young man never had the opportunity to return to Barbados with his family to pay homage and celebrate with his beloved family there.

His brave migration to America paved the way and established a precedent for his family and its present belief that the world we live in today is truly an international arena. After graduating college, his grandson Troy Bolden landed a promising entry level position with a Fortune 500 firm in New York City. Months later, while vacationing in Cancun, Mexico, he decided that the country with its rapidly developing economy offered the ideal environment for his anticipated foray into the real estate industry. Without any second thoughts, he decided to establish residence in Cancun. Troy had heard many stories about his grandfather and was not afraid to embark upon establishing himself in a foreign culture and attempt to master a new language. Chesterfield had already set the precedent, and his efforts were not in vain. Like other ancestors he encoded valuable information into the DNA of his descendants. He proved that one can succeed anywhere, that's it is really about courage and the will to excel against all odds.

World War II was in full bloom at the time of Chesterfield's death. It was a scary period in American history, with the frequent barrage of air raid drills in towns and cities across this great land, with city sirens often blaring and constant nightmares about the war among the youth. On the radio one could listen to broadcasts of the war. Many children became mesmerized about the possibility of falling into one of those vast caverns that they imagined bombs created upon explosion on the terrain. Even though the actual fighting was occurring in Europe, life in America was still traumatic for everyone.

During the War, from 1942-1945, **Evelyn Brown** taught at Georgetown School, located between Society Hill and Darlington, in the Mont Clare section of Darlington County. In 1946, she began a short stint at Galilee School in the western sector of the county. The historic school, located on Highway 401 between Lamar and Darlington near Cypress Crossroads, was in desperate need of devoted teachers and she responded to the challenge. She remained there for four years while the citizens of Mont Clare clamored vehemently for her return. During the 1950s she was back in Mont Clare serving at the Round O School. From the early 1960s until her retirement in 1973 she taught at Brockington Elementary School in the West End community of Darlington. The first three schools were small, one room, rural, segregated facilities. As a teacher, one was obligated to also serve as nurse, social worker, humanitarian, community organizer, activist, confidant, and substitute mother.

To put it in the proper perspective, these were rural schools located on rural roads, and considering the present state of the roads in South Carolina, one can only imagine the difficulties to even get to them by automobile in the 1940s. The entire initiative was wrought with challenges and required efforts and sacrifices that she readily accepted and dealt with.

The role of the rural educator was indeed an arduous complicated task during that era. The hours were long. On many occasions when it was time to turn the lights off at night she was up grading papers only to arise before dawn to get her own young boys prepared for the day's activities. Present day Americans cannot begin to imagine what it was like at the small, rural, "separate but unequal" black, segregated schools. Segregated schools were inferior then and still are today. Simply stated, in most cases there were zero supplies. Sometimes items as basic as wood for the stoves, chalk and erasers were not available, and don't even talk about books.

If some books were available they were mostly of the secondhand, outdated variety, castoffs from the white schools. The situation required that sometimes students had to share books for the entire school year. In retrospect, this was not ideal, however it was not necessarily a negative, unconducive to the learning process. As a student you realized that your possession time with the book was limited, forcing you to become focused, proactive and productive.

She provided paper and pencils at times when the school did not. On many occasions she shared or gave up her lunch to hungry students because there were no cafeterias or food services on site. Despite her busy schedule, she always found time to visit parents at their home to address school related issues involving her students. Perhaps the greatest sacrifice of all was facing the threat to her safety which was constantly compromised on some of those dark, pothole-laden, rural, roads at night after those conferences.

Evelyn's primary assets were her deep compassion for people, exceptional communicative skills and an innate ability to command respect. In her chosen field they served her well. They fostered understanding and trust, key ingredients for establishing a creative learning environment in the classroom. Contrary to the posture that many teachers adopt in the classroom, many of her former students espouse that she made a conscious effort to build a personal relationship with all of them. She harbored no prejudices and consistently treated each student equally, regardless of race, color, sex, or religion, during a tenure that spanned the pre-integration and post integration eras. As an educator she believed that she had a direct responsibility to each of her students, to make their lives better.

After a heroic effort managing and encouraging her two sons for four years as a single parent, in 1947, at the age of thirty-eight, Evelyn wed Ernest Brown, aka Newtie Brown. He was a welcomed addition to the family as he brought stability to its existence.

Newtie was the son of Mr. Jimmy and Mrs. Florie Samuel Brown, longtime Darlington natives. He was educated in the Darlington County public schools and was a member of Macedonia Baptist Church. Newtie was very proud of the fact that he was a World War II veteran, wounded in combat in Germany and honorably discharged in 1945. He played a role in securing this country's sovereignty at the international level.

Many community galvanizing events occurred in Darlington during 40s and 50s. One that was very significant to Evelyn, from her educational perspective, was the destruction by fire of Mayo High School in the early hours of a chilly, pre-dawn morning in 1947. Evelyn's family resided directly across the street from the school and as such had front row seats. Although she was not employed at Mayo she often expressed how depressing it was to witness the destruction of this important facility. To observe the flames continue to increase in size and the fiery embers descending on the homes surrounding the school was very disheartening. Many neighbors gathered in her yard to watch the firemen's futile but brave attempt to save the structure. It was only by the grace of God that many private residences did not go up in flames also.

As the intensity of the flames mounted and the walls began to crumble, tears began to flow. The fire raged for hours. The astute observers were devastated, as they knew the community was in trouble. They knew that a breakdown in the education process in the already struggling, small, African-American community would place the entire community in a very difficult situation. In addition, even though the school was "separate but unequal," it was the only major social institution, outside the churches in the community.

Many community activities revolved around the school. The loss represented a major blow to the community.

The initial reaction of the city's governing body did not help. Rather than purchase new bricks to immediately rebuild the school, city leaders decided the prudent move was to implement a project to clean all the charred old bricks that survived the devastating fire, so they could be utilized in the construction of the new school. It took the city nearly four years to reconstruct Mayo High School, seriously impacting the educational and social development of the children as well as the community.

Nevertheless, the Board of Education, **Evelyn** and a core of dedicated educators as well as concerned citizens in Darlington were galvanized on the same page, reasoning that drastic creative initiatives had to be implemented to prevent a major interruption in the educational process in the black community. They did not sit idly by waiting for a new structure to be erected. It was determined that since there was no classical classroom space on site, students would be sequestered at numerous venues in the community during that period until the school was rebuilt. Temporary classrooms were established at the community center, the VFW hall, black churches, and even private homes to implement very critical educational continuity. Evelyn played a major role as the city worked to overcome the very difficult problem.

Evelyn Brown's primary vocation was education. But like other industrious women during that era, she did all she could to help defray the financial obligations of her family. When she was not teaching, she did seamstress work, a trade she practiced during her stay in New York City. Her specialty was customized men's shirts, men's briefs, and women's blouses and dresses. She also specialized in the mending of socks, to extend their period of usefulness. She even taught her sons that procedure, one that they later utilized many times during their lives. Evelyn frequently worked into the wee hours of the night practicing her craft and would still get to her regular job on time and prepared to teach.

Evelyn and Newtie were dedicated parents who believed in maintaining a comfortable, active, positive, learning atmosphere at home. It was not until the late 1940s that they had in-house running water in their home. Nevertheless it never seemed like a hardship.

313

The saying, "what you don't know, you don't pine for," is real. The family was busy constantly; the focus was on personal development, education and scholarship. Evelyn assured that. During the summer months, they sometimes worked with family members on their farms. Sometimes her sons would stay at their Uncle Leo Bacote's farm for a week at a time getting a bird's eye view of farm life. Some years, during the summer, she would afford them the luxury of a visit to Philadelphia to experience the pleasures and difficulties of city living with their Uncle Jake and Aunt Viola. These trips provided a much needed exposure to the broader picture of big city culture, art, history, and philosophy, all of which were very instrumental in their development.

Even though the family lived "uptown," she was enamored with country living and one's connection to nature, wild life, and the forest. Many times during the year she would venture into the forest area "across the branch," with her sons, to pick blueberries and wild scuppernong grapes, to harvest pecans from trees that had somehow sprouted there, or to harvest pine needles, commonly called pine straw in the South. If the harvests were substantial, the boys would market the extra delicacies in the neighborhood in pint or quart containers. Darlingtonians would pay good money for blueberries and grapes that they would use to make pies and jelly. The pine straw was utilized as mulch around the rose bushes and red berry bearing nandina plants in her garden.

Many of the duties and chores of maintaining, cleaning and assisting around the home were executed by her oldest son. Evelyn often reiterated that when Chesterfield, went to the Golden Shores in 1943, the mere five year old, told her at the funeral as they were walking out of the church, "don't worry mom, I will take care of you." She said from that point forward he was like the man of the house, performing many important tasks, including raking the yard, cutting the grass with a swing blade, making a fire in the stove before daybreak so everyone could arise in a warm environment, bringing in wood and coal for the stoves, and cooking grits, eggs and bacon breakfasts for the family.

Evelyn had a small, tight knit family and a strong relationship with her brother Harold. Harold was employed at the War Department in Philadelphia, Pennsylvania, in the storage division, as an ammunition packer making a modest $7.36 per diem. Nevertheless he capitalized on his opportunities and exploited them with as much overtime work as possible, receiving compensation at 2-3 times the normal per diem rate. He and his wife returned to Darlington for Christmas and other holidays, looking very prosperous and always with numerous gifts and tidings of joy.

Their gifts were always significant, provoking and fulfilled a purpose. Some classics were stylish clothing, black Louisville Slugger baseball bats, baseball gloves, as well as Kodak box cameras, which were state of the art at that time and immensely appreciated and utilized. The camera gift when her oldest son was about eight years old turned out to be very significant. As he would reflect years later, in many regards it was a very effective teaching tool. As a youngster, it taught him how to visualize people and things beyond the surface: how to focus on and embrace the real beauty of nature, while incorporating the immense value of photography in his young mind. It literally unlocked his eyes and helped him recognize the value of savoring the moment and capturing that moment for all eternity. This was a classic example of how one can positively impact a young person's life with the proper stimulus. It is a model that can be exploited today in interacting with and mentoring young people in general.

In 1948, Harold resigned from the War Department to return to Mechanicsville to the land where he spent his childhood, and longed for again. He had become dissatisfied with the hustle and bustle of city life. He wanted to feel free, to feel the call of the wild, to raise his own foods and work the land again. On the other hand, his wife, Viola, wanted to remain in the City of Brotherly Love which she had grown very fond of. She had experienced her saturation level of rural farm life as a youngster in Hartsville, South Carolina, and had transformed into a sophisticated city girl.

Nevertheless, they relocated to Mechanicsville hoping to work it out. They were a classic example of two adults growing in different directions during a stage of their relationship/marriage. Viola tried valiantly to make the adjustment. They farmed Kelly Place, which he had been renting for many years to Mr. Priestly Pierce. She worked her butt off, but the transformation kept gnawing at her innermost self. Many mornings she would arise, put on her makeup and adorn herself with her beautiful jewelry, with nowhere to go. She did not drive, hence was dependent on him to take her everywhere. It was a very difficult time for Viola, especially after sundown in Mechanicsville when the primary outside light was from the moon above. They were constantly at odds and on each other's nerves until she finally left in 1951-1952, returning to Philadelphia and its urban lifestyle.

The divorce had a ripple effect because they were such a stalwart, positive, motivating, force in Evelyn's close-knit family. The breakdown of their family had a profound effect on everyone. Her sons viewed their uncle differently, as the younger Chester detested him for the hateful, disgusting manner in which he treated Viola. His relationship with **Evelyn** also deteriorated, but even more significantly, he went through a metamorphosis. He was no longer a positive, loving and giving man as he attempted to lessen the impact of his demise with the overuse of alcohol. Evelyn's older son never hated him, but later would admit that he consciously distanced himself from his uncle, which in retrospect, he felt was a tremendous mistake that he still regrets today. He felt he should have exhibited a greater presence, even though he tried, that he should not have accepted his uncle's failure to attempt to make a healthy transition into a new life style.

Early in life, Evelyn Brown bought into the concept that education and knowledge is power and this thought process prevailed throughout her lifetime. She was driven to pursue her educational goals. On weekends and during the summers of the late 1940s and early 1950s, this highly motivated, young mother was off to Morris College, in nearby Sumter, South Carolina, or South Carolina Agriculture and Mechanical College, taking college courses. Those efforts serve as a testament to this "Butterfly's" tenacity, persistence and dedication. They culminated with the attainment of a Bachelor of Science degree in elementary education in 1956 from Morris College.

It was a day that would be remembered for a long time. The commencement speaker was Dr. R.W. Puryear, president of Florida Normal and Industrial Memorial College. Evelyn's entire family drove up from Darlington to acknowledge her accomplishment and relish the special day with her.

This achievement served as inspiration for her sons as they actually witnessed their mother graduating from college. Both of them later attained advanced degrees in their own professions. They saw that through hard work and dedication one could achieve, that they could possibly do likewise. These two young men witnessed firsthand that their mother's accomplishment did not happen overnight. It took planning, hard work and execution. More importantly, they comprehended that her success was the product of a genuine commitment.

Evelyn was married to an ambitious, strong, caring gentleman, and they worked as a team. He was the ultimate entrepreneur. After graduating from a government sponsored training program for veterans, as a brick mason, he never performed any construction work. Instead they launched a small, community, mom and pop grocery store, where they marketed items like bread, eggs, ice cream, candy, skins, sodas, hot sandwiches, can goods, a few fresh vegetables, potato chips, milk, cold drinks etc.

The busiest time at the store was the lunch hour traffic from Mayo High School. Arthur would come over from school at that time to assist him with sales and to help control the crowds. Some students would attempt to pilfer, especially during the chaotic lunch period, because the small store would be packed and it was difficult to watch and serve everyone promptly. It did not become clear how rampart the thievery was until many years after they had closed down the operation, and it was difficult to fathom, because Newtie was such a generous man, he would share the shirt off his back if you needed it. He provided credit to some patrons (actually even to the families of some of the thieves) who had financial woes, sometimes knowing that he possibly would not collect. That's the kind of man he was. It is said that God puts us in odd places sometimes with a plan of action for us. Even with the thievery and numerous late night break-ins the venture was successful, as it provided a useful service to the community and prepared the family for future endeavors. They shared and in return received much more than they gave, just as the scriptures relate and many believe.

After nearly a year of thrashing the idea around, being the entrepreneurs that they were, they launched a farming effort in 1951. This venture was essentially a three prong initiative to generate revenue. The rational was: we have this land out in the country, (land originally deeded to **Minnie** by her father, **Elias Bacote,** and now under Evelyn's ownership) that we are renting, why not maximize its utilization? The plan consisted, firstly of renting the bulk of the agricultural area to a local farmer, secondly, planting three acres of tobacco and two acres of corn on another five acres, and last but not least, growing hogs for retail in the marketplace.

A receipt dated in 1951 documents their purchase of a dark brown, 1,200 pound mule from J.L. Weinberg for $100. The mule, which was used for preparing the land and hauling materials at the farm, was housed at Junius's stable for use across the branch.

Newtie embraced this momentous challenge with no prior experience as a farmer, or hog grower, relying on assistance and guidance from his in-law relatives **Jake, Junius, Buddy, Handy** and all the other members of the Bacote clan on Bull Road. They were always there for him, all of them, like always they were family. They were constantly available for consultation; free consultation no less. Of course, **Evelyn** was in the forefront of much of the planning as she had lived her pre-adult years on a farm.

She acquired adaptability skills as a child, learning from her parents as they weaved their way through the hectic agricultural environment. As an adult, her own family was much like your typical struggling family in the South in many regards. However, what differentiated them from many was her philosophy which, simply stated, was: you take what God has afforded you and use it to the best of your ability; you endeavor to take control of the situation, not let the situation take control of you. You adapt as you navigate the obstacles.

An analogy can be drawn to the mentality of a productive running back on the gridiron. First of all you must make the first attacker miss. As your eyes simultaneously survey the remainder of the field, you prepare for the next attacker or hit because you know its coming and you cannot give him a clean look. You must make him miss also.

They constructed a state of the art tobacco barn to cure the tobacco on site and then transported it to their storehouse on Chestnut Street for grading and packaging, to ultimately sell at the warehouses in Darlington. Although very successful financially, this exciting venture was also very grueling. Inexperience and long days took its toll on **Evelyn** and **Newtie**, mentally and physically. That sturdy old curing barn which is still standing today, is verification of and a reminder of what transpired across the branch.

Raising hogs was a year-round venture, as there was constant consumer demand. Let me take you there for a moment. The large pig pen, also known as a pig sty, constructed of heavy-duty hog wire reinforced with oak logs at the lower level, was purposely situated behind Junius' tobacco barn in full view of his living quarters. Its location across the branch would have been an open invitation to opportunistic thieves who were so inclined. It was positioned under two large pecan trees to provide protection for the animals from the sun, and contained three partially covered, isolated sections to separate sows and her newborns from the general population. In addition, a large well which served as an abundant source of essential, fresh, clean water was nearby.

As the hogs were not pasture fed, their nutritional needs were fulfilled with fresh household and restaurant scraps that Newtie collected from local restaurants including his parents', and transported daily from town. In addition they were fed homegrown corn and supplemental commercial feed.

The ambitious, well-conceived plan consisted of maintaining a stable of three good, fertile, brood sows and a healthy active one to two year old boar. Sows were "in heat" for three-four days. The gestation period for a sow was about four months. There was an excellent market at that time for six to eight week old piglets, or weaners as they were called, and with a litter averaging about ten piglets and three sows delivering two litters a year they were able to turn over about sixty-seventy piglets during a good year.

It was not a simple straight-forward task growing healthy, alert hogs for slaughter. There were countless emergencies and health issues that demanded resolution. In addition to the piglet market, the thrust also encompassed having a constant supply of mature four-five month old hogs, of about 180-250 pounds in weight, ready for market during the Thanksgiving and Christmas holidays as the demand and hence the prices were higher during those months. They were either auctioned or sold to butchers and restaurants in the area.

The farming and hog raising initiative encompassed about five years before abandonment. They had a good run and more importantly banked a little cash.

Chestnut Street was finally paved in 1951-1952. Before then it was your typical, southern, two lane, rutty, dirt/sand street in the black section of town where kids in the neighborhood caught grass hoppers and sand crabs to be sold as fish bait. People who fished would pay nice money for those insects. The street had to be plowed periodically with large earth moving machines to level out the ruts which made for a smoother ride in cars or on bicycles.

Evelyn's neighbors on Chestnut Street were all hard working people. Starting with Reverend J. P. Pearson-Pansy Pearson and son Joshua, Mr. Henry Williamson-Charlena Williamson and children, Charles, Ralph, Patricia and Betty, the Alexanders with children "Cat, Rat and Possum," Janie Wilds and her crew of Imogene, Harold, Ruth, Billy, Leroy, Franklin, Peter, and their grandmother, the Gibsons, parents of the late, noted South Carolina civil rights leader Dr. William F. Gibson, Mr. James McIver - Mrs. Helen McIver and children James Jr., Ralph and Betty, and Coach Virgil Wells' family on the other side of Mayo High School, they were the proverbial village that raised the children.

Last, but not least, Mr. Charlie Chestnut and Mrs. Annie Chestnut, a six grade teacher lived across the street from Evelyn. Mr. Charlie, as he was affectionately called, was a blacksmith, welder, wheelwright and undertaker, a multi-faceted man who could repair anything. Whenever neighborhood children had something broken they would take it to Mr. Charlie for repairs. He jokingly referred to them as "botherations," but he never turned them away.

A receipt dated June 8, 1929, shows he was paid $155 by Minnie to utilize his skills as an undertaker and bury Shadrack.

Evelyn understood that sustained advancement in personal behavior and attitudes requires sustainable changes at the institutional and systemic levels of the communities in which we reside. She was very active socially, politically and spiritually in the community and stressed the importance of such involvement throughout her life. In addition to the education system her life was divided primarily between three other important organizations, the NAACP, her sorority and the Missionary Board at Macedonia Baptist Church.

As an educator, the landmark *Brown v. Board of Education of Topeka Kansas Decision of 1954* was a major victory for her. Evelyn believed that the best way to achieve social and political change was to engage in more academic discourse, not limit it by isolation. She often voiced that one reason this decision was so significant, although this nation still struggles with finding means of providing equitable public education as well as equal access to health care, and equal employment across all economic and racial barriers, "is because it afforded a much needed opportunity for all races to interact more closely." These interactions fostered much needed exposure and understanding, and highlighted racial similarities as well as differences. She said "it served to soften the scar tissue from the centuries of racial discrimination, bigotry, hatred, resentment and ignorance and defused many myths that have retarded America's development as a nation of the people." History will reflect that this Decision played an overwhelming role in the election of Barack Hussein Obama as the 44th President of the United States of America in November 2008, and the eventual passing of his controversial $938 billion Health Care Reform Act in 2010.

During the pre-modern civil rights era when many blacks in the South were acquiescing and assuming a relatively moderate posture, **Evelyn**, was very active in the Darlington chapter of the National Association for the Advancement of Colored People (NAACP). The Darlington chapter was a collaborative effort with the fearless Mann Stanley at the helm. Evelyn Brown was one of his lieutenants.

During the period when the Universities of Mississippi, Alabama, Georgia, South Carolina and Arkansas were being challenged and integrated, the civil rights organization diligently considered using classmates Carrie Brown and Evelyn's son Arthur to integrate the University of South Carolina in 1955. During a highly spirited meeting, Evelyn in her initial enthusiasm offered him as a sort of sacrificial candidate for that crucial test, willing to put her son's life and well-being on the limb for the cause. However, when they got home and discussed the possible worst case scenarios from a family point of view, the fear of physical retaliation by the Ku Klux Klan and economic reprisals by the city and state were too overwhelming. Everyone realized it was a potentially explosive step and Evelyn was concerned about her job and the safety of her family. There is no doubt that she would have been terminated from her position as an educator. Arthur respectively declined and instead enrolled at

Morehouse College in Atlanta, Georgia. Carrie attended Talladega College in Talladega, Alabama.

In retrospect, when we look back, that exercise served a very useful purpose after all. Although that NAACP chapter was unsuccessful in providing a team to integrate the university, so as not to be outdone, it decided to launch two new initiatives; an expanded role in voter registration in the county and the elimination of the denial of black voting rights in the South. This strategy would prove to be very essential and beneficial, instantly and over a period of years as it produced a strong bloc of voters in the county, and an increased interest in the political process by the next generation and following generations of blacks.

The Darlington branch of the NAACP reshaped the civil rights struggle in the "Back Swamp" during the 1960s. The efforts of these brave committed individuals were rewarded by the passage of the 1965 Voting Rights Act, which outlawed restrictions denying African-Americans the right to vote.

Evelyn was also a very active member of the Alpha Pi Chi Sorority. Their mission was to promote education and provide venues for uplifting the community. The Darlington chapter which included members such as Elouise Harrison, Josephine Lee, Ruth Hudson, Reholda Norwood, Louise Rogers, Dorothy White, Fannie M. Davis, Mary E. Bines, Lavicie McDowell, Theola Wilson, Lena Manning, Eleese McCrey and Iva Mae Woods, were a group of dedicated, successful, influential women in Darlington. History will show that they were a very beneficial community group that provided a much needed service.

Like the two preceding generations of Kellys and Bacotes, her family was also a God-fearing, church going family in the Bacote and Kelly tradition. Every Sunday was church time, 10am-2pm, which included Sunday School and the regular service. Her sons experienced revival meetings and were exposed to the arts and confidence building at Macedonia Baptist Church. **Evelyn Brown** served God in many capacities at Macedonia, having served with fervor on the Missionary Board for decades. During the last few years of her life she received communion at home every month from a representative of the church. Once she became unable to attend services, Ronald Jackson, Reverend Flora McCurry, and Herbert McCurry graciously served her in that capacity.

There were numerous events that tested **Evelyn's** character, fortitude and faith during her challenging life. One of the more life-altering challenges occurred in 1952 when her son, Chester, contracted measles or chickenpox, one of the viral-driven diseases, that ultimately damaged one of his kidneys. She had the most difficult time trying to contain him and getting him to obey doctor's orders. The Darlington/Florence medical community did not expect her son to survive as the problem appeared to be beyond their level of expertise.

Her insight, diligence and perseverance saved his life and allowed him to experience many years of enjoyable existence. After having gone through one negative experience at McCloud Hospital in Florence, South Carolina in 1943 with her husband Chesterfield, she decided to take her son to the noted Duke Hospital in Durham, North Carolina, to be treated by some of the premier medical minds nationwide. Dr. Sparks of Darlington help set it up. Chester was a patient there for two months and **Evelyn** stayed the entire time with her young son, while the medical staff saved his life. Sometimes she would stay in his room all night, sleeping in a bed provided by staff. The doctors projected he would only live to be about twenty-five or thirty years old and would probably develop mental and physical difficulties. Well, Chester survived another fifty years. Although he had his share of physical ailments, like the rest of us mere mortals, during his lifetime he made significant artistic and educational contributions to mankind. His teachings and art will undoubtedly withstand the rigorous test of time and serve us well into the future. Evelyn responded to a very challenging situation, made the good decisions and saved his life when many would have simply wilted under the pressure and accepted the status quo.

Like her parents had done for her, Evelyn spared no expense to get her offspring prepared for the future. Even though the medical profession had predicted a very short life for her son, she persevered in her resolve to prepare him for a future of productivity, regardless of its length.

In 1956, she enrolled Chester in Mather Academy, a private school in Camden, South Carolina, to improve his academic performance. As a youngster he suffered with a speech impediment which hampered his performance at Mayo High School. One year at the private school corrected his difficulties, converted him into a force, a dedicated honor student. He returned to Mayo to attain his high school diploma with honors. This academic excellence continued throughout his productive college and post-graduate school years.

As a team, Evelyn and Newtie continued their journey. She held the steady position as a teacher with the guaranteed income, while Newtie took on numerous ventures, in their quest for financial security. After the stint as a farmer, he later owned and managed a night club on Old Mont Clare Highway called the Dew Drop Inn.

This venture to a certain degree represented a unique challenge to the family. Evelyn was not too enamored with that situation because after all she was a teacher in the small town and her credibility prevented her presence at such an establishment. Although teachers did not command high salaries, their vocation represented a highly important position in African-American culture in the south during the pre-integration era of the 1930s, 40s and 50s. In Darlington, like other Southern communities, they were afforded the ultimate respect. As such, Evelyn was a role model for many students as well as parents. With that came the responsibility of setting a good example. Because of the culture of the South she had to be careful about the places she frequented and was seen; her image was essential for her mystique.

As a result Newtie eventually divested himself of the night club and began managing Brown's Paradise. This establishment was a mom and pop restaurant on South Main Street that was owned by his parents. They were advancing in age and the business was becoming too much for them to handle. It was a family business that was already two generations in existence and was a classic forerunner of the sports bar of today. There was always a basketball, football, or baseball game on the "black and white" nineteen inch television for the many who would gather daily to watch the games, to socialize, play spades, whist or checkers, to enjoy themselves. Newtie had his hands into a little bit of everything there. Meals were offered, bootleg or regular whiskey was for sale, and off-site baseball or football gaming was available. No gambling or card games like poker, etc.

were allowed at the restaurant. A lot was happening, you had to be able to wheel and deal if you were running the shop.

Evelyn sincerely believed the activities at this establishment also clashed with her position as a public servant and her presence at the business decreased dramatically over a short period. Again, she felt it compromised her credibility. It was a personal thing, there were no complaints registered by the community, parents, or the school board against the restaurant or her. Her position was how could she in good faith lecture students about changing the culture, confront the illegality of racial injustice, or attempt to uplift the community from a social standpoint, when one of her business ventures bordered on impropriety? The business which operated in a sort of grey area created a rift in the family that never really was resolved. Nonetheless, Evelyn continued on her apparent mission to institute change in the community.

They were fortunate indeed, as their entrepreneurial efforts afforded them the financial capability to also send their last son, Chester, to Hampton University in 1959, and provide everything required of them.

Evelyn's model for fostering personal growth and elevating expectations captured the imagination of the community and her family. It was successfully passed on to her offspring, and the ensuing generation as well. All of her children and grandchildren finished college and attained advanced education, inspired by a scholastic tradition established decades earlier in the family and exemplified by their grandmother.

Her sons embraced her philosophy and were smitten by the proven power of knowledge. They spent an inordinate amount of time at educational events and in the presence of teachers as young men. Both earned master's degrees in their respective disciplines. Arthur's wife, Jackie, obtained advanced degrees in education from Montclair State College and Columbia University while simultaneously raising their family. They were always burning the midnight oil at home. Upon receiving an MBA in Management from Fairleigh Dickinson University in Rutherford New Jersey in 1976, they made certain that their three young children were there to see their father walk proudly across the stage, after having seen him stay up late many nights studying and writing. When one closely studies the photographs that were taken that day, it is clear that the seeds had been planted in minds of the next generation once again. You can see pride in their eyes, you can see I like this in their demeanor, you can see the passage of a family tradition that was ignited generations earlier, being processed by their brain cells.

Evelyn Brown was an excellent educator by many criteria. Firstly, she sincerely cared about her students, all her students. She did not care about the tint of their skin, the knottiness of their hair or apparent pedigree of their family. It appears that she had a knack for seizing the opportunity to transmit her belief in them as individuals. Secondly, she graded test papers quickly and got the results back to the students quickly while the subject material was still warm in their brains; and thirdly, at home where she was free to fully express her innermost feelings, she never made disparaging remarks during all those years about any student. This suggests that she had faith in these children. I am sure she was exposed to some provoking hell-raisers but she never came home with negative stories about little Johnny. Those patterns translated into motivation, motivation on the part of the student to learn the subject matter; motivation to reward the teacher for her efforts. In retrospect I suggest that maybe that is the reason so many of her students held her in such high esteem, because they knew that in addition to her high expectations, she had a sincere interest and confidence in them.

She received the Distinguished Educator Award in Darlington on two occasions, and her efforts at the small, rural, Darlington County Schools, like those of many of her peers, merit the praise and distinguished tributes her former students still espouse. The overall value and contribution of these educators to society at-large is greatly under-represented and under-appreciated.

Evelyn truly believed in the power of information and the power of awareness. She was well versed on many subjects as she was an avid reader, even into her nineties this driven Bacote/Kelly icon would stay up all night reading. She lost her hearing but never her thirst for knowledge. Reading the classics, the Bible and medical articles were her favorite pastime activities. Her library at home contained three versions of the *Bible* in addition to such classics as Robinson Crusoe, Robin Hood, The Adventures of Tom Sawyer, The Adventures of Huckleberry Finn, Thomas Mann's Dr. Faustus, The

Gathering Storm by Winston Churchill and Ralph Ellison's Invisible Man, to name a few. She always subscribed to *Ebony, Time,* and *Life* magazines. **Evelyn** introduced hundreds of students to outstanding authors and the importance of reading such works.

At home, she constantly stressed the importance of reading to her sons. Her library also contained complete sets of Funk & Wagnalls New Encyclopedia, The World Book Encyclopedia, and The Champlin Encyclopedia, as well as The World's Greatest Thinkers series.

Her innovative classes taught young, rural, African-American children, once mostly destined for the agricultural fields, skills beyond what the usual school curriculums offered. Ralph Brown, one of her former students from the 1960s, and Vietnam veteran, often avowed his commitment to his former teacher. Ralph Brown once eloquently stated "Mrs. Brown taught me beyond the classroom, she changed my perception of life, and taught me what compassion and caring really means."

That is a powerful statement to make about a person. To support that statement with action is even more powerful. Up to Evelyn K. Brown's departure from earth, like her family and three close friends, Ralph Brown and his family were there for her, for many years assisting in caring for her, bringing her home-cooked dinners from their kitchen, taking her to the doctor, checking on her and assisting her from morning through night, anytime they would be available. He checked her temperature, checked her blood pressure, checked her blood sugar levels many, many times and it is very ironic that on her final November morning, Ralph was the person who unlocked the back door, came into the house, checked her pulse and determined she had gone to the Golden Shore. I guess what we witnessed here is the ultimate power of an effective, devoted educator. They are very significant individuals in our lives and in the overall scheme of things. They are loved. Ralph Brown, no relation to Ernest Brown, cared about this educator. **Evelyn Kelly Bolden Brown** went to the Golden Shore on November 18, 2007, at age ninety-eight.

What merits her special attention as the "Butterfly" in this treatise? She did not, against all odds, acquire hundreds of acres of real estate, discover a cure for AIDS or become a world-renowned figure.

You can attempt to quantify a teacher's performance and success rate but there are many variables you cannot account for or control when it comes to measuring the total extent and effectiveness of their teachings. For example, is the atmosphere at the student's home conducive to learning? Do the parents participate in enhancing the educational process of their children? Do they monitor homework assignments or assist with their children's homework? Do they talk to the children about what's happening at school? Does the student comprehend the importance of striving to be the best student they can be? Does he/she appreciate the long term importance of a thirst for knowledge? Evelyn attempted to impact these variables and others, via presentations in and out of the classroom setting. She assumed the responsibility of establishing appointments to visit the parents of at-risk students at their homes, since many were not involved in PTA activities. Her booklets of teaching plans indicate that she instituted surprise workshops within the classroom dealing with daily living, by utilizing tools acquired over the years in the education process. Ultimately it is the students themselves who provide the true measure of an educator's effectiveness.

It is one thing to be a teacher, it's another thing to be an effective educator as Evelyn was. Effective educators take education to another level. They do more than teach the subject material, they teach more than science, reading and mathematics. They teach life, and ultimately they shape lives. Martin Luther King Jr. once said his mentor, Benjamin E. Mays, "made him understand the relevance of living."

There are countless individuals who during the course of their existence are placed in a position where they can significantly impact the lives and futures of people other than themselves in a positive manner. However the bulk of these individuals fail to capitalize or maximize their potential for a variety of reasons, many of which they have no control of, but often because they simply lack the desire. The dissimilarity between them and the difference makers is that the latter accept the challenge and elevate their talents to another level. It requires an extra effort, another gear, sacrifices, longer hours and ultimate dedication to your craft.

It is very clear that Evelyn possessed an abounding compassion for her students and this quality keyed her success. She shaped the lives of hundreds of young people in Darlington, South Carolina, over a career that spanned four decades. Her life-long dedication to the public education process, the fight for civil rights, as well as her position as an activist and mentor paved the way for many.

Few of us are fortunate enough to achieve such a noble goal during our lifetime. History will reflect that this dynamic woman played an important role in preparing a family and a community for the future.

EPILOG

The discourse that you have just perused has by no means exhausted the subject of the lives and past contributions of these ancestors or the future accomplishments of their progeny. It is not and was never intended to be an exercise in the history of slavery although it does contain a great deal of historical data and information regarding this important era in world history. It is a classical story of African-American life in South Carolina and represents a microcosmic progress report based on the documentation available to the author, on the "Three Iron Horses and the Butterfly" at this time.

Though not exhaustive, this treatise breaks new ground vis-à-vis Bacote and Kelly genealogy and family history and directs the general public's attention to African-American family life during the Slavery, Reconstruction and Antebellum periods of American history. The caveat is that it is from a black prospective. Hopefully it will serve as a catalyst for greater subsequent research by young contemporary Kelly and Bacote descendants, and encourage more pursuits of this genre by academicians and historians throughout this land.

What began as an ambitious recording of some facts from a cache of handwritten notes and observations regarding some facets of Kelly and Bacote family history has resulted in a researched document that is part history and part inquiry into love and faith. Having outlined the facts available to me, I rest my inquiry. I will leave it here and allow this treatise to, to a certain degree, demonstrate the ambiguity of history. It affords the reader an opportunity to play historian, to delve deeper and perform additional research in the quest for the further truths.

During nearly five years of historical research, from January 2008 through November 2012, I embarked on a mission to interview as many senior contemporary Kelly and Bacote family members as possible, that would speak freely with me. During this period over one hundred telephone and live interviews were conducted. Before each interview the subjects were informed that I was gathering information to be included in a treatise on Kelly and Bacote family history. I believe that was important in eliciting the frankness and candor a project of this nature requires.

Some were reluctant to convey their thoughts and recollection of information that had been passed on to them by family lore, but most were very cooperative. Less than a dozen descendants declined to reveal their knowledge. Some cooperative subjects were in their sixties, some were seventy, some were eighty and older, some were male, most were female, and I found myself constantly fascinated by their revelations about their accounts of the "will to survive against all odds," and the adoration of their own personal journeys within the context of family. Family history can be a very touchy subject as many families are inflicted with a host of internal struggles and strife.

Through the ancestors featured in this treatise we have seen that Kelly and Bacote family history, as it should, mirrors the history and advancement of America during this period. The story has some relatively unique and distinctive aspects, but to a large degree it is synonymous with the history of our country. Their history is irrevocably intertwined with the diverse chapters of American life and demonstrates many facets of the resiliency that America is noted for.

During the 1800s, through the Civil War, up to the turn of the century the world of the black man, simply put, was essentially limited to the plantation or the small rural area in which he resided. Elias Bacote and Matilda White were at the same plantation before they wed. John Kelly Sr. and Hannah Harrison both resided at Roseville Plantation before marriage as well as John and his first wife Nancy Brockinton. Matilda White and Hannah Harrison resided at the same plantation during their period in bondage. Miraculously some forty years after slavery ended, Matilda's daughter wed Hannah's son in that same, small, rural community.

From the turn of the century up to World War II the world enlarged greatly with the advancements in railroad and airplane transportation and massive migrations to the North and West for greater employment opportunities and a more resourceful life. Evelyn Kelly, a 4th generation Kelly/Bacote, met her spouse Chesterfield Bolden not in Darlington, South Carolina, but nearly eight hundred miles away in Harlem, New York.

Through the Civil Rights Movement and the technology driven 1980s and 1990s the world has continually expanded as computer technology has advanced and man's knowledge of the universe has soared to unprecedented heights. Troy Bolden, a sixth generation Kelly/Bacote/Bolden, on September 9, 2009, wed Czech native Alena Kudelova. They met and worked, not in Darlington, not in New York, but in Mexico before they wed and produced two beautiful daughters, Alexis Bolden and Alyson Summer Bolden.

When one observes the Kelly and Bacote descendants today, the many cousins and in-laws, it is very clear that God has truly blessed us, has allowed the efforts of our predecessors to bear fruit that nourishes us on a daily basis. Their brave sustained efforts have not been in vain and it is our charge as descendants to continue in that same tradition, so that centuries later mankind will recall and appreciate our efforts and contributions.

The four ancestors featured in this treatise, Elias Bacote, John Kelly Sr., Shadrack Kelly, and Evelyn K. B. Brown, established their own limits, were driven to overcome numerous barriers and, against all odds, struggled to position themselves in the higher percentile at what they did. This cursory investigation into their lives reveals that each of them had a clearly defined life purpose that they selected for themselves through the grace of God. They embraced their challenges with unbreakable determination stabilized by a steadfast dedication of intensity and discipline.

Frederick Douglas, the noted black abolitionist, once said "if there is no struggle, there is no progress." This is true not only as it relates to a nation, but also as it relates to a family. Progress in these Kelly and Bacote families has not been a simple process by any stretch of the imagination. The slave ships that imported the early ancestors through the treacherous middle passage were not conveying simple laborers, but strong men and women deeply anchored in a faith and destiny, too intense for the average mortal to even comprehend.

For centuries these unheralded ancestors nurtured and laid the groundwork for the family, and indeed the nation, by overcoming enormous obstacles, leading reforms and destroying barriers that allowed the four icons featured in this treatise as well as contemporary generations to actually aspire and achieve horizons unimaginable to the dreamer. Their efforts continue to serve as a source of inspiration for many of us today. The result of their exemplary struggle is extraordinary progress, although many barriers still exist today, as America continues to strive for equal opportunity and empowerment for its melting pot of citizens.

We celebrate the vision and achievements of the "Iron Horse," Elias Bacote, who had the courage and foresight to initiate endeavors that would broaden the economic, academic, as well as social opportunities of succeeding generations. His bold efforts required inspiration, confidence, intelligence and faith. What I take most from the life of Elias is the significance of long-term planning and charting your own course in this marathon called life. As his descendants move forward individually and even as a family we remain cognizant that nearly 150 years ago this man essentially formulated the contemporary socio-economic paradigm of the Bacote family. His teachings and philosophy continue to impact most of our lives on an ongoing basis.

The other "Iron Horse," John Kelly Sr., as well as Elias taught us how to respond when events beyond one's control leaves a sense of emptiness in places that we think can never be refilled. Shadrack Kelly and the "Butterfly," Evelyn K.B. Brown, echoed the virtue of persistence from the beginning of their lives to the end. I have learned so much from the lives of these improvident ancestral souls who bestowed us with everlasting multi-dimensional gifts.

Although no treatise of this nature, considering the perspective of time and the inherent nature of the intent, can be all inclusive and exquisitely definitive, two things are certain; firstly, a small portion of the journey of the Kelly and Bacote families featured herein has been officially documented and recorded, and secondly, numerous uncertainties vis-à-vis their history have been discharged and new information uncovered in an attempt to color the landscapes of these African-Americans.

Continuity is the key to accurate in depth family history. The unexpected discovery of the heretofore unknown first family of John Kelly Sr. caused me a lot of anxiety initially, but ultimately it fostered a fuller appreciation of the complexity of this undertaking. It obligated me to question are there other clans connected to this family out there in the "Naked City" that we are unaware of? Is it possible that he had other alliances? How in-depth is any reconstructed family history? What percentage of the actual genealogy can one expect to account for? These are all valid queries.

Many of the constraints that decreased the probability of identifying early ancestors like the scantiness of early birth and death records for example, or census reports excluding blacks before 1870, etc. were cited in the body of this work. Now if we consider the so-called plantation culture and factor in the ambiguity due to entire clans falling through the cracks for non-obvious reasons and avoiding detection, or the noted "mandingo" and miscegenist phenomena and their dubious effect on family identity and continuity, then these reconstructions becomes significantly more complex.

We are all aware of the history of the utilization of mandingos to go from plantation to plantation and father children to generate a work force and provide income for the land owner in the lucrative slave trade industry. These children became property of the plantation, were reared by the mother and were sold at the owner's discretion. Some plantations, large and small, had their own in-house mandingo. This type of activity offers an explanation for the common practice during that era of offspring being given the surname of the mother, which was for identification purposes solely. This was the name recorded in plantation records. It was about economics, with the males serving solely as sperm donors. In these cases their names, as fathers, were either not registered or simply misrepresented.

Within this framework, the effects on familial continuity were far reaching. Females became the primary conduit of that continuity. On some plantations they could adopt any surname desired. On some plantations, if they wed, the woman had the option of adopting the surname of her husband. On many plantations there was a consistent institutionalized effort to disrupt any concept of family in order to exercise more dominance over the enslaved. From a record keeping standpoint this disregard of family and continuous surnames severely compromised the continuity of family history.

The impingement of mandingo and miscegenation phenomena on plantation life and the difficulty in truly assessing the extent to which these forays impacted early African-American ancestral beginnings makes it very problematic to assess the true scope of reconstructions of this nature. It does not take a rocket scientist to understand that the impingement of a singular mandingo act, two centuries removed, could amount to thousands of descendants today whose heritages may be dubious.

These and other variables highlight the importance of accurate, dynamic, oral African-American family history in the overall scheme of things. In addition to its value as a source of true history, it also serves as a launch pad for ambitious research efforts to reconstruct the past utilizing the many internet search machines available today. The importance of documenting as much of this history as possible while the brains of those who possess the knowledge are still functional cannot be overstated. For the sake of humanity, this important information must not be further compromised or allowed to vanish.

The question often arises among contemporary scholars as to whether it is a moot point to uncover only a tip of this iceberg? Is there real value in knowing only 5, 10, or 20 per cent of the real history while 80, 90, or 95 per cent remains obscure? To this query again I submit, "Yes." As stated in the Preface, it is incumbent upon us to document as much truth and educated speculation as possible; to uncover as many lost clans as conceivable. We must celebrate the successes of reconstructions of this nature and continue toiling for the big breakthrough. The thorough, exhaustive examination of Colonial British records, plantation records, church records, local and national archives is a difficult, time consuming process, but we are cognizant that history has a way of unfolding, that documents will emerge from the depth of the black hole containing clarity and truth. With continued efforts, at some point, the pieces of the puzzle will tumble into place.

This historical account should serve as inspiration to members of the human race throughout the universe, whose ancestors waged the courageous battle to first survive and then succeed, against all odds. It is a patriotic story which embodies the American dream and is a dynamic example of personal courage. The "Three Iron Horses and the Butterfly" looked fear of failure squarely in his beaded eyes and declared with sincere conviction that they would not be denied.

Such a defiance of dramatic odds must have meaning for all of us. Why they survived and flourished when many peers failed or refused to even collectively mount a serious challenge is one of those mystical phenomena we all must examine during the course of our existence. How we respond as individuals, I think, defines our character and illustrates what we are made of.

It appears to me that the solution to some of the paramount problems that plague America today, namely the under-achievement of many African-Americans, the alarmingly dramatic high school dropout rates, day-to-day survival mentality and teen pregnancy can begin with a very simple faith-based initiative. We as a people, starting at the individual level, are not obliged to accept the preset limits that society attempts to thrust upon us. Television and other media, including many educational establishments, are constantly bombarding us with "stuff" that does not foster breaking out. It is indeed difficult but through faith, education, discipline and unwavering belief in oneself, I believe we can develop alternatives to many dilemmas of contemporary society.

Even though **Evelyn Kelly Bolden Brown** began her educational process in a one-room shack (thanks to Plessy v Ferguson), her parents envisioned a greater role for her and planted the seed that she could attain a higher level of excellence. Without internal conflict this concept has carried forth into succeeding generations. Speaking as a Molecular Biologist, from a biological viewpoint, it appears that the trick is to integrate the behavioral concept into the ancestral DNA, and once it's intermingled it will be duplicated or copied.

Mankind has inhabited the planet for thousands of years and our stay will be a hundred years, if we're lucky. We are only here for a very short period of time, yet every generation, every person leaves a contribution, a legacy, a footprint, no matter how small or how large, they leave a footprint. The evolution and development of the Bacotes and Kellys is an on-going process and as such many believe that the best is yet to come, that God still has important plans for us.

Arthur H. Bolden

The question I pose to you, America, to the youngsters in these two families, to the preteens, the teenagers, the thirty year olds, the forty year olds, the sixty year olds: how large will your footprint be? **Elias Bacote, John Kelly Sr., Shadrack Kelly, Evelyn K.B.** **Brown** and numerous others born during a time when there were no cars on the road, no 747s soaring overhead, no computers, no cell phones, iPods, iPads, Blackberrys, or iPhones have left huge footprints and achieved lofty goals. How large will your footprint be?

SOURCES OF INFORMATION

Ancestry.com

Bennett, Lerone Jr. *Before the Mayflower.* 6th ed. Chicago, 1995.

Bennett, Lerone Jr. *Forced into Glory: Abraham Lincoln's White Dream.* Chicago, 2000.

Bureau of Vital Statistics, State Board of Health, State of South Carolina.

Chicora Research Contribution 217, Brief Overview of an Archaeological Survey of a Florence County, South Carolina Tract.

Coker, C.L. *History of Railroads in the Pee Dee Section.*

Darlington County Court Records

Darlington County Historical Commission

Darlington County, South Carolina, 1860 Census. Compiled by Horace Fraser Rudisill.

Darlington, South Carolina newspaper, *The News and Press.*

Darlingtoniana. A History of People, Places and Events in Darlington County, South Carolina. Edited by Eliza Cowan Ervin and Horace Fraser Rudisill. 1964.

Documents of Evelyn K.B. Brown

DuBois, W.E.B. *Souls of Black Folk.* 1903.

DuBois, W.E.B. *Black Reconstruction.* New York, 1935.

Family Bible

Family Members, Clarin Bacote, Gladys Bacote Hunter, Sammie Bacote, Patricia Bacote James, Rosa Kelly Robinson, Lee Bacote, Mary Norkhird, Rose Mattison and Donald Ruff.

Family Wills

Fogel, Robert W. and Stanley L. Engerman. *Time on the Cross: The Economics of American Negro Slavery.* 1974.

Franklin, John Hope. *From Slavery to Freedom: A History of Negro Americans.* 1947.

Franklin, John Hope. *Mirrors to America.* 2005.

Franklin, John Hope, and Loren Schweninger. *Runaway Slaves: Rebels on a Plantation.*

Guyton, Vivian H. "African American Bacot and Brockington Family History." Pamplet at the Darlington County Historical Commission.

James, Lillian Clarke. "Uncle Ket, A Kind Gentle Giant." Pee Dee Magazine, May-June 2001.

"Kansas Fever," Legacy Magazine article, Spring 2009 Issue,

Kelly, Catherine, et al. "The Legend To Live The Legacy." Family Reunion Booklet. 2003.

Land Deed Records, Darlington, South Carolina District

Macedonia Baptist Church Records

Mechanicsville Baptist Church Records

Michener, James A. *The Source.* New York. 2002 edition.

Records of the Freedmen Bureau of Refuges, Freemen and Abandons, South Carolina.

Scott Wilds, Darlington County, South Carolina Historian

South Carolina Genealogical Society Inc., Old Darlington Chapter, Robert DeFee, 2001 Copyright.

United States 1870 Census Report

Unveiling ceremony of Roseville Plantation Slave Cemetery historical marker, November 13, 2004.

Willcox BJ, Donlon TA, He Q, Chen R, Grove JS, Yano K, Masaig KH, Willcox DC, Rodriguez B, Curb JD. "FOXO3A genotype is strongly associated with human longevity," Proc. Natl. Acad. Sci. U.S.A. **105** (September 2008) (37) 13987-92.

Yinger, Milton J. *A Minority Group in American Society.* New York, 1965.

APPENDIX

Figures 3-7 were reproduced from the book *Darlingtoniana*, with permission of the R.L.Bryan Company. They were color enhanced for visual effects.

TABLE 3

Schedule of negro Slaves and other Chattels to be partitioned & divided

#	Name	#	Name	#	Name	#	Name
1	Jack	42	January	86	George	128	Toby
2	Abram	43	Caroline	87	Billy	129	Alfred
3	Daniel	44	Mapey	88	Franky	130	P. Moses
4	Adam	45	Lucinda	89	Dinah	131	Moses
5	Phillip	47	Hyziah	90	Betsey	132	O. Adam
6	Esau	48	Dick	91	London	133	
7	Jerry	49	Julius	92	Caroline	134	
8	Dave	50	Rose	93	Margaret	135	
9	Harry	51	Isaac	94	Esau	136	
10	Victoria	52	Doctor			137	
11	Elizabeth	53	Betty	95	Toney		
12	Mary	54	Patty	96	Suey		
13	Anson	55	Peggy	97	Alexander		
14	Rose	56	Caty	98	Annie		
15	John, carp	57	Ned	99	Tigbon		
16	Nancy	58	Louisa	100	Hopkins		
17	Lewis	59	Mariah	101	Lucy		
18	Tom	60	Bob	102	Leona		
19	Jonas	61	Amy	103	Dorcas		
20	John	62	Jackson	104	Ben		
21	Bilious	63	Judy	105	Susannah		
22	Leah	64	Rachael	106	Oliver		
23	Bob	65	Charles	107	Simon		
24	Cornelius	66	Joe	108	Minder		
25	Hannah	67	Lott	109	Jane		
26	Matilda	68	Cloe	110	Jane		
27	Lydia	69	Daphney	111	April		
28	Peter	70	Richard	112	Isabella		
29	Ted	71	Frank	113	Kitty		
30	Ann	72	Dinah	114	Sylvia		
31	Hetty	73	Glasgow	115	Patience		
32	Mapey	74	Martella	116	Henry		
33	Daphney	75	William	117	Ann		
34	Temple	76	Albert	118	Nat		
35	Ned	77	Charlotte	119	Mary		
36	Cato	78	Ada	120	Cow Daniel		
37	Phillis	79	Venus	121	Joseph		
38	Peggy	80	Lucy	122	Bob, Sam		
39	Delila	81	Sarah	123	Billy		
40	Lambert	82	Polly	124	Isabel John		
41	Tim	83	Horace	125	Washington		
		84	Tigitte	126	Little Sam		

together with the neg slaves born since the making of the inven of Mary H Brooking & deceased

Mules. name
Rock, Frank, Joe, Blue.
48 head of Cattle, then
2 yoke of oxen
148 Hogs.
Side Board, Rocking ch
winnow fan, ox cart

1857

INDEX

A

Abyssinian Baptist Church, 306
Adam Clayton Powell Boulevard, 306-07
African Methodist Episcopal Church, 80
Africans from West Africa, 29
Al-Biruni, Abu'l-Rayhan Muhammad, 19
Aliases, 218-19, 277-78
Allen, Richard Rev., 80
Alligator Branch, **31**, 33, **35**, 83-4, 87
Alpha Pi Chi Sorority, 322
Amending of Kelly genealogy, 193-94
American Civil Liberties Union (ACLU), 104
American Indian slavery, 45, 158, 161
Ancestral surnames, 167
Andrews, John L. Jr., 164
Angelou, Maya, 22
Antibiotics, 114
Antrum, Viola, 125
Atlanta, Georgia, 101, 134

Augusta, Georgia, 102
"Aunt Sue Kelly," 223

B

Back Swamp Country, 28, **32**, 41, 153, 181, 229
Back Swamp settlers, 28-9, 41, 54
Bacot, Benjamin and Sara, 42, 46, 81
Bacot, Cyrus I, 48, 54, 56, 59, 83
Bacot, Cyrus II, 48, 56-7
Bacot Family Papers, 193
Bacot, Mary Allston, 157
Bacot, Peter Hannibal, 48, 157
Bacot, Peter Samuel, 48, 157, 184, 207
    papers, 210
    planter, 158
Bacot, Pierre, 40, 47
Bacot plantations, 40, 48
Bacot, Richard Brockinton, 40, 48
Bacot, Samuel I, 48
Bacot, Samuel II, 48
Bacot Slave Graveyard, 98
Bacote, Beatrice, 113, 116

Bacote, Benjamin Earl, 131
Bacote, Bennie, 92, **107**, 127-130
Bacote, Boyd, 84, 109, 121-22, 266
Bacote, Brock, 84, 92, 109,
Bacote, Carl, 138
Bacote, Chad, 142
Bacote, Chaney, **107**, 113, 116
Bacote, Clarin "Bunny," 137
Bacote, Cleo, 133
Bacote, Coker, 134, 137
Bacote, Cynthia, 136
Bacote, Elias, 12, 42, 69, **106**
   accountability of, 54
   activist activity of, 62-64
   appearance before Congressional
      Committee, 63-65
   background of, 46
   Baptist Church and, 71
   beginning of family of, 61, 66
   change of surname, 54, 77
   children of, 61, 73-4, 76-7, 86
   common thread among
      children, 78
   courage of, 63, 66
   date of birth, 47
   death of, 98
   diphtheria epidemic and, 75
   early post-slavery residence of,
      62-3
   estate off Bull Road, **86**
   industriousness of, 79
   influenced by, 50, 53
   interracial heritage of, 46
   land amassment, 83
   leadership ability of, 65, 69
   location of properties, 62, 81, 83-
      85, 88
   loss of children, 76

   management style of, 69
   marriage of, 61
   modus operandi of, 71, 82
   plantation address of, 47-8, 50, 60
   railroad crossties, production of,
      73, 83, 96
   railroad entrepreneur, 69, 72-3
   real estate accolades of, 94
   residences of, 62, 88-9
   runaway activity of, 48-9
   siblings of, 46
   skilled craftsman, 95
   social activism of, 100
   socialization of, 67
   visionary expertise of, 93
   wedding gift to offspring, 97
   woodsman skills of, 95-6
   work ethics of descendants, 93
Bacote, Elihu, 81, 91-2, 143
Bacote, Elijah "Buddy," 139
   children of, 140
   homestead of, 140
   marriage of, 140
   Stuart pecan trees and, 141
Bacote, Ezekial, **107**
Bacote Handy, 121-22
Bacote, Harry, 112
Bacote homesteads, **35**, 36, 109-10
Bacote, Josephine, 113, 261
Bacote, Junius, 92, 115
   bloodhound chewing tobacco
      and, 114
   children of, 113
   diphtheria and, 113
   tuberculosis and, 114
Bacote, LaMorris, 121
Bacote, Laverne, 116
Bacote, Leo, 92, **107**, 109, 119

children of, 116
    marriage, 116
    national hero, 118
    patriotism of, 117
    World War I and, 118
Bacote-Kelly family, **17**
Bacote, Leola, 135
Bacote, Mae Ruth, **107**, 130
Bacote, Marjorie, 142
Bacote, Mary, 122
Bacote, Mary Ida, 121
Bacote, Matilda White, 60,
    daughter of, 56-7
    death certificate of, 56
    interracial heritage, 56
    marriage of, 61
    mulatto status, 56
    plantation address, 59
Bacote, Maxine, 121-22
Bacote, Minnie, **106**, 119, 124, 291
Bacote, Nannie, 92, **107**, 127
Bacote, Norris, **106**, 121
Bacote, Patricia, 140
Bacote, Rosebud, 113, 116
Bacote, Rose "Posey," 131
Bacote, Royal, **107**, 115
Bacote, Sammie, 109, 130-31, 138
Bacote, Sarah, 76, 92, **106**, 144
Bacote, Sylvia, 131
Bacote, Theodore, 131
Bacote, Waddell, 116, 120
Badin, North Carolina, 178
Bailey, Lanie, 178
Baldwin, James, 16
Barbados, 301, 307
Barber Scotia College, 179
Barbezon Fashion School, 237
Battle of Bull Run, 36, 184

Benedict College, 189
Berlin, Isiah, 69
Big Mama and Big Papa, 226
    children of, 227
Black activism, 100
Black codes, 60, 215
Black Creek, 48-9
Blackfoot Indians, 46
Black land ownership, 215
Blacks in the wars of America, 45
Bloodhound Chewing Tobacco, 114
Bolden, Arthur H. (author), **106**
    career of, 124
    children of, 125
    defiant acts of, 100-104
    marriage of, 124
Bolden, Arthur H. II, 125
Bolden, Carl, **150**, 302
Bolden, Chester, 125, 307, 323
Bolden, Chesterfield, 124, 301
    death of, 309
    employment of in NYC, 307
    family in Barbados, **150**, 302
    genealogy of, **303**
    letter from mother, **305**
    life in Harlem, 306
    pugilistic career, 306
    stowaway, 301
    wedding of, 304
Bolden, C. Lindsey, 302
Bolden, Ermine, **150**, 302
Bolden, Ethelene Sargent, **150**, 302
Bolden, Gwen, **150**, 302
Bolden, Jacqueline Matthews, 124
Bolden, Melville, **150**, 306
Bolden, Troy, 125, 310
Brockinton, Mary Hart, 192, 207

slave inventory of, 158, 159, 205, 208, 345
Brockinton, Richard, 157, 192
Brockington, Billow, 194, 206, 211
Brockington, Cato, 164
    body servant, 184
    children of, 183
    Civil War hero, 184
    lay preacher, 185
    Major William Cannon and, 184
    relationship to Vivian
        Guyton, 185
Brockington Elementary School, 310
Brockington, George, 186, 201, 204
Brockington, Ida, 201, 297
Brockington, Isaac P. Rev., 80
Brockington, John (N), 194, 201
Brockington, Lewis, 194
Brockington, Nancy, 193, 205
    children of, 193, 205
    death of, 206
    elder Kelly matriarch, 194, 206
    entombed at, 206
    marriage of, 193
Brockington, Sarah, 186, 201
Brockington, Tom, 194
Brockington, Ulysses, 127
Brockington, Willow, 194
Brown, Carrie, 321
Brown, Ernest, 312
Brown, Evelyn K.B., 12, **147**, 168, 257, 297, 304
    Abyssinian Baptist Church
        and, 306
    birthday of, 257
    career as seamstress, 301, 313
    children of, 124, 307
    college education, 300

community activities, 322
community legacy of, 324, 327
community priorities, 320, 322
death of, 327
Distinguished Educator Award
    of, 326
Duke Hospital and, 323
educator, 313, 328
endurance of, 297
entrepreneurial ventures of, 317-19, 323-25
family griot, 230
Jake's visits, 315
Macedonia Baptist Church
    and, 322
marriage to Chesterfield, 304
marriage to Ernest Brown, 312
NAACP affiliation, 320-22
neighbors on Chestnut Street, 320
nicknamed Toonie, 297
primary assets of, 311
relationship with brother, 314
relocation to New York, 300-01
residences in Harlem, 307
return to Darlington, 307
social life in NYC, 306
son's bout with measles, 323
teaching positions, 300, 310
views on education, 297, 300, 315
views on integration, 321
Brown, Florie, 312
Brown, Jimmy, 312
Brown, Ralph, 327
Brownsville, South Carolina, 244
Brown v. Board of Education of
    Topeka Kansas, 67, 100, 320
Buddy Lane, 85
Bull Road, 85-6, 109

Butts, Calvin O., 306
Bynum, Lilly Mae Samuel, 182-83

C

Cardoza, Frances L., 61
Carolina, John, 190, 217, 276, 278
    aliases of, 219, 277-78
Cashua Ferry Road, 35, 81, 89-0, 143,
    160, 211
Cemeteries, 98, 256
Census of Colfax Township, 153,
    218-20
Charleston, South Carolina, 26-7, 29
Chattel Mortgage, 265, **268**
Cheraw and Darlington Railroad, 72
Chestnut Street, 126, 174, 291, 308
    paving of, 320
Civil Rights Act of 1866, 55
Civil Rights Bills, 299
Civil War, 36, 45, 55, 184
Clark Atlanta University, 179
Clarke, Ada Bacot, 165-66, 185
Clarke Cemetery, 164
Clarke's Crossroads, 36
Clemson University, 142
Coggeshall, A.C., 86
Colfax, 33, **34**, 41, 153 155, 169, 212
Colfax Township Census, 218-19
"Colored Cemetery," 201
Colored Community College, 300
Commissions in Equity, 55, 207,
    213-14
Compromise of 1877, 62
Confederate States of America
    (CSA), 36
Cotton picking, 258
Cover-up by omission, 160
Cox, Annie Kelley, 238

D

Daniel Lumber Company, 291
Daniels, Barbara Wilds, 188
Daniels, Hattie Carol, 227
Daniels, Johnathan, 189
Dargan, Ned, 38
Darlington area map, **31**
Darlington County, South Carolina,
    30, **32**, **35**, 38, 153, 158
Darlington Memorial Cemetery, 98-9
Davis, Roland, 103
Deeds, 281-284
Defee, Robert M., 276
Dillon, South Carolina, 223, 243
Diphtheria, 75, 215
Diphtheria epidemic, 75
Director of Farming, 278
Dixie Cup Company, 38
Dodd Frank Wall Street Reform Act,
    125
Dred Scott Decision, 47, 52, 55, 207
DuBois, W.E.B., 53, 97

E

Early ancestors, 25, 28, 52, 194
Early Kelly generation, 194
Effingham, South Carolina, 186
Egg story, 308
Elevator man/Handyman, 307
Elihue Bacote Estate, 90, **91**
Emancipation Proclamation, 50-1
Emory University, 132
European Bacots, 47-8
Extended family relationships, 232

F

Federal Crop Mortgage, 265, **266**
Ferguson, John Howard, 79
Fields, Hattie, 261
Fifteenth Amendment, 55, 61
First family, 193
Florence, South Carolina, 30, 101, 158,
    163, 186, 204, 229, 282
Flue-cured tobacco, 39
Fourteenth Amendment, 56, 60
Frank, Robert, 202-03
Franklin, John Hope, 22, 49
Fred Stems Place, 236
"Free agents," 210
Freedmen's Bureau of Refugees,
    Freemen and Abandons, 37,
    58, 212
    document of, 59, 211-12
French Huguenots, 47
French settlers, 28, 48
Freshets, 143
Friendship Baptist Church, 174
Fruit trees, 110

G

Galilee School, 310
Gant, Brandy, 228
Gant, Patricia Mack, 228
Gay, Sherel Kelley, 238
Georgetown Road, **35**, 113, 167,
    229, 253
Georgetown, South Carolina, 204
Georgia State University, 179
Genealogical Extracts, 276
Goodson, Theron, 101
Graham, Elizabeth, 126

Grandfather clauses, 299
Great Depression, 292
Gregg, Mary Robinson, **148**, 239
Greyhound Bus Lines, 101
Greyhound Bus Station, 80, 101, 175
Guyton, Vivian H., 156, 185

H

Hampton, University, 125, 132
Hankins, Anne Ruth, 127
Harding, Ometa, 302
Harlem, New York, 306-07,
Harlem Renaissance, 306
Hayes, Rutherford B., 62
Headrights, 94
Health Care Reform Act of 2010, 321
Hedgehog, 69
"Heir" property, 90, 143
Henderson, Donald, 175
Henderson, Elizabeth Kelly, 174-75
Hercules Chemical Company, 245
Herring Creek, 213, 251, 256
Herring (red), 256
Herrington, Brenda, 188
Herrington, Myles, 189
Herrington, Shayla, 188
Herrington, Winfred, 188
Herrington, Winfred Jr., 188
Hilton Head, South Carolina, 97
Historical time capsule, 144-45
Hog raising, 319
Honda Corporation, 164
Hood Cemetery, 98
Hopewell, Virginia, 245
Horse and Buggy, 263-64
Howard, A.J., 33
Howard, Richard, 33

Howard University, 125
Hudson, Orlando, 39
Human genome, 180
Hunter, Gladys Bacote, 88, **106**, 121
Hunter's paradise, 85
Hyman, Celia, 275, 283, 289

I

Iconic Butterfly, 14, 316, 327
Iconic Iron Horses, 13, 14, 162, 312
Independent farmer, 186, 212, 216, 288
Indigo, 29
Inherited behavioral traits, 230
In-house water, 292
Integration of public swimming
    pool, 104

J

Jackson, Ronald, 323
Jackson, Sarah, 180
Jackson, Susie, 223
Jackson, Thomas J. "Stonewall," 184
James, Lillian Clarke, 184
James, Patricia Bacote, 141
Jarrott, Mary Allston, 207
Jim Crow, 270
John Kelly Memorial Scholarship
    Fund, 235
Johnson C. Smith University, 133
Jones, Anceline, 177
Jones, Columbus, Jr., 177
Jones, James Kirmire, 177

K

Kappa Alpha Psi Fraternity, 133,
    306, 308
Kelley, Frank J., **150**, 237
Kelley, James (Boisey) Jr., **148**, 236
    children of, 237
    marriage of, 237
    residences of, 236
Kelley, John, 225
Kelly, Alfred, 210, 229, 234, 282
    career of, 235
Kelly and Bacote relationship, 222
Kelly, Bessie Linda, 245
Kelly, Binah, 171-72
Kelly, Boyd, 186
Kelly, Carolina, 180
Kelly, Carolina #1, 190-92, 221
    elder Kelly patriarch, 191
    presence at Roseville
        Plantation, 191
    Mechanicsville church records
        of, 191
Kelly, Carolina #2, 180-81, 191, 221,
Kelly, Caroline, 210
Kelly Cemetery, 256
Kelly, Chamberlain, 187
Kelly, Dellie, 177
Kelly, Dublin, 170-72, 180, 198, 221
Kelly, Elizabeth, 174, 235
Kelly, Elvira, 168, 187, 189
Kelly, Esau, 210, 279
Kelly, Eugenia Russell, **148**, 172-73
Kelly, Evelyn, 236
Kelly, Frank, 223, 237
Kelly, Frankie, 178
Kelly genealogy, **200**
Kelly, George, 173

Kelly, George Paris Sr., **147**, 171-
72, 175
Kelly, Georgianna, 210, 244, 248
Kelly Graveyard, 157, 256
Kelly, Hannah, 186, 229
Kelly, Hannah Harrison, 195, 209, 219
    a legend, 216
    as slave inventory, 208
    children of, 210
    death, 229
    marriage of, 209
Kelly, Harold "Jake," 90, 125
Kelly, Harry, 210, 281
Kelly, Horace, 126-27
Kelly, James Jr., **148**
Kelly, James Sr., **147**, 226, 234
Kelly, James W. Rev., 168, 172-73
Kelly, Jerry Rev., 169, 245
    career of, 246
    marriage of, 246
    offspring, 246
Kelly, Jessie Lee, 245-47
Kelly, Jessie Mae, 232, 245
Kelly, John Sr. #2, 227
    children of, 234
    death of, 235
    marriage of, 234
    Memorial Scholarship, 235
    religious emphasis, 235
    residences of, 234
    World War II and, 234
Kelly, John III, 236
Kelly, John Jr., (first), 210, 219,
223, 279
Kelly, John Sr., 12, 50, 155, 158, 190,
233
    aliases of, 213, 277-78
    birthplace of, 156, 192

boundary of existence, 222
    children of, **18**, 156, 205, 208,
210, 219
    death of, 229
    enslaved value of, 205-06
    financial skills, 212
    John Carolina estate and, **253**
    management style, 230
    marriages of, 193, 209, 219
    Mary H. Brockinton's will
        and, 207
    real estate purchase, 212
    registered as John Carolina, 213
    will of, 276, 285
Kelly, Lewis, 171, 195, 198, 207
Kelly, Lizzie, 241
    CEO, 235
    children of, 234
    tenacity of, 235
Kelly, Lydia, 210, 219
Kelly, Margrett, 181
    children of, 182
    residence of, 182
Kelly, Margrett (second), 187
Kelly, Marie, 181, 183
Kelly, Mary Pierce, **147**, 226, 234
Kelly, Meshach, 210, 219, 243, 281
Kelly, Nancy Robinson, 170, 180
Kelly, Nelly Mae, 244, 249
Kelly Place, **214**, 223, 230, **255**, 257,
278, 284
Kelly, Rena, 240
Kelly Reunions, **151**, 231
Kelly, Rosa, **148**, 241, 264
    children of, 238
    death of, 238
    family focus, 238
Kelly, Rose, 226

Kelly, Samuel, 168, 174-75
Kelly, Sarah Jackson, 180
Kelly, Shadrack, 12, **147**, 210
  battle with the court system, 55,
    286-87
  children of, 124, 251, 257, 271
  death of, 300
  farming aptitude, 278
  forerunner of independent black
    farmer, 279
  importance of education to, 263
  investments uptown, 291
  Kelly Place and, 285, 289
  key acquisitions, 282, 284
  land purchases, 229, 281, 283-
    84, 291
  loans, 283
  marriages of, 124, 250, 257
  modus operandi of, 253, 284,
    289-90
  nature of home site, 250, 292
  occupation of, 251
  retirement, 291
  sale of timber, 265
  self-trained agronomist, 290
  signature of, 265, 288-89
  true test of, 285
  virtuosity of, 290
Kelly slave quarters, 161
Kelly surname, 153
Kelly, Susie, 227
Kelly, Susie Jackson, 223
Kelly Town, 29
Kelly, Vivian, **149**, 174, 176
Kelly, Wilbur Shadrack Jr., 245
  at age 13, 245
  children of, 245-46

Hercules Chemical Company
    and, 245
  Hopewell, Virginia and, 245
  water boy on train, 245
  World War II service, 245
Kelly, Wilbur Shadrack Sr., 244
Kelly, Willow, 220
Kelly, Wilson, 240-41
Kilal, Abdul-Rasheed, 127
"Kings Highway," 33
Kirvens, Vermella, 174
Ku Klux Klan, 63, 66, 79, 271

L

Lamar, South Carolina, 235
Land acquisitions, 83-5, 212, 215,
    281-283
Land ownership, 83-5, 215
Land preservation, 93, 97
Land rental, 279
Large families, 272-73
Leavenworth section, 182
Lee Bell School, 77
Legal paperwork, 283-85
Lewis, Dorla, 38
Livingston College, 179
Long, Lewis, 125
Long, Sydne Bolden, 125
Longevity (age), 110, 115, 180
Louthers Lake, 25, 33, 256
Lyric soprano, 179

M

Macedonia Baptist Church, 79-0,
    312, 322
Mack, Ada, 228

Mack, Clara Kelly, 228, 241, 257
Mack, Patricia, 228
Marian, South Carolina, 30, 207
Marian, South Carolina Equity
    Bill, 207
Marlboro County, South Carolina, 243
Marriage terminology, 195
Mass migration, 112, 229, 243, 270-71
Mather Academy, 323
Mayo High School fire, 312
Mays, Benjamin E., 37, 328
McCown Clarke Company, 36
McCurry, Flora, Rev., 323
McCurry, Herbert, 323
McGown, 62
McKinnon, Henry, 226
McKinnon, Henry Jr., 226
McPhail, Ann Marie, 179
McPhail, Jessie, 178
McPhail, John Wesley, 150, 178
McPhail, Lanie Bailey, 150, 178
McPhail, Mae, 178
McPhail, Paul H. Jr., 179
McPhail, Paul H. Sr., 178
Mechanicsville, 25, 32, 41, 160,
    169, 263
Mechanicsville Baptist Church,
    163, 263
    documents of, 156
Michener, James, 209
Midwifes, 217
Milling, Chapman J., 29, 257
Molasses maker, 129
Monarch Butterfly, 14
Money management, 211
Mont Clair, 175, 310
Morehouse College, 37-8, 101, 133,
    179, 227, 306, 322

Morgan State University, 175
Morris College, 174, 316
"Mr. Jakes," 213, 230
Mulatto, 73-4
Mush, 185

N

NAACP, 320-21
National Register of Historic
    Places, 166
New England Plan, 30, 33
New Haven, Connecticut, 136
"Newly found ancestral Kelly
    family," 194
News and Press tidbits, 258-59
New York University, 123
Norfolk State University, 132
Norkhird, Mary Bacote, 122
North Carolina A&T University, 174
North Carolina Central University,
    133, 179
Norwood, Jimmy, 38
Notable Darlingtonians, 39
Nut trees, 110

O

Obama, Barack Hussein, 44, 66, 321
Old Darlington businesses, 293-94
Old family addresses, 144-45
Old family telephone numbers, 144-46
Old Georgetown Road, 162, 210, 213,
    233, 255
    spiritual energy of, 155
    location of St. Paul School on, 261
Old Society Hill Road, 175

P

Paine College, 116
Palmetto, South Carolina, 169, 202-03
Patriotism, 117
Pearson, Joshua, 103
Pee Dee Light Artillery Unit, 36
Pee Dee River, 28, 89, 161, 163
Perkins, Julia Kelly, 237
Perseverance, 154
Peterson, LaWana Rene, 169, 247
Pierce, Johnny Jr., 256
Pierce, Mary, 226, 234
Pinckney, Charles Cotesworth, 25
Pink horse named Joe, 144
Plantation Work Agreement
      Contracts, 46, 59
Pleasant Grove Baptist Church, 99,
      125, 261
Pleasant Grove Cemetery, 99
Pleasant Grove School, 78
Plessy, Homer, 79
Plessy v. Ferguson, 79, 100, 299
Pocket Road, 35, 36, 109
Post-Traumatic Stress Disorder, 118
Powell, Adam Clayton Jr., 306
Powell, Adam Clayton Sr., 306
Protection of legacies, 263
Puryear, R.W. Dr., 316

Q

Quadruplets, 210, 218-19, 220,
      223, 278

R

Railroad crossties, 72, 85
Railroad Industry, 13, 72

Railroad lines, 72
Rainey, Joseph, 61
"Redshirts," 62-3
Richardson, Jaret-Daniels, 227
Richardson, Phyllis, 279
Riverdale, 41, 153, 226, 253, 263
Riverside Drive, 304
Roadside markers (historic), 150, 163-
      64, 166
Robinson, Albert, 239
Robinson, Blair, 240
Robinson, Nancy, 175, 180
Robinson, Shirley, 239
Rolling Store, 111-12
Roseville Plantation, 149, 155,
      158, 206
   agricultural center, 163
   birthplace of John Kelly Sr., 156
   harvests at, 162
   layout of manor, 161
   legacy, 233
   national historic landmark,
      151, 163
   plantation grounds, 161
   river bottom land, 162
   slave quarters, 161
   spiritual energy of, 165
   uncertainty at, 206
Roseville Plantation Clarke
      Family, 185
Roseville Plantation Slave Cemetery,
      98, 150, 157, 164, 206
Round O School, 310
Ruff, Benjamin, 133
Ruff, Cleo, 130, 133, 145
Ruff, Donald, 133
Ruff, Rhonda, 133
Ruff, Ronald, 133
Ruff, Ronelle, 133

Runaway slave phenomenon, 48-9
Rural schools, 310-11

S

Samuel, Darrell, 183
Samuel, Estelle Nettles, 183
Samuel, Frank, 182
Samuel, Frank Jr., 182
Samuel, Washington, 182
Sargent, Maude, 145, 302
Schweninger, Loren, 49
Sealy, Richard, 302, 304
Sears and Roebuck, 101
Share Cropping, 68, 280
Shaw University, 116
"Sit ins," 101
Slave Cemetery at Roseville
    Plantation, 98, 157, 164
Slavery and usage of aliases, 213, 218
Slavery in America, 25, 28, 42-44, 49,
    52, 160
Slave trading sites (historic), 165
Smallpox, 26
Snake colonies, 87
Society Hill, South Carolina, 32, 28-9
Sonoco Products Company, 38
South Carolina Circuit Court
    Districts, 27
South Carolina Fed. Home
    Administration, 131
South Carolina Indian Tribes, 26
South Carolina Land Grants, 28, 94
South Carolina Militia, 47
South Carolina State College, 103,
    121, 130, 300
Spanish Harlem, 304
Splendor, 209

Springville, 29, 84
Stanley, Mann, 321
St. Augustine, 209
Stevens, Array, 64
St. John School, 300
St. Paul School, 113, 239
    description of, 261-62
Street plow story, 308
Stubbs, Leroy, 292

T

Tate, Josephine Martha, 113
Tax list, 219, 275-277, 279, 281
"The Square," 260
Thirteenth Amendment, 55, 210
Tobacco barns, 88, 318
Toonie, 201, 297, 307
Transfer of Title, 281-82
Tuberculosis, 114-15
Tucker, Carl, 163-64

U

University of North Carolina, Chapel
    Hill, 210
U.S. Civil Service Commission, 116
U.S. Supreme Court, 53, 99, 299

V

Voorhees College, 123

W

War Department, 314-15
Warren, Brenda, 188
Washington, DC, 44, 104, 116

Water carrier, 260-61
Waters, Muddy, 100
Watkins Liniment, 111
Watkin's Man, 111
Webster University, 189
Welch settlers, 31
Wells, Virgil, 39
Whipple, Paul, 282-83, 288-89
Whiskey still, 85
White, Matilda, 55-7, 222
White "only" water fountain, 101
Whittemore Township, 34, 61-2
Wilberforce University, 227
Wild animals, 87, 256
Wilds, Barbara, 188
Wilds, Doctor, 202
Wilds, Franklin, 149, 176
Wilds, Janie, 202

Wilds, Nicole Renee, 176
Wilds, Scott, 7, 41, 57, 65, 156, 193, 210
Wilds, Vivian Kelly, 149, 176
Wilmington and Manchester Line, 30, 72
Wilson, John Silvanos Jr., 37
Wings of Kelly family, 168-69, 180, 190-91, 199
Winthrop University, 189
Witherspoon Island, 31, 33
Wright, Hannah, 201

Y

Yingers, J. Milton, 299
Young brides, 209

Arthur Harcourt Bolden is a retired biochemist and molecular biologist. At the renowned National Institutes of Health and the Roche Institute of Molecular Biology he studied inositol biosynthesis, DNA and protein synthesis, as well as DNA methylation, having published over 30 articles in those genre.

Researchers at those institutions have had a profound effect on healthcare world-wide, saving millions of lives. The author is proud to be a part of that legacy, that achievement.

He is a graduate of Morehouse College, Howard University and Fairleigh Dickerson University.

He is married to the former Jacqueline Matthews of Martinsville, Virginia, and they currently reside in Coral Springs, Florida, where they are avid golfers, travelers, gardeners and community volunteers.